WWE SUPERSTARS "LEGENDS"

W9-BDL-645

Mick Foley
Shane Riches
Co-Creators

Shane Riches
Script

Paris Cullins
Artist

Jim Salicrup
Editor

SUPER GENIUS

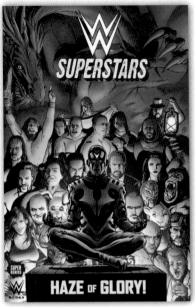
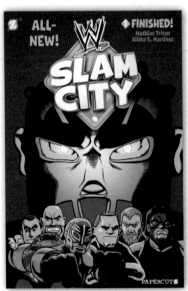
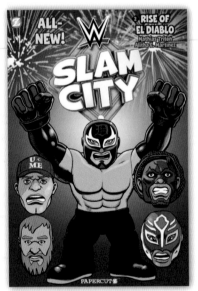

SUPERSTARS

#3 "Legends"

Mick Foley
Shane Riches
Co-Creators

Shane Riches
Script

Paris Cullins
Artist

Jim Salicrup
Editor

SUPER
GENIUS

New York

**Co-Created by MICK FOLEY, the
legendary WWE Hall of famer and
three-time WWE Champion, turned
multiple best-selling author of four
memoirs Mankind:Have a Nice Day!:
A Tale of Blood and Sweatsocks,
Mick Foley is Good: And the Real
World is Faker than Wrestling, The
Hardcore Diaries, and Countdown
to Lockdown: A Hardcore Journal
and SHANE RICHES, a film and
television writer and producer, as
well as graphic novel writer and
publisher.**

WWE SUPERSTARS #3 "Legends"

Mick Foley, Shane Riches – Co-Creators

Shane Riches
Script

Paris Cullins

{Alitha E. Martinez (Pages 1 & 51)
Joe Jusko (Page 5)
Simon Williams (Page 29)
Jolyon Yates (Page 73)}
Art

Alitha E. Martinez – Front Cover Art
JayJay Jackson – Front Cover Color
Jolyon Yates – Back Cover Art & Color

Laurie E. Smith
{JayJay Jackson (Pages 1, 51, & 73)
Joe Jusko (Page 5)
Simon Williams (Page 29)}
Color

Janice Chiang (Pages 9-28)
Chris Nelson (Pages 31-50, 53-72, 75-94)
Letters

Dawn K. Guzzo – Design and Production
Michael Petranek – Production
Jeff Whitman – Production Coordinator
Michael Petranek – Associate Editor
Jim Salicrup
Editor-in-Chief

Originally published as WWE SUPERSTARS #9-12 comics, by Super Genius, an
imprint of Papercutz, 160 Broadway, Suite 700, East Wing, New York, NY 10038.

ISBN: 978-1-62991-176-2

Printed in the US
February 2015 by Avenue 4 Communications
Cenveo Publisher Services
2901 Byrdhill Road
Richmond, VA 23228

Super Genius books may be purchased for business or promotional use. For information on
bulk purchases please contact Macmillan Corporate and Premium Sales Department at
(800) 221-7945 x5442.

Distributed by Macmillan
First Printing

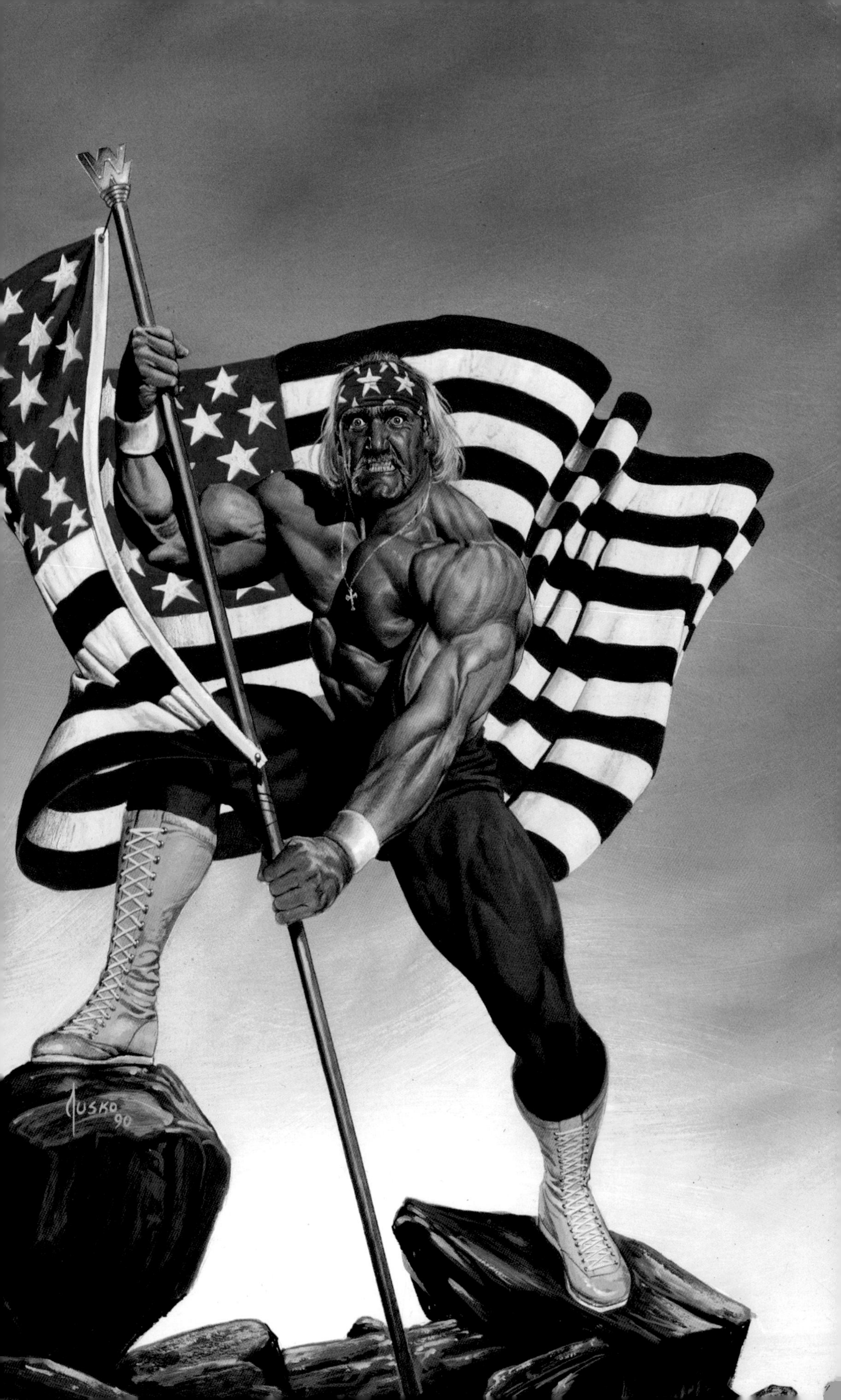
JUSKO
'90

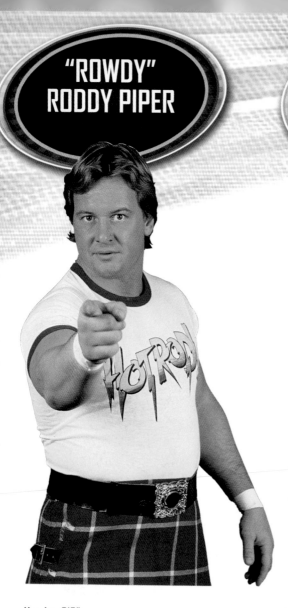

"ROWDY" RODDY PIPER

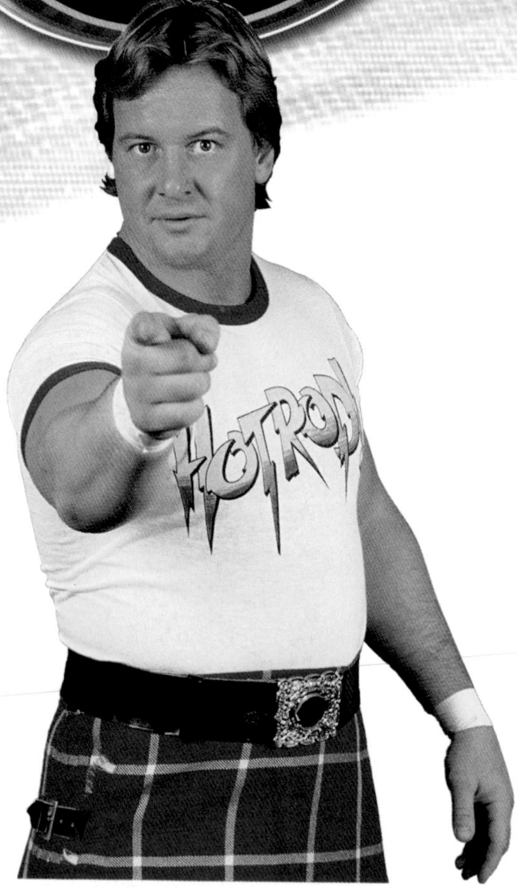
HOT ROD

Height: 6'2"
Weight: 230 lbs.
From: Glasgow, Scotland
Signature Move: Sleeper Hold
Career Highlights: Intercontinental Champion; World Tag Team Champion; WCW United States Champion; 2005 WWE Hall of Fame Inductee

DANIEL BRYAN

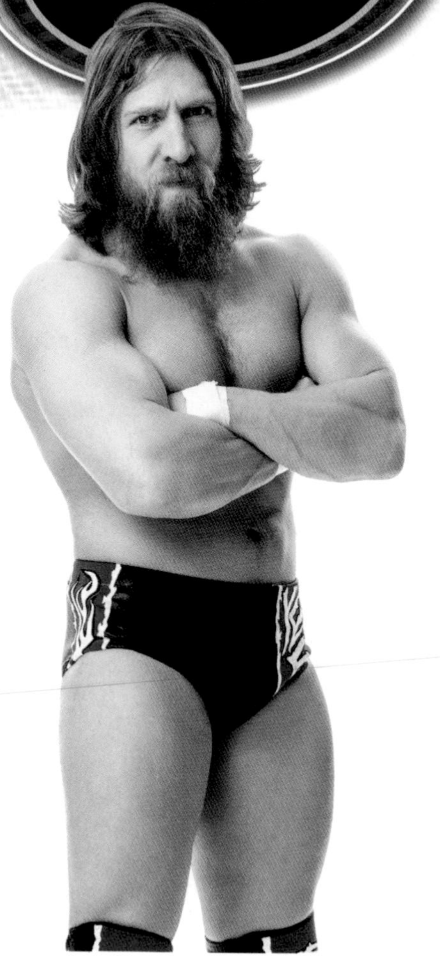

Height: 5'10"
Weight: 210 lbs.
From: Aberdeen, Washington
Signature Move: "Yes!" Lock
Career Highlights: WWE World Heavyweight Champion, WWE Tag Team Champion; World Heavyweight Champion; United States Champion; 2011 SmackDown Money in the Bank winner

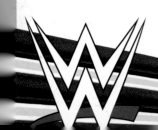

"STONE COLD" STEVE AUSTIN

HULK HOGAN

Height: 6'2"
Weight: 252 lbs.
From: Victoria, Texas
Signature Move: Stone Cold Stunner
Career Highlights: WWE Champion;
Intercontinental Champion; World Tag Team
Champion; 1996 King of the Ring; Royal
Rumble Match winner (1997, 1998, 2001);
WCW U.S. Champion; WCW Tag Team Champion;
2009 WWE Hall of Fame Inductee

Height: 6'7"
Weight: 302 lbs.
From: Venice Beach, California
Signature Move: Leg Drop
Career Highlights: WWE Champion;
WCW Champion; World Tag Team Champion;
two-time Royal Rumble match winner;
2005 WWE Hall of Fame Inductee

PART ONE "SECRET *RAW*"

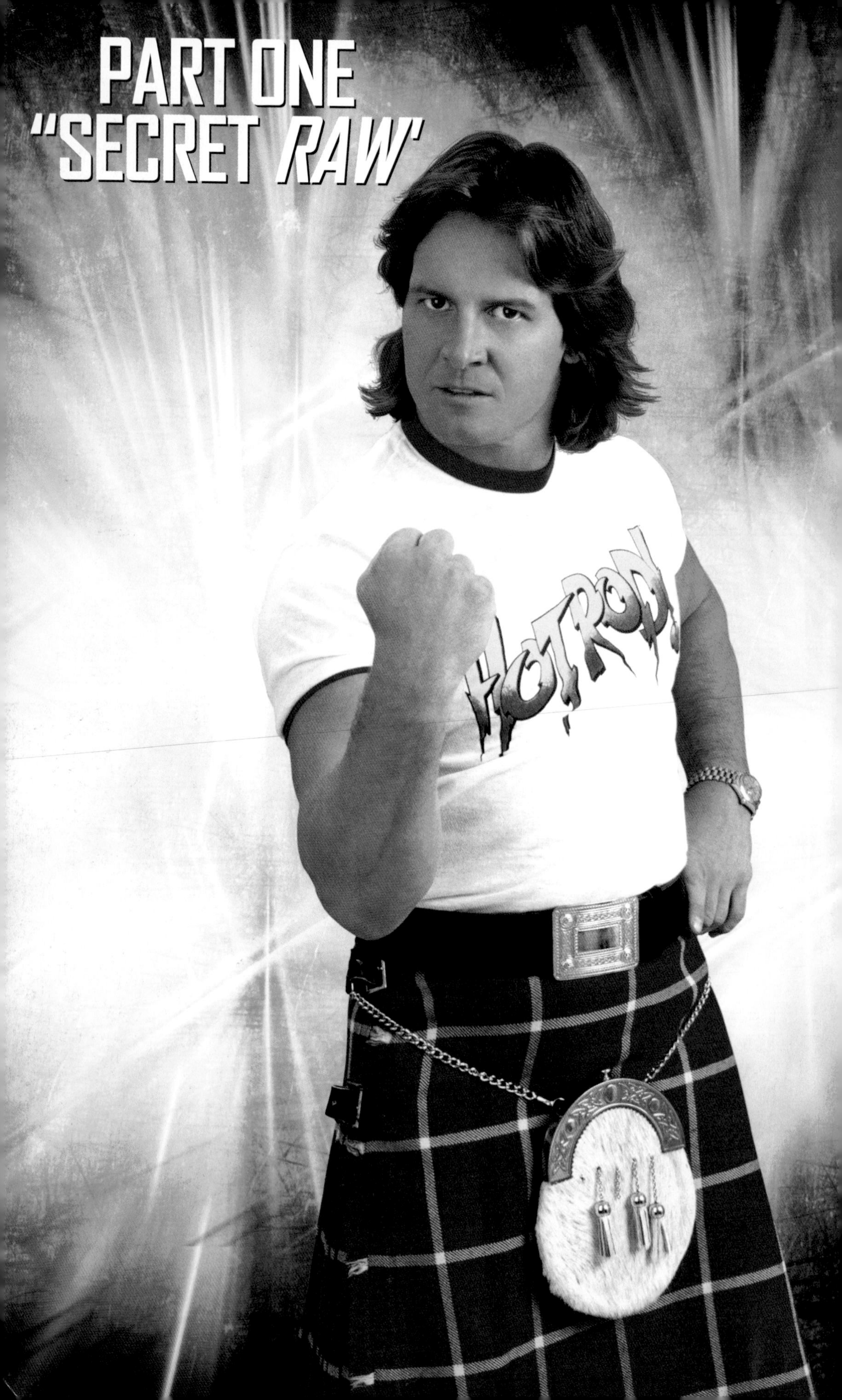
HOT ROD!

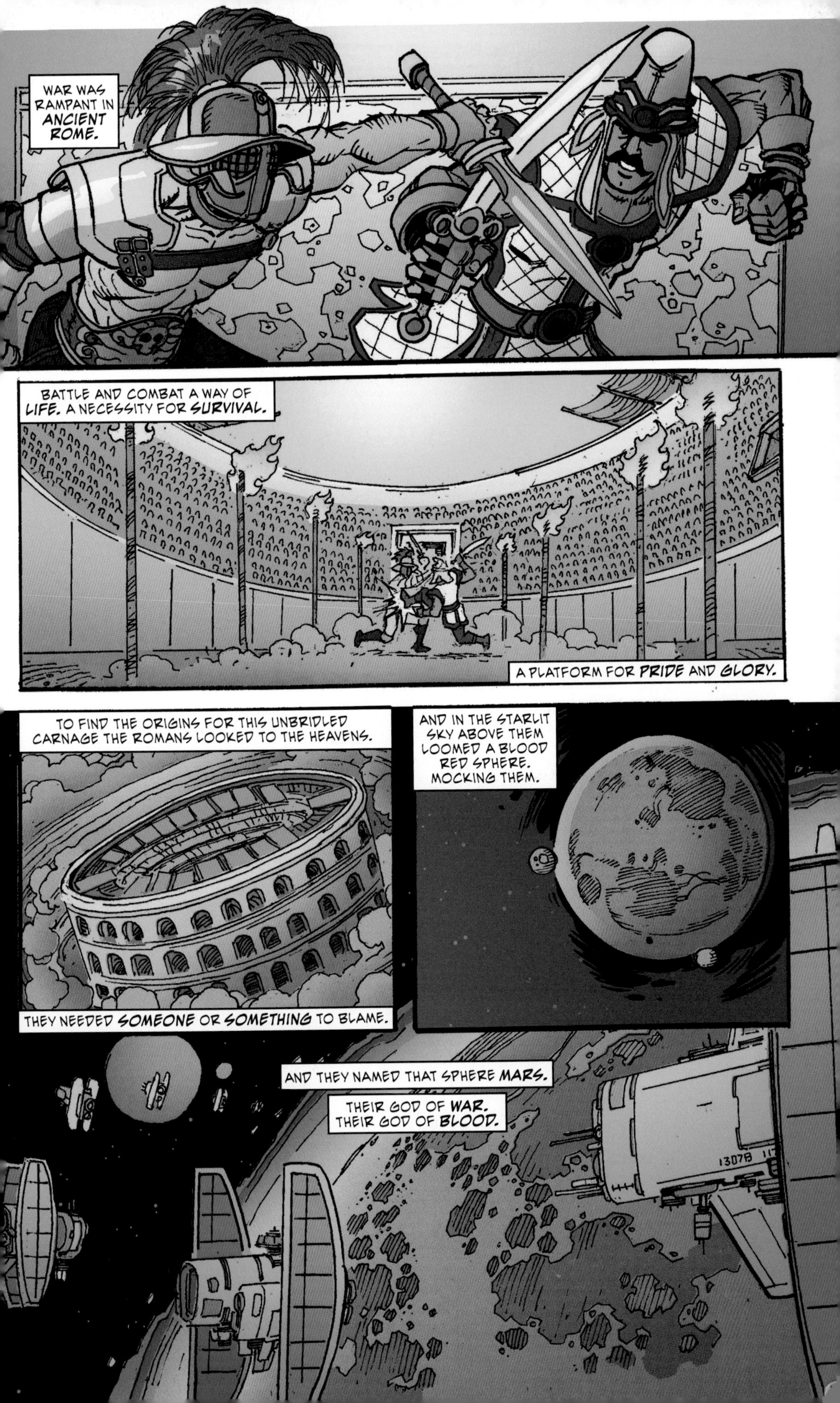
WAR WAS RAMPANT IN ANCIENT ROME.
BATTLE AND COMBAT A WAY OF LIFE. A NECESSITY FOR SURVIVAL.
A PLATFORM FOR PRIDE AND GLORY.
TO FIND THE ORIGINS FOR THIS UNBRIDLED CARNAGE THE ROMANS LOOKED TO THE HEAVENS.
THEY NEEDED SOMEONE OR SOMETHING TO BLAME.
AND IN THE STARLIT SKY ABOVE THEM LOOMED A BLOOD RED SPHERE. MOCKING THEM.
AND THEY NAMED THAT SPHERE MARS.
THEIR GOD OF WAR. THEIR GOD OF BLOOD.
13078

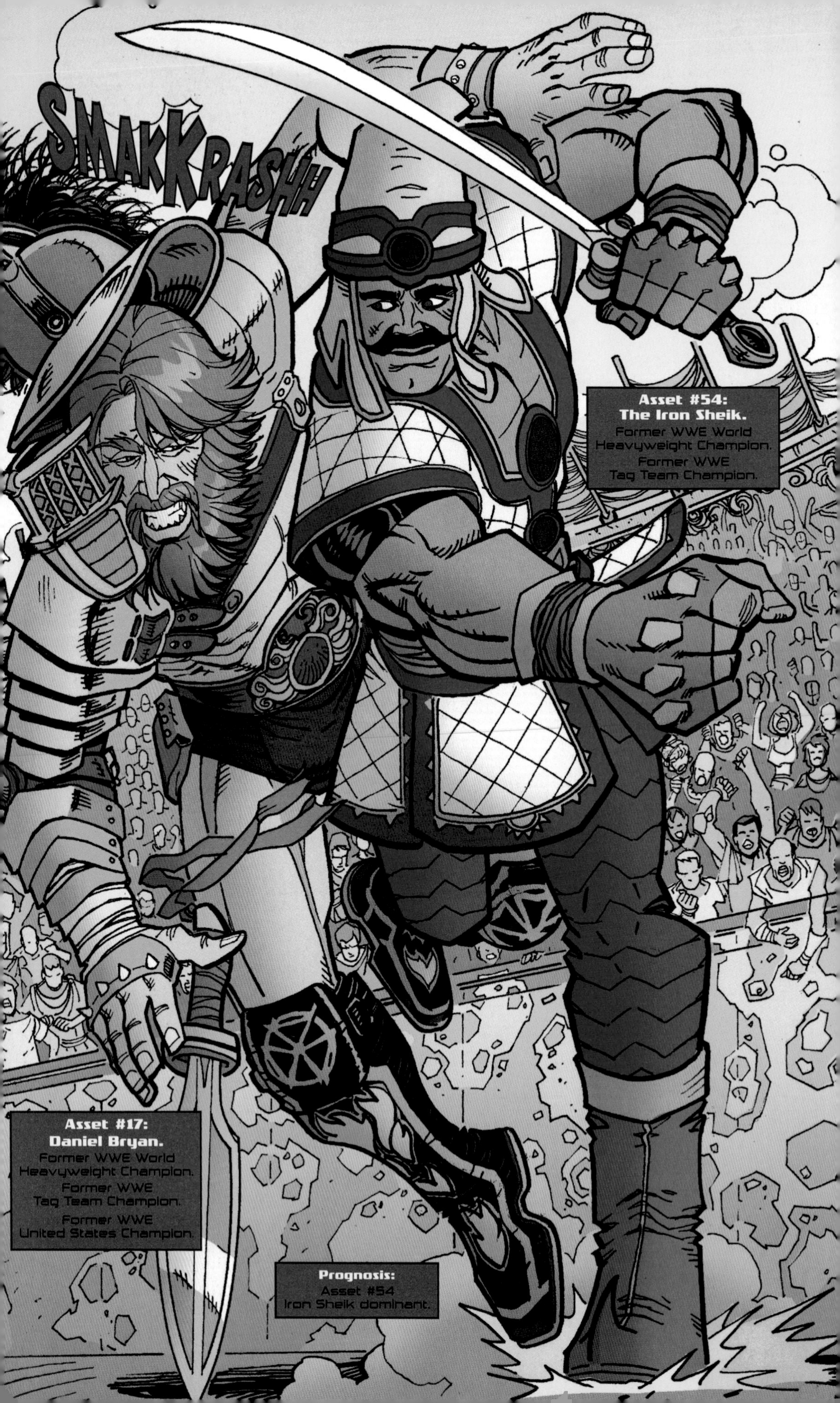
SMAKKRASHH
Asset #54:
The Iron Sheik.
Former WWE World Heavyweight Champion.
Former WWE Tag Team Champion.
Asset #17:
Daniel Bryan.
Former WWE World Heavyweight Champion.
Former WWE Tag Team Champion.
Former WWE United States Champion.
Prognosis:
Asset #54
Iron Sheik dominant.

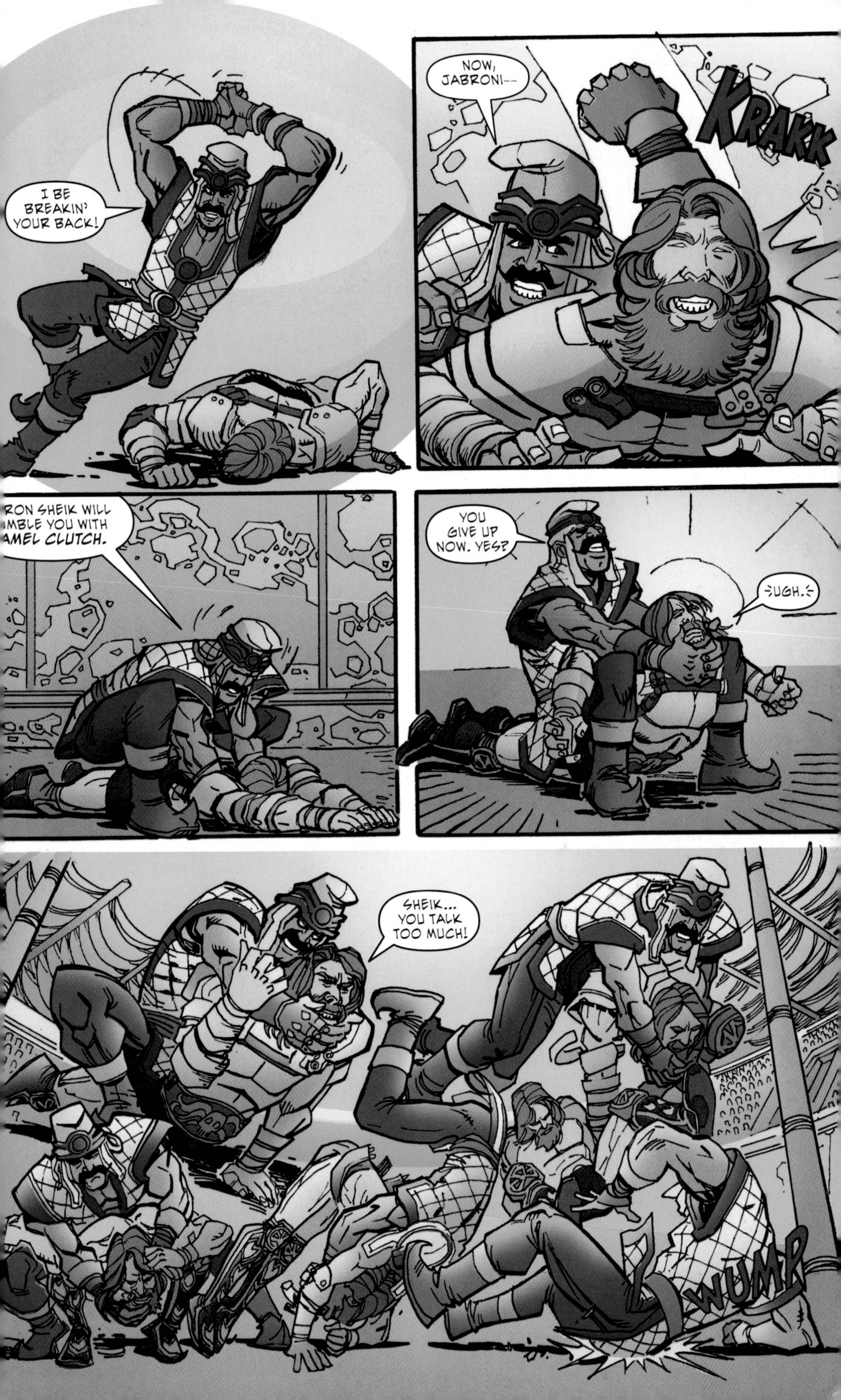
I BE BREAKIN' YOUR BACK!
NOW, JABRONI--
KRAKK
RON SHEIK WILL
MBLE YOU WITH
AMEL CLUTCH.
YOU GIVE UP NOW. YES?
UGH.
SHEIK... YOU TALK TOO MUCH!
WUMP

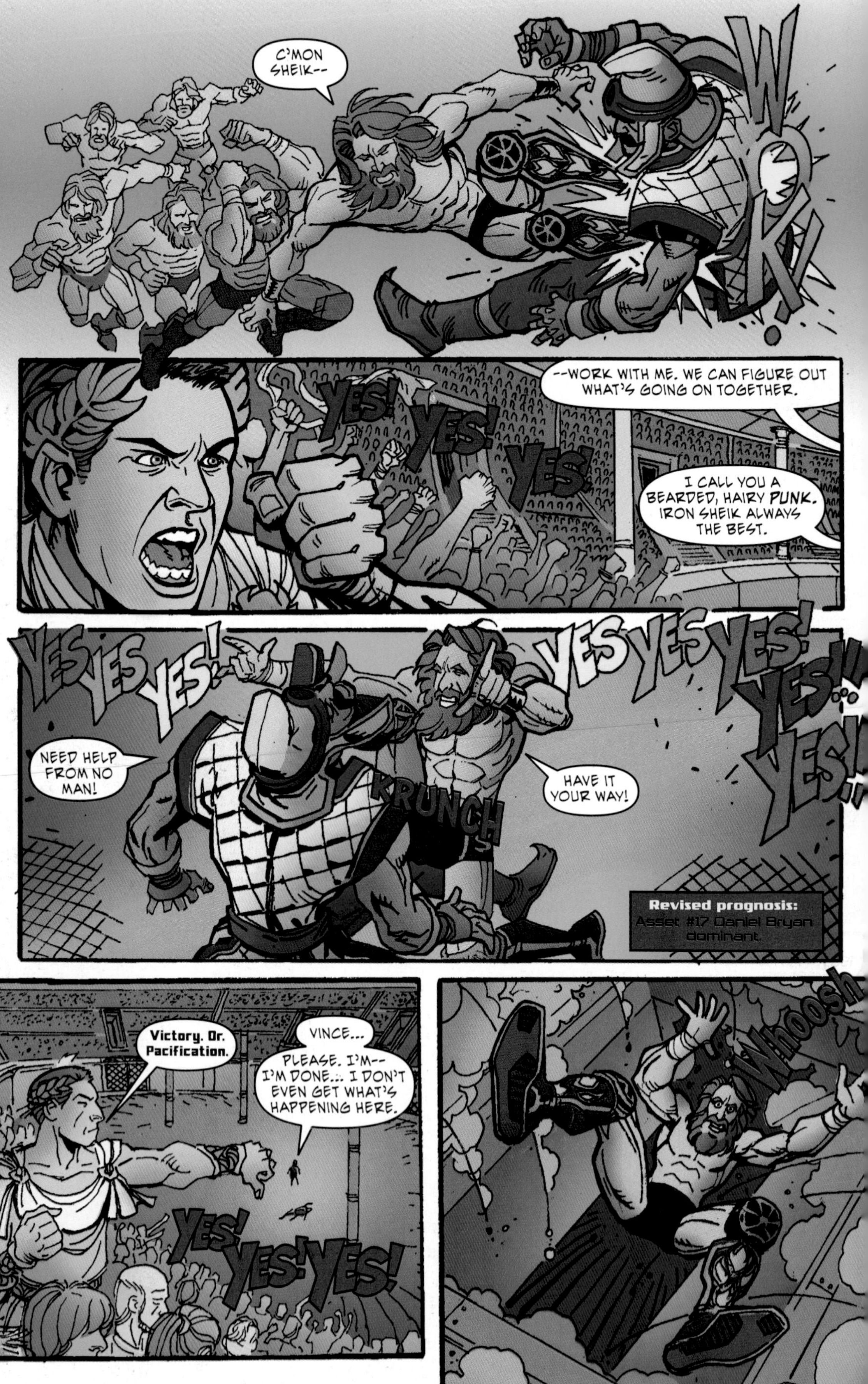
C'MON SHEIK--
WHAK!
--WORK WITH ME. WE CAN FIGURE OUT WHAT'S GOING ON TOGETHER.
YES! YES! YES!
I CALL YOU A BEARDED, HAIRY PUNK. IRON SHEIK ALWAYS THE BEST.
YES YES YES!
YES YES YES! YES!! YES!!
NEED HELP FROM NO MAN!
KRUNCH
HAVE IT YOUR WAY!
Revised prognosis:
Asset #17 Daniel Bryan dominant.
Victory. Or. Pacification.
VINCE...
PLEASE. I'M-- I'M DONE... I DON'T EVEN GET WHAT'S HAPPENING HERE.
YES! YES! YES!
Whoosh

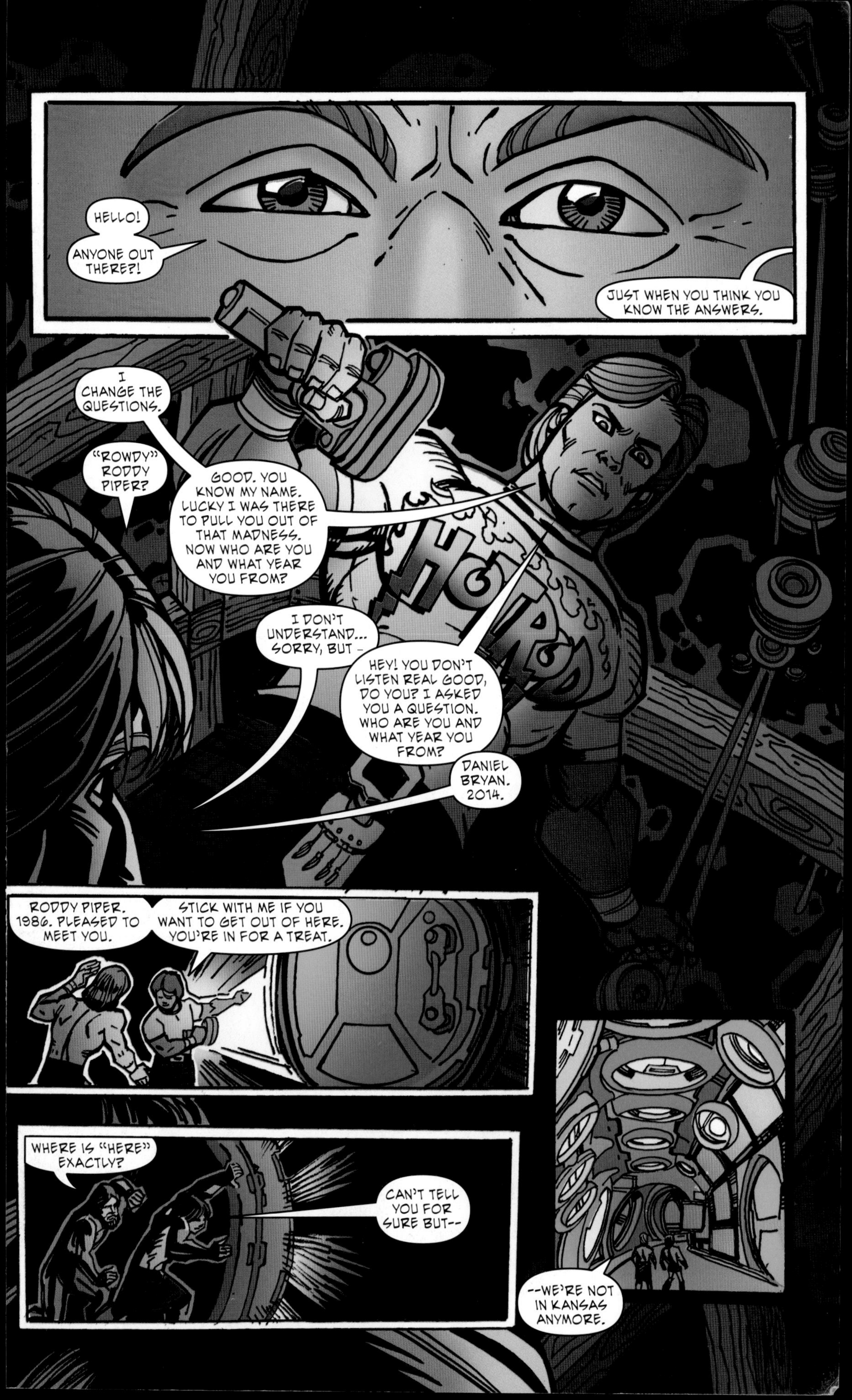
HELLO!
ANYONE OUT THERE?!
JUST WHEN YOU THINK YOU KNOW THE ANSWERS.
I CHANGE THE QUESTIONS.
"ROWDY" RODDY PIPER?
GOOD. YOU KNOW MY NAME. LUCKY I WAS THERE TO PULL YOU OUT OF THAT MADNESS. NOW WHO ARE YOU AND WHAT YEAR YOU FROM?
I DON'T UNDERSTAND... SORRY, BUT -
HEY! YOU DON'T LISTEN REAL GOOD, DO YOU? I ASKED YOU A QUESTION. WHO ARE YOU AND WHAT YEAR YOU FROM?
DANIEL BRYAN. 2014.
RODDY PIPER. 1986. PLEASED TO MEET YOU.
STICK WITH ME IF YOU WANT TO GET OUT OF HERE. YOU'RE IN FOR A TREAT.
WHERE IS "HERE" EXACTLY?
CAN'T TELL YOU FOR SURE BUT--
--WE'RE NOT IN KANSAS ANYMORE.

Analysis:
Assets Piper and Bryan have escaped the primary functionality of the game.

Asset #4:
Roddy Piper.
Former WWE
Intercontinental Champion.
Former WWE
World Tag Team Champion.

TAKE A LOOK AT THIS.

Conclusion:
Threat to program minimal. Allow free range to maximize spontaneity of outcomes.

YOU RECOGNIZE THESE TWO?

THE **ULTIMATE WARRIOR** AND JOHN CENA.

BUT NONE OF THIS MAKES ANY SENSE. HOW COULD THEY BE FIGHTING EACH OTHER?

SAME WAY YOU AND I ARE TALKING EVEN THOUGH YOU SAY YOU'RE FROM THIRTY YEARS IN MY FUTURE. DOESN'T REALLY MATTER.

I THINK TO MYSELF, WELL... WHY DID SOMEONE MAKE ALL THIS? KIDNAP US FROM DIFFERENT ERAS. PIT US AGAINST EACH OTHER. SIMPLE--

IT'S ENTERTAINMENT.

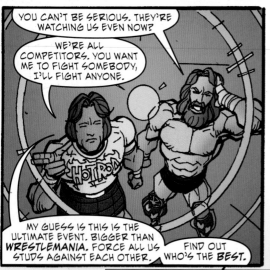

YOU CAN'T BE SERIOUS. THEY'RE WATCHING US EVEN NOW?

WE'RE ALL COMPETITORS. YOU WANT ME TO FIGHT SOMEBODY, I'LL FIGHT ANYONE.

MY GUESS IS THIS IS THE ULTIMATE EVENT. BIGGER THAN **WRESTLEMANIA.** FORCE ALL US STUDS AGAINST EACH OTHER.

FIND OUT WHO'S THE **BEST.**

WE NEED TO SAVE THE OTHER WWE SUPERSTARS. BUT HOW DO WE STOP SOMETHING THAT MONITORS OUR EVERY MOVE?

FOR SOME REASON THEY LET YOU GET TO ME, PIPER. TELL ME EVERYTHING YOU KNOW.

THAT'S NOT MUCH. I WENT TO BED IN MY HOTEL ROOM, ONLY TO WAKE UP IN--

"--EASTER ISLAND. COULDN'T MAKE HEADS OR TAILS OF THAT. BUT I WASN'T ALONE.

I'M AFRAID I'VE GOT SOME--

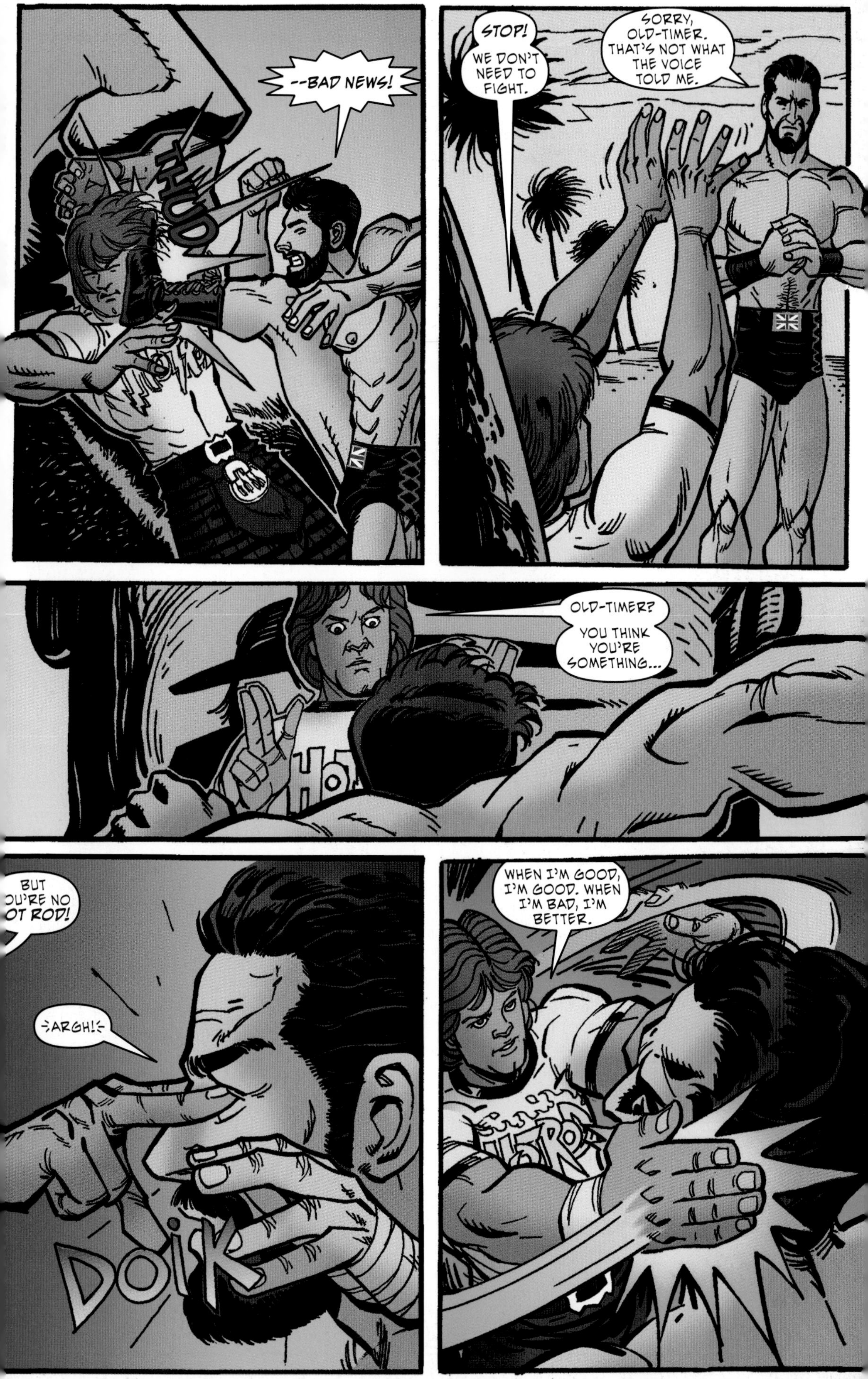
--BAD NEWS!
THUD
STOP!
WE DON'T NEED TO FIGHT.
SORRY, OLD-TIMER. THAT'S NOT WHAT THE VOICE TOLD ME.
OLD-TIMER?
YOU THINK YOU'RE SOMETHING...
BUT OU'RE NO OT ROD!
ARGH!
DOiK
WHEN I'M GOOD, I'M GOOD. WHEN I'M BAD, I'M BETTER.

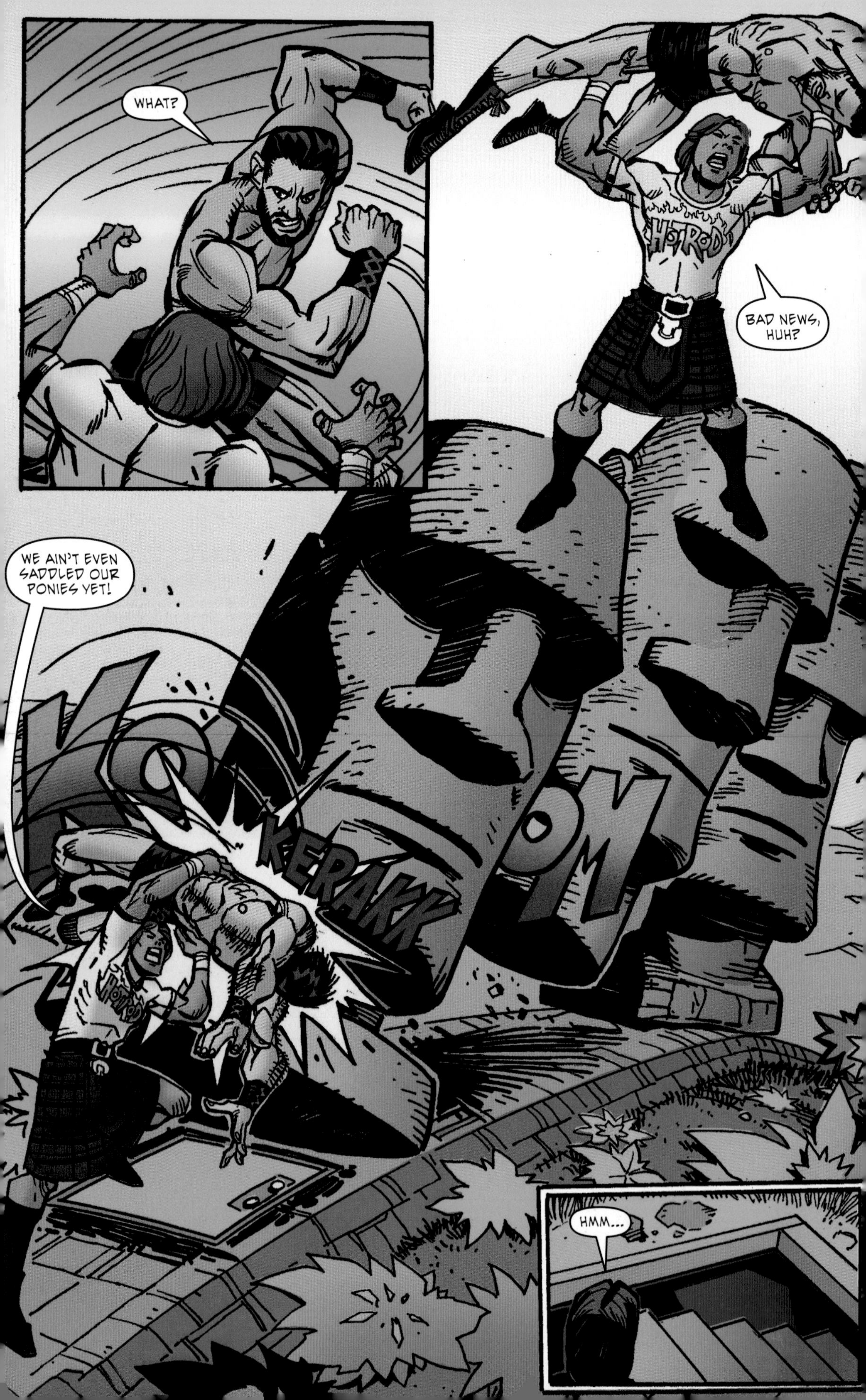
WHAT?
BAD NEWS, HUH?
WE AIN'T EVEN SADDLED OUR PONIES YET!
VOOM
KERAKK
HMM...

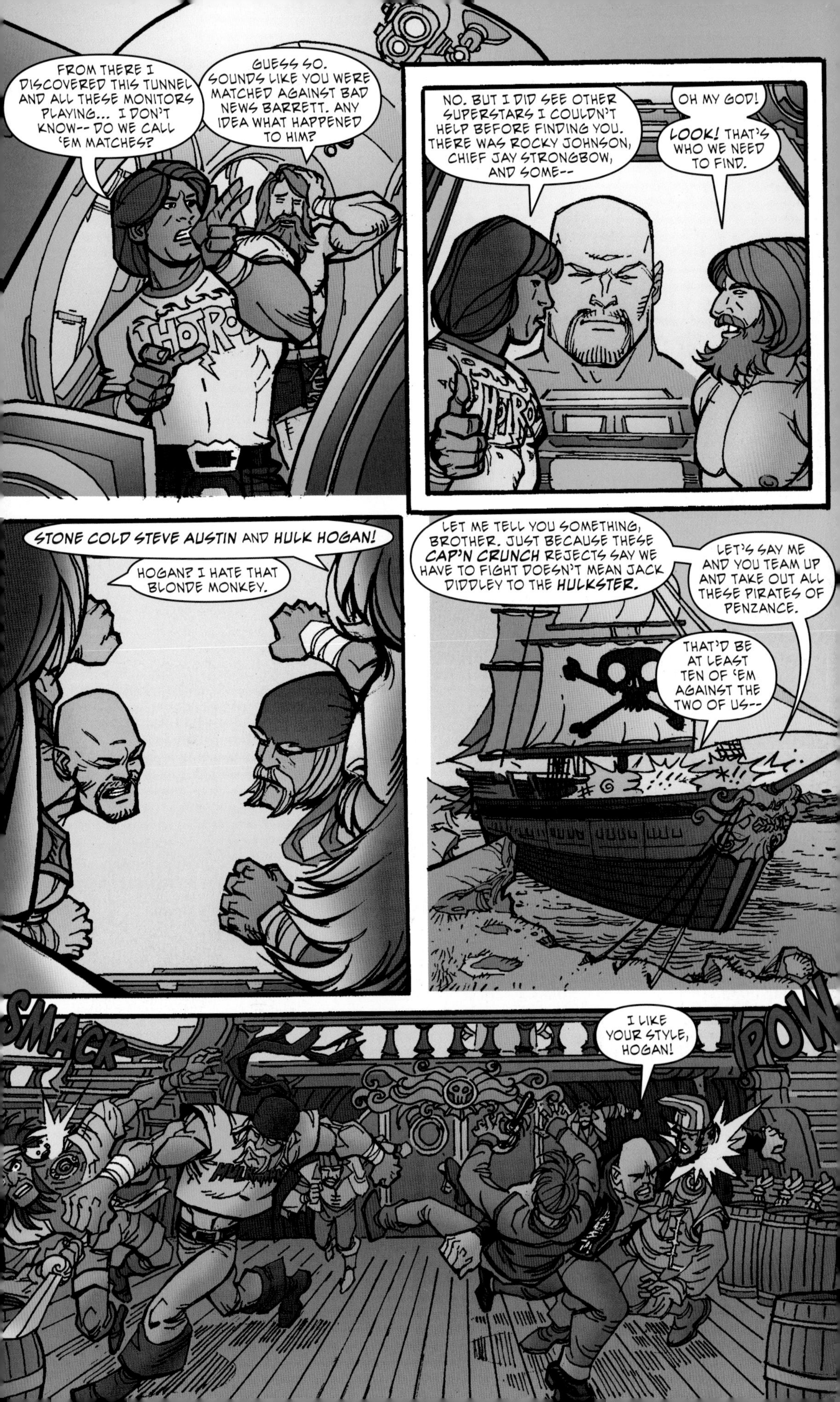
FROM THERE I DISCOVERED THIS TUNNEL AND ALL THESE MONITORS PLAYING... I DON'T KNOW-- DO WE CALL 'EM MATCHES?
GUESS SO. SOUNDS LIKE YOU WERE MATCHED AGAINST BAD NEWS BARRETT. ANY IDEA WHAT HAPPENED TO HIM?
NO. BUT I DID SEE OTHER SUPERSTARS I COULDN'T HELP BEFORE FINDING YOU. THERE WAS ROCKY JOHNSON, CHIEF JAY STRONGBOW, AND SOME--
OH MY GOD!
LOOK! THAT'S WHO WE NEED TO FIND.
STONE COLD STEVE AUSTIN AND HULK HOGAN!
HOGAN? I HATE THAT BLONDE MONKEY.
LET ME TELL YOU SOMETHING, BROTHER. JUST BECAUSE THESE CAP'N CRUNCH REJECTS SAY WE HAVE TO FIGHT DOESN'T MEAN JACK DIDDLEY TO THE HULKSTER.
LET'S SAY ME AND YOU TEAM UP AND TAKE OUT ALL THESE PIRATES OF PENZANCE.
THAT'D BE AT LEAST TEN OF 'EM AGAINST THE TWO OF US--
SMACK
I LIKE YOUR STYLE, HOGAN!
POW

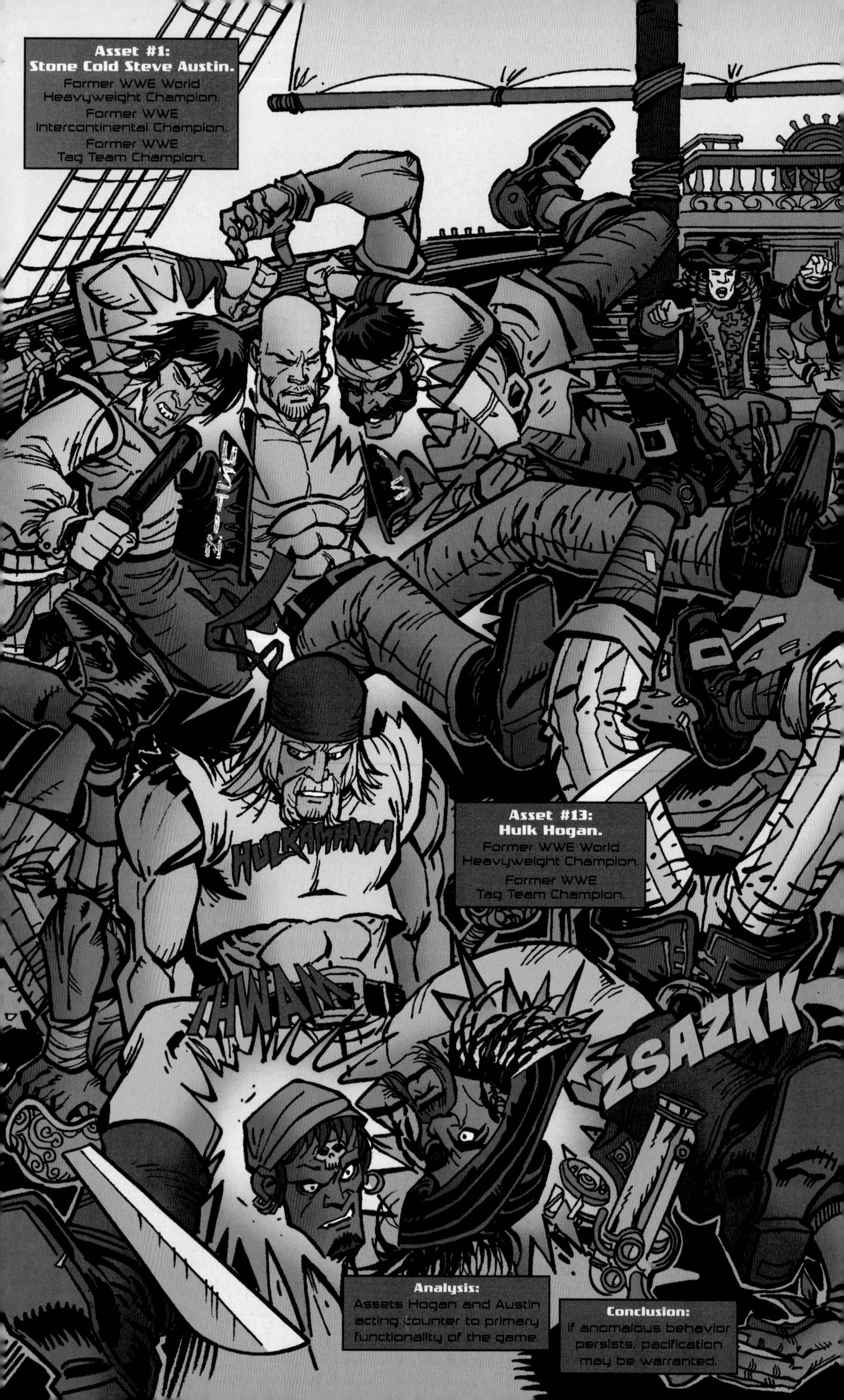
Asset #1:
Stone Cold Steve Austin.
Former WWE World Heavyweight Champion.
Former WWE Intercontinental Champion.
Former WWE Tag Team Champion.
Asset #13:
Hulk Hogan.
Former WWE World Heavyweight Champion.
Former WWE Tag Team Champion.
HULKAMANIA
THWAM
ZSAZKK
Analysis:
Assets Hogan and Austin acting counter to primary functionality of the game.
Conclusion:
If anomalous behavior persists, pacification may be warranted.

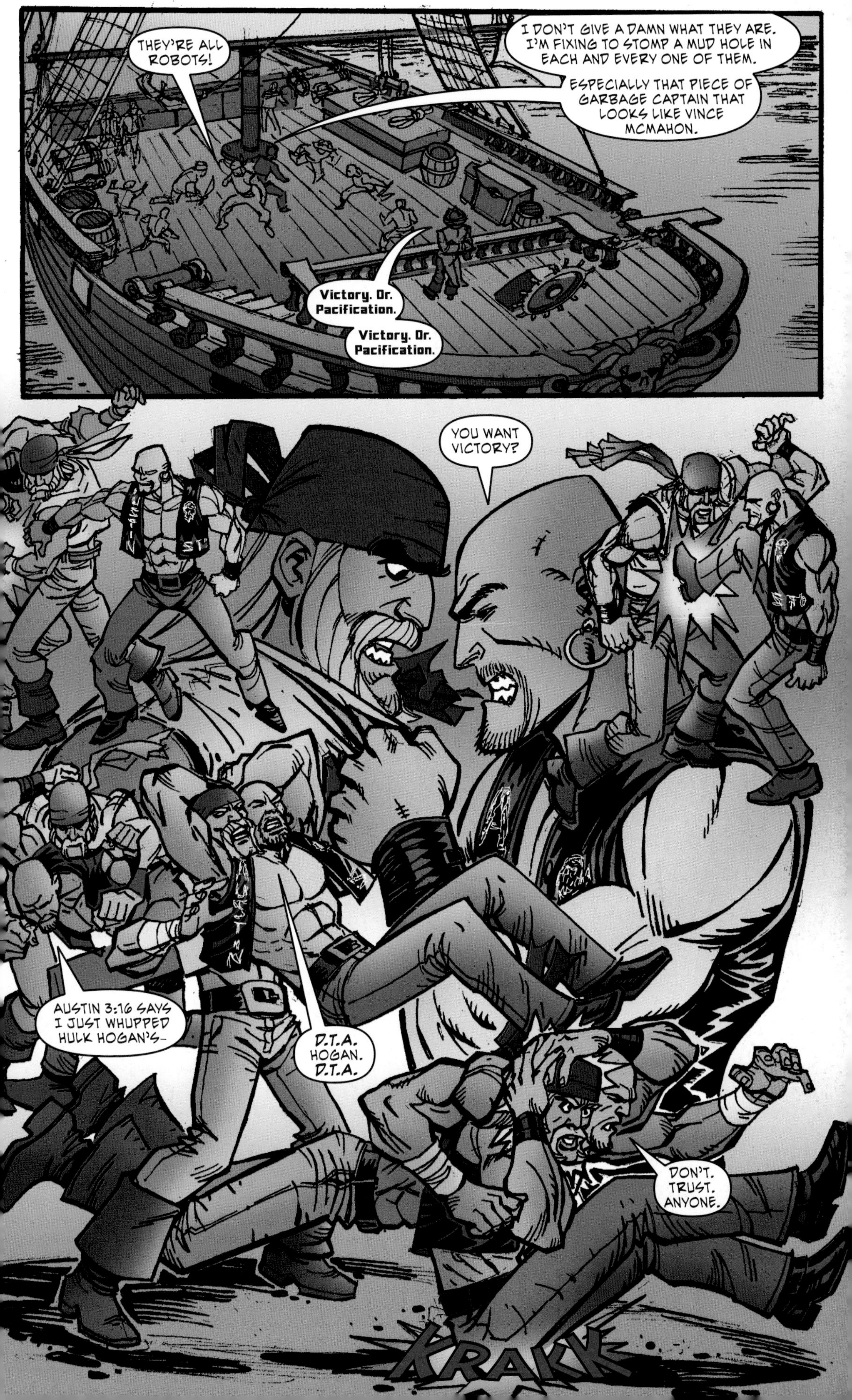
THEY'RE ALL ROBOTS!
I DON'T GIVE A DAMN WHAT THEY ARE. I'M FIXING TO STOMP A MUD HOLE IN EACH AND EVERY ONE OF THEM.
ESPECIALLY THAT PIECE OF GARBAGE CAPTAIN THAT LOOKS LIKE VINCE MCMAHON.
Victory. Or. Pacification.
Victory. Or. Pacification.
YOU WANT VICTORY?
AUSTIN 3:16 SAYS I JUST WHUPPED HULK HOGAN'S-
D.T.A. HOGAN. D.T.A.
DON'T. TRUST. ANYONE.
KRAKK

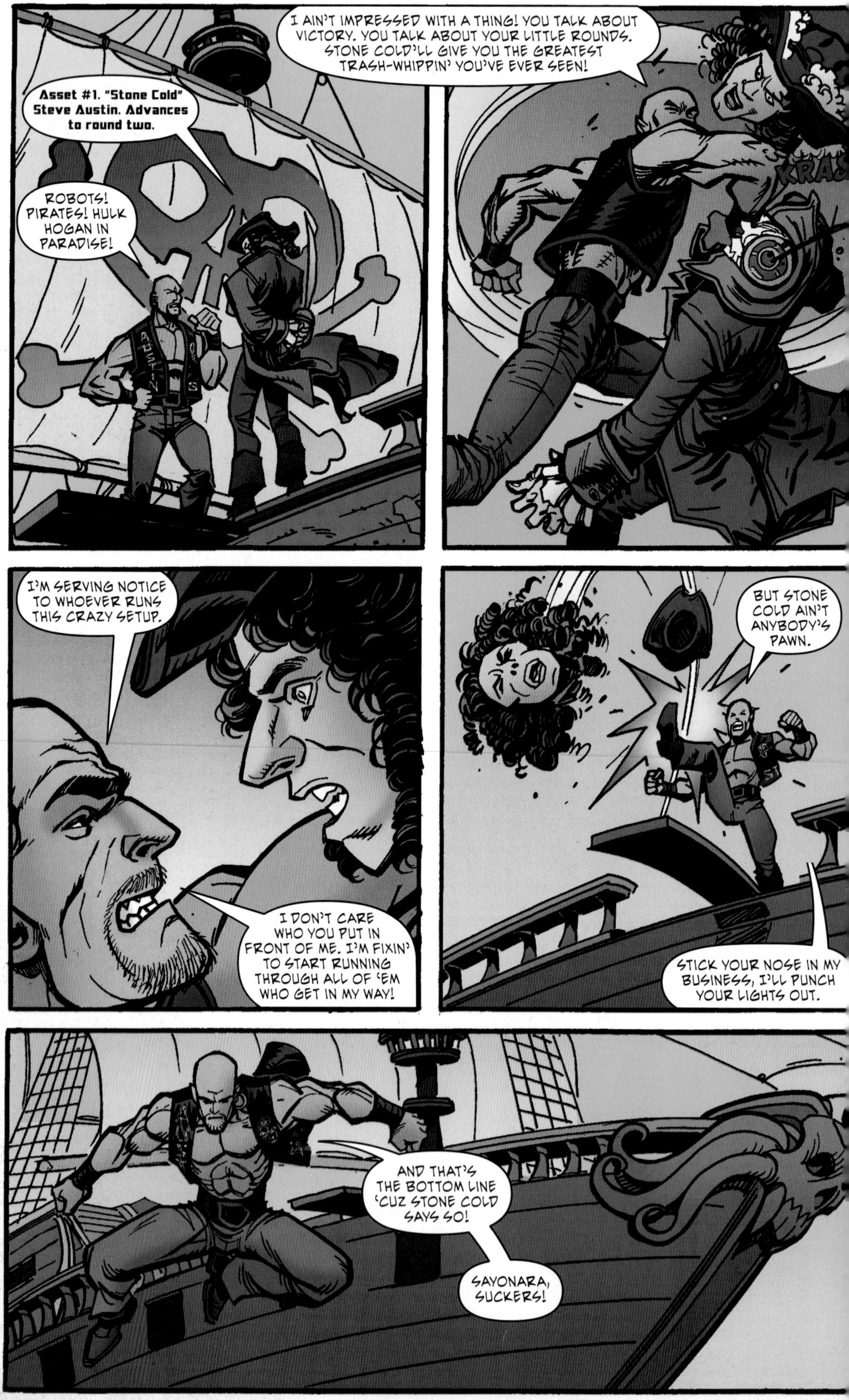

Asset #1. "Stone Cold" Steve Austin. Advances to round two.
ROBOTS! PIRATES! HULK HOGAN IN PARADISE!
I AIN'T IMPRESSED WITH A THING! YOU TALK ABOUT VICTORY. YOU TALK ABOUT YOUR LITTLE ROUNDS. STONE COLD'LL GIVE YOU THE GREATEST TRASH-WHIPPIN' YOU'VE EVER SEEN!
KRAS
I'M SERVING NOTICE TO WHOEVER RUNS THIS CRAZY SETUP.
I DON'T CARE WHO YOU PUT IN FRONT OF ME. I'M FIXIN' TO START RUNNING THROUGH ALL OF 'EM WHO GET IN MY WAY!
BUT STONE COLD AIN'T ANYBODY'S PAWN.
STICK YOUR NOSE IN MY BUSINESS, I'LL PUNCH YOUR LIGHTS OUT.
AND THAT'S THE BOTTOM LINE 'CUZ STONE COLD SAYS SO!
SAYONARA, SUCKERS!

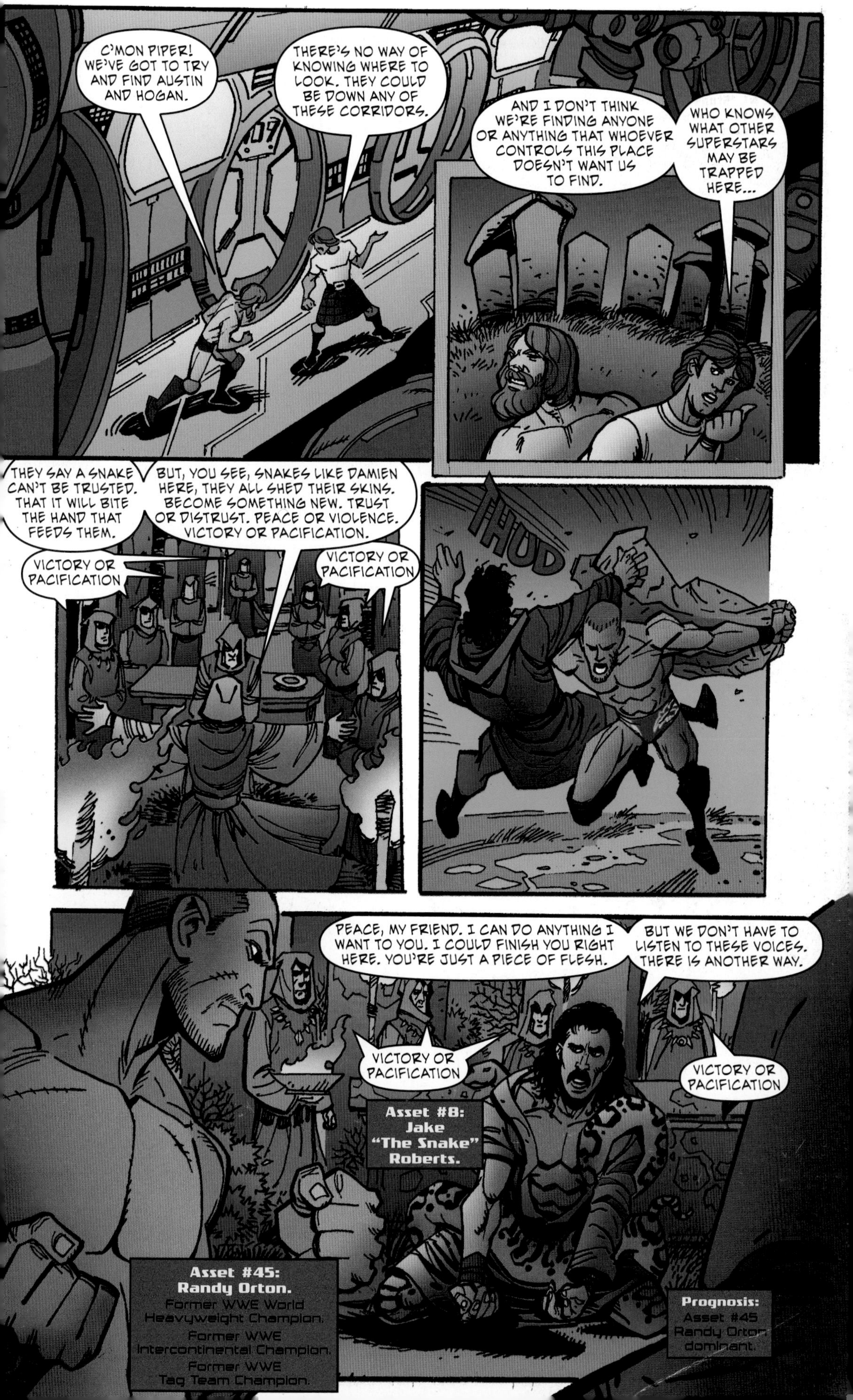

C'MON PIPER! WE'VE GOT TO TRY AND FIND AUSTIN AND HOGAN.
THERE'S NO WAY OF KNOWING WHERE TO LOOK. THEY COULD BE DOWN ANY OF THESE CORRIDORS.
AND I DON'T THINK WE'RE FINDING ANYONE OR ANYTHING THAT WHOEVER CONTROLS THIS PLACE DOESN'T WANT US TO FIND.
WHO KNOWS WHAT OTHER SUPERSTARS MAY BE TRAPPED HERE...
THEY SAY A SNAKE CAN'T BE TRUSTED. THAT IT WILL BITE THE HAND THAT FEEDS THEM.
BUT, YOU SEE, SNAKES LIKE DAMIEN HERE, THEY ALL SHED THEIR SKINS. BECOME SOMETHING NEW. TRUST OR DISTRUST. PEACE OR VIOLENCE. VICTORY OR PACIFICATION.
VICTORY OR PACIFICATION
VICTORY OR PACIFICATION
THUD
PEACE, MY FRIEND. I CAN DO ANYTHING I WANT TO YOU. I COULD FINISH YOU RIGHT HERE. YOU'RE JUST A PIECE OF FLESH.
BUT WE DON'T HAVE TO LISTEN TO THESE VOICES. THERE IS ANOTHER WAY.
VICTORY OR PACIFICATION
VICTORY OR PACIFICATION
Asset #8: Jake "The Snake" Roberts.
Asset #45: Randy Orton. Former WWE World Heavyweight Champion. Former WWE Intercontinental Champion. Former WWE Tag Team Champion.
Prognosis: Asset #45 Randy Orton dominant.

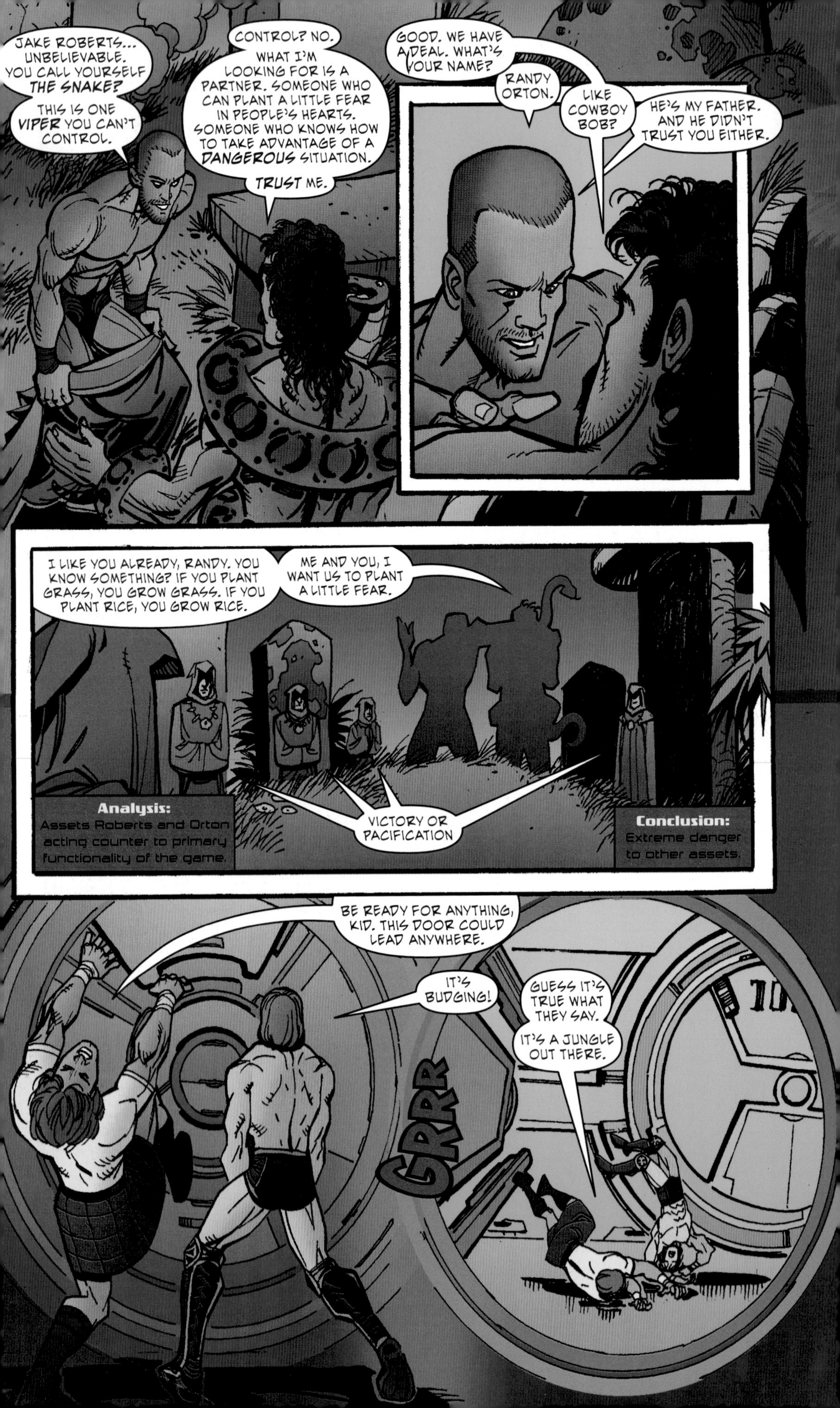

JAKE ROBERTS... UNBELIEVABLE. YOU CALL YOURSELF *THE SNAKE?*
THIS IS ONE *VIPER* YOU CAN'T CONTROL.
CONTROL? NO.
WHAT I'M LOOKING FOR IS A PARTNER. SOMEONE WHO CAN PLANT A LITTLE FEAR IN PEOPLE'S HEARTS. SOMEONE WHO KNOWS HOW TO TAKE ADVANTAGE OF A *DANGEROUS* SITUATION.
TRUST ME.
GOOD. WE HAVE A DEAL. WHAT'S YOUR NAME?
RANDY ORTON.
LIKE COWBOY BOB?
HE'S MY FATHER. AND HE DIDN'T TRUST YOU EITHER.
I LIKE YOU ALREADY, RANDY. YOU KNOW SOMETHING? IF YOU PLANT GRASS, YOU GROW GRASS. IF YOU PLANT RICE, YOU GROW RICE.
ME AND YOU, I WANT US TO PLANT A LITTLE FEAR.
Analysis:
Assets Roberts and Orton acting counter to primary functionality of the game.
VICTORY OR PACIFICATION
Conclusion:
Extreme danger to other assets.
BE READY FOR ANYTHING, KID. THIS DOOR COULD LEAD ANYWHERE.
IT'S BUDGING!
GRRR
GUESS IT'S TRUE WHAT THEY SAY.
IT'S A JUNGLE OUT THERE.

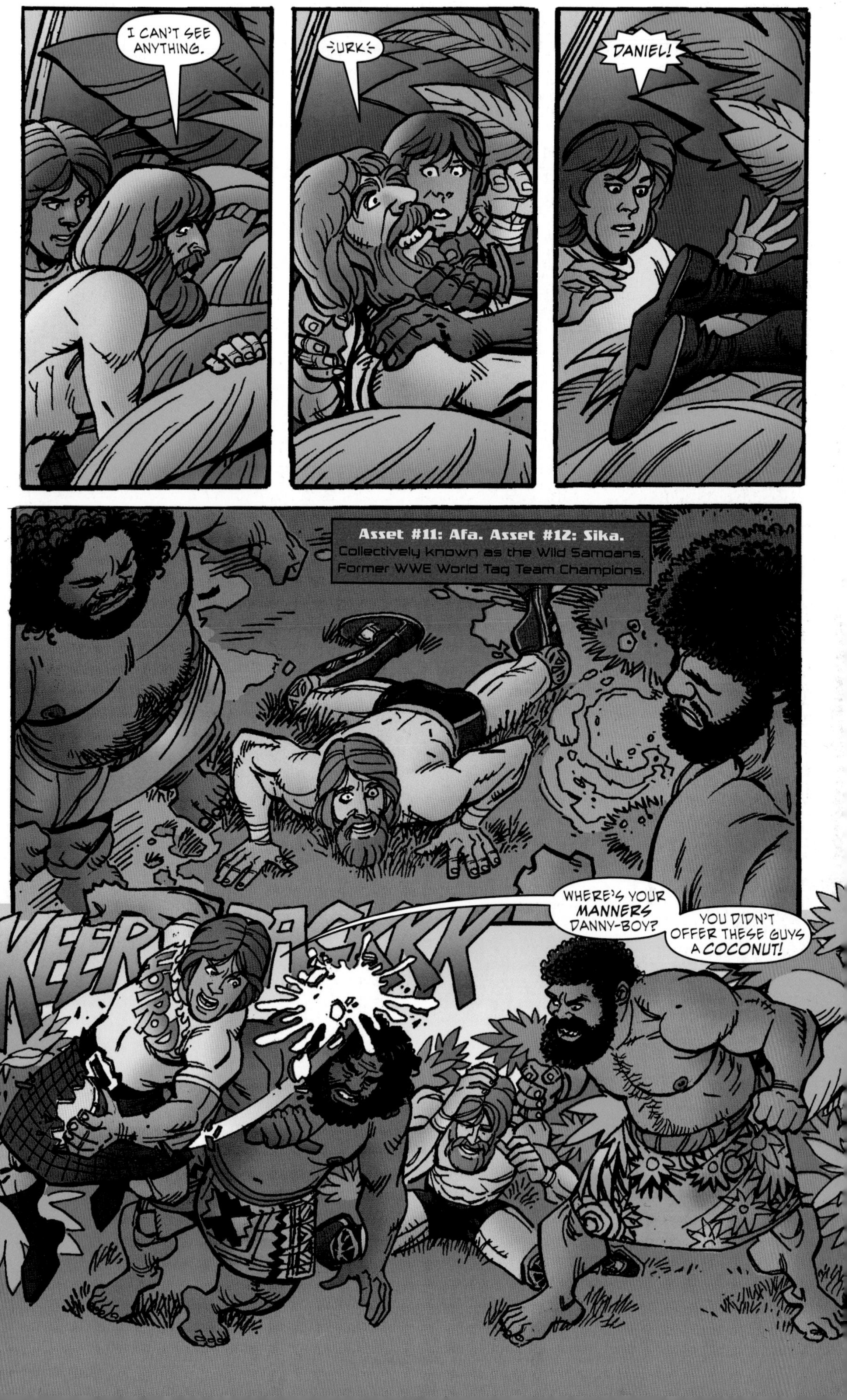

I CAN'T SEE ANYTHING.
URK
DANIEL!
Asset #11: Afa. Asset #12: Sika.
Collectively known as the Wild Samoans.
Former WWE World Tag Team Champions.
WHERE'S YOUR MANNERS DANNY-BOY?
YOU DIDN'T OFFER THESE GUYS A COCONUT!

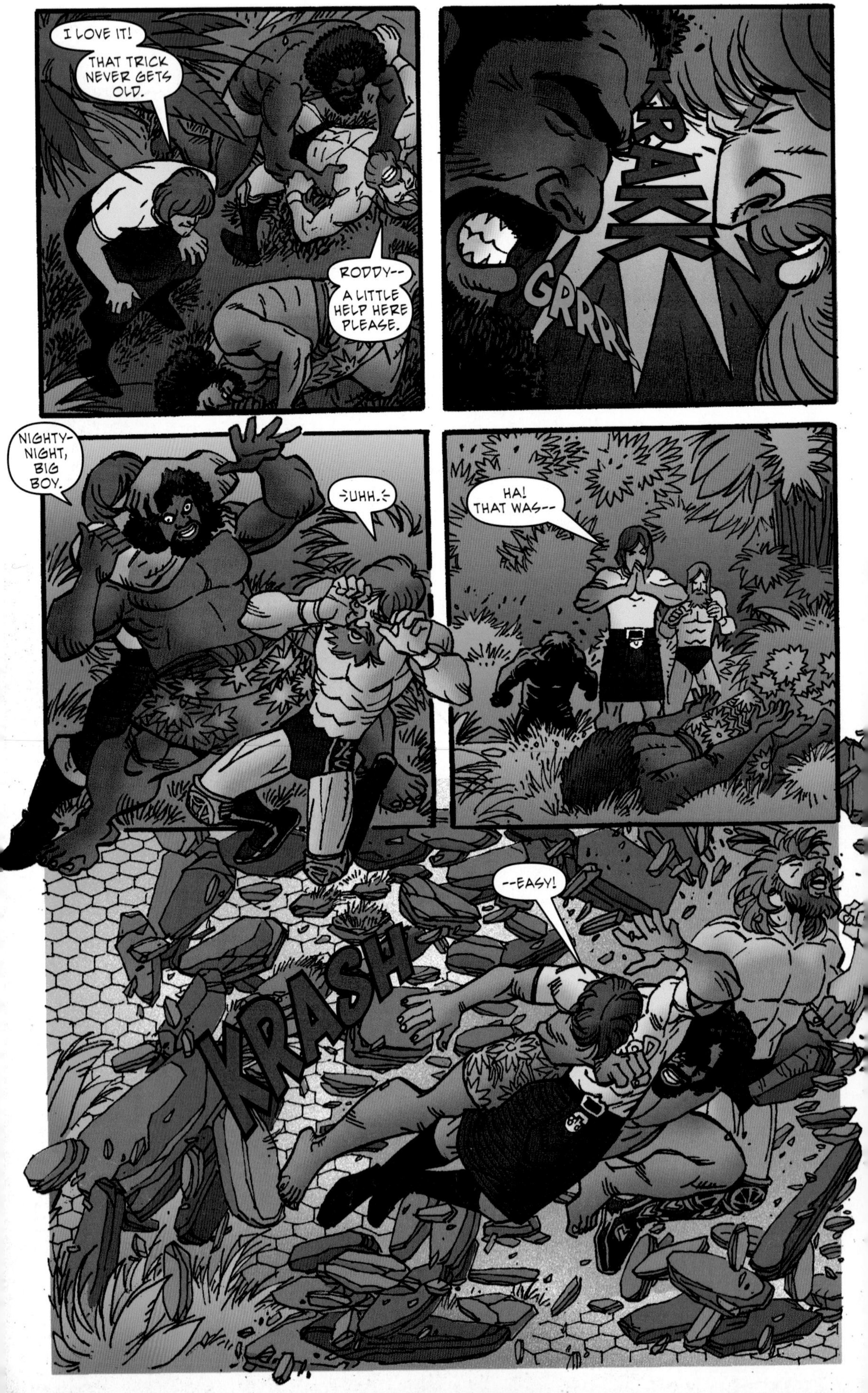

I LOVE IT!
THAT TRICK NEVER GETS OLD.
RODDY-- A LITTLE HELP HERE PLEASE.
KRAK
GRRRR
NIGHTY-NIGHT, BIG BOY.
UHH.
HA! THAT WAS--
--EASY!
KRASH

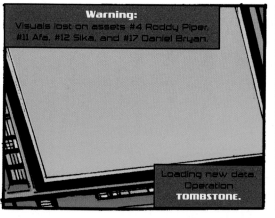

Warning:
Visuals lost on assets #4 Roddy Piper, #11 Afa, #12 Sika, and #17 Daniel Bryan.

Loading new data. Operation **TOMBSTONE.**

Asset #2:
Undertaker.
Former WWE World Heavyweight Champion.
Former WWE Tag Team Champion.
Former WWE Hardcore Champion.

O.K. CORRAL

WHOOSH

¥UGH.¥

NOW LISTEN UP MAGGOTS!

WHAT THE–?!

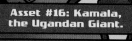

Asset #16: Kamala, the Ugandan Giant.

Asset #60: Big Show.
Former WWE World Heavyweight Champion.
Former WWE Intercontinental Champion.
Former WWE Tag Team Champion.
Former WWE United States Champion.
Former WWE Hardcore Champion.

Asset #58: Yokozuna.
Former WWE World Heavyweight Champion.
Former WWE Tag Team Champion.

Asset #19: Diesel
Former WWE World Heavyweight Champion.
Former WWE Intercontinental Champion.
Former WWE Tag Team Champion.

Asset #30: Vader.
Former WCW World Heavyweight Champion.

Asset #47: Gorilla Monsoon.

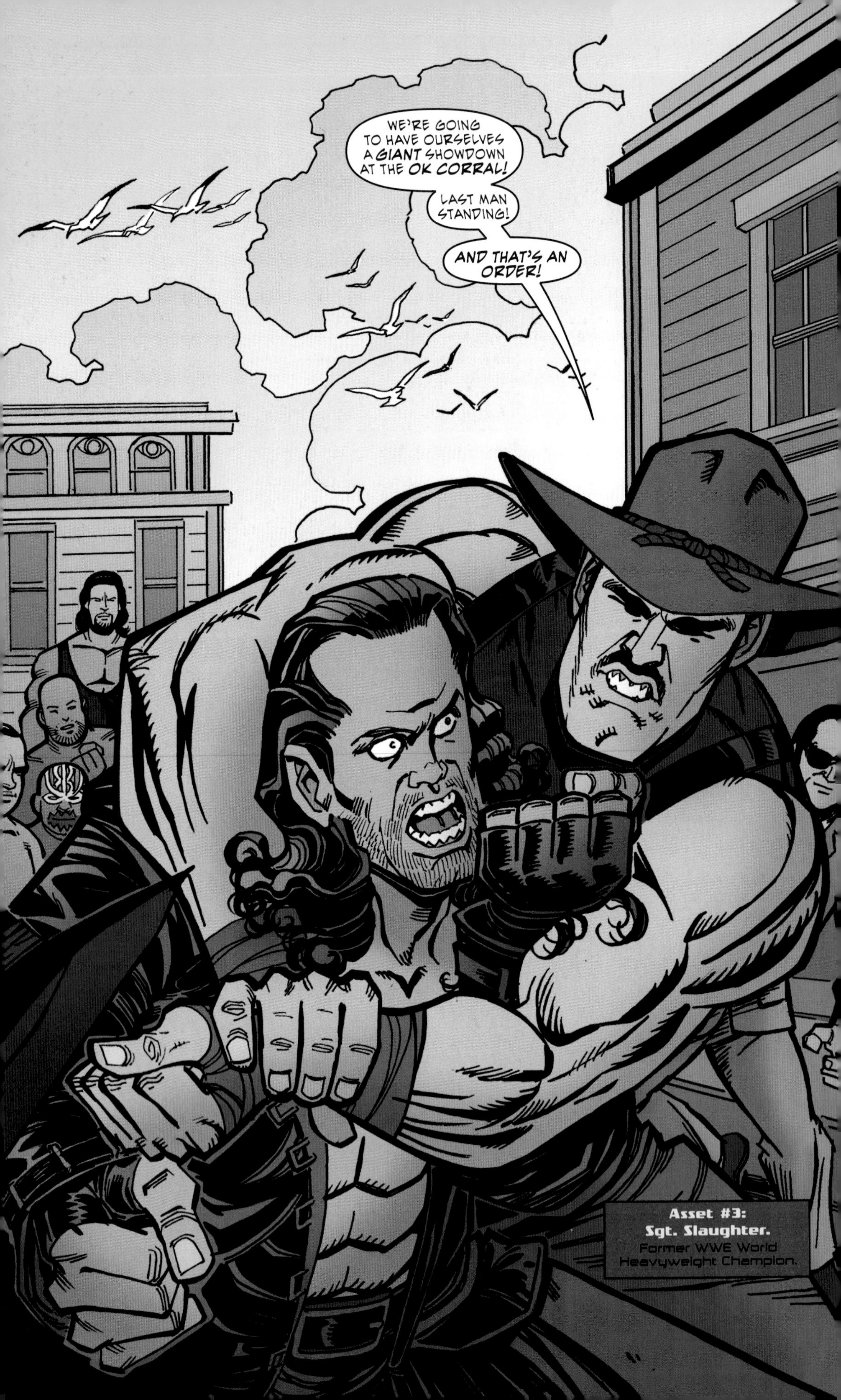
WE'RE GOING TO HAVE OURSELVES A GIANT SHOWDOWN AT THE OK CORRAL!
LAST MAN STANDING!
AND THAT'S AN ORDER!
Asset #3: Sgt. Slaughter.
Former WWE World Heavyweight Champion.

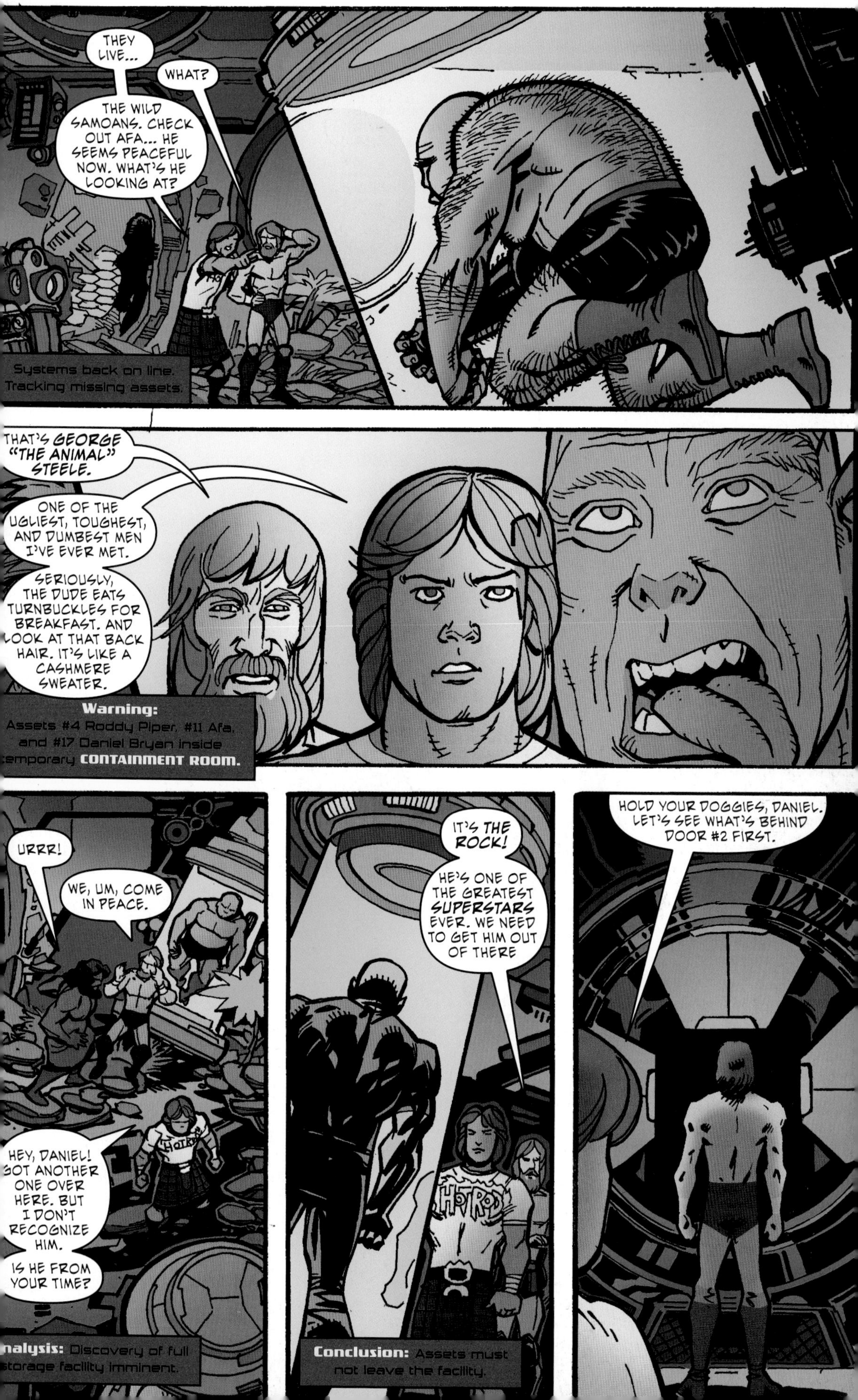
THEY LIVE...
WHAT?
THE WILD SAMOANS. CHECK OUT AFA... HE SEEMS PEACEFUL NOW. WHAT'S HE LOOKING AT?
Systems back on line. Tracking missing assets.
THAT'S GEORGE "THE ANIMAL" STEELE.
ONE OF THE UGLIEST, TOUGHEST, AND DUMBEST MEN I'VE EVER MET.
SERIOUSLY, THE DUDE EATS TURNBUCKLES FOR BREAKFAST. AND LOOK AT THAT BACK HAIR. IT'S LIKE A CASHMERE SWEATER.
Warning: Assets #4 Roddy Piper, #11 Afa, and #17 Daniel Bryan inside temporary CONTAINMENT ROOM.
URRR!
WE, UM, COME IN PEACE.
HEY, DANIEL! GOT ANOTHER ONE OVER HERE. BUT I DON'T RECOGNIZE HIM.
IS HE FROM YOUR TIME?
Analysis: Discovery of full storage facility imminent.
IT'S THE ROCK!
HE'S ONE OF THE GREATEST SUPERSTARS EVER. WE NEED TO GET HIM OUT OF THERE
Conclusion: Assets must not leave the facility.
HOLD YOUR DOGGIES, DANIEL. LET'S SEE WHAT'S BEHIND DOOR #2 FIRST.

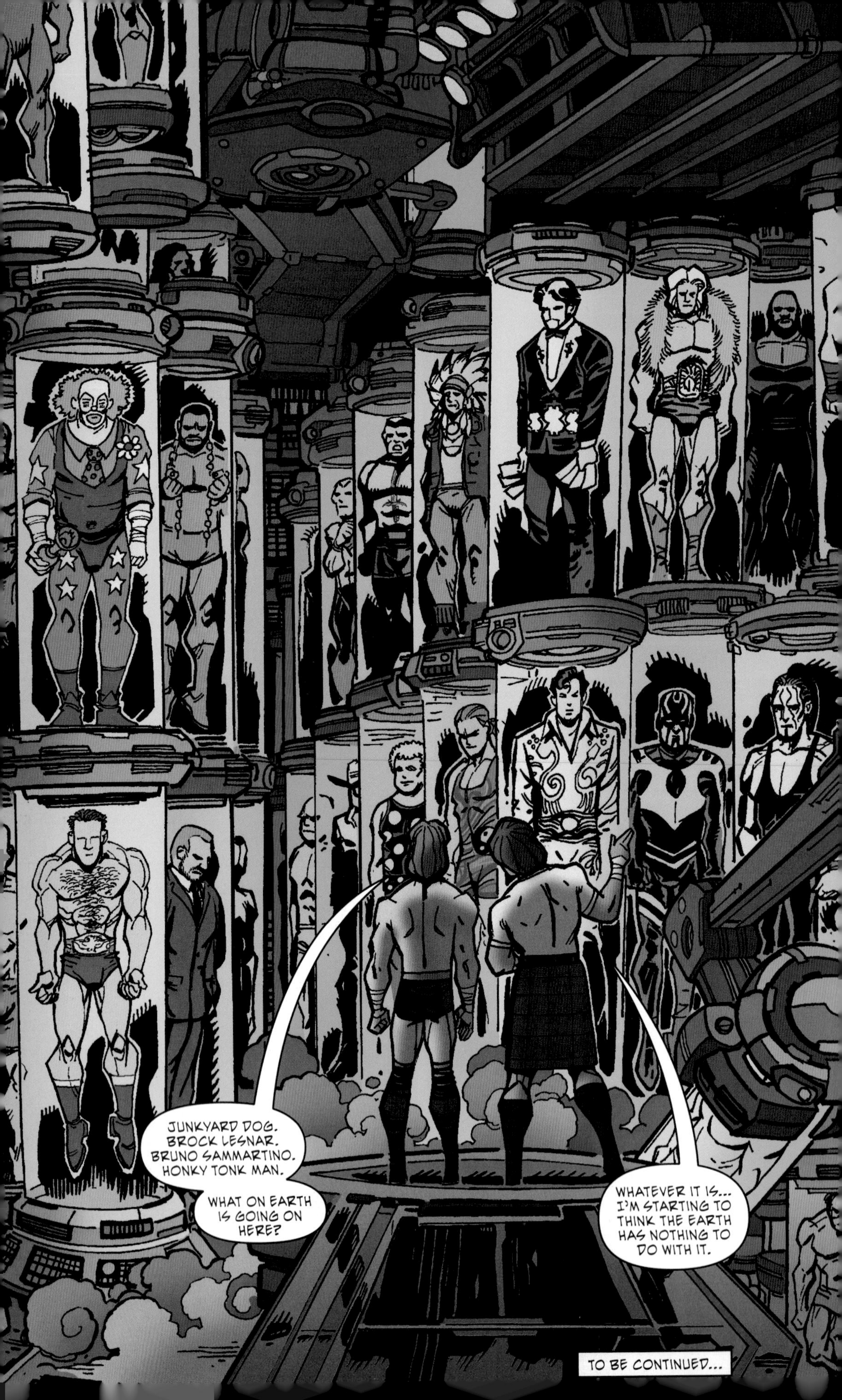

JUNKYARD DOG. BROCK LESNAR. BRUNO SAMMARTINO. HONKY TONK MAN.
WHAT ON EARTH IS GOING ON HERE?
WHATEVER IT IS... I'M STARTING TO THINK THE EARTH HAS NOTHING TO DO WITH IT.
TO BE CONTINUED...

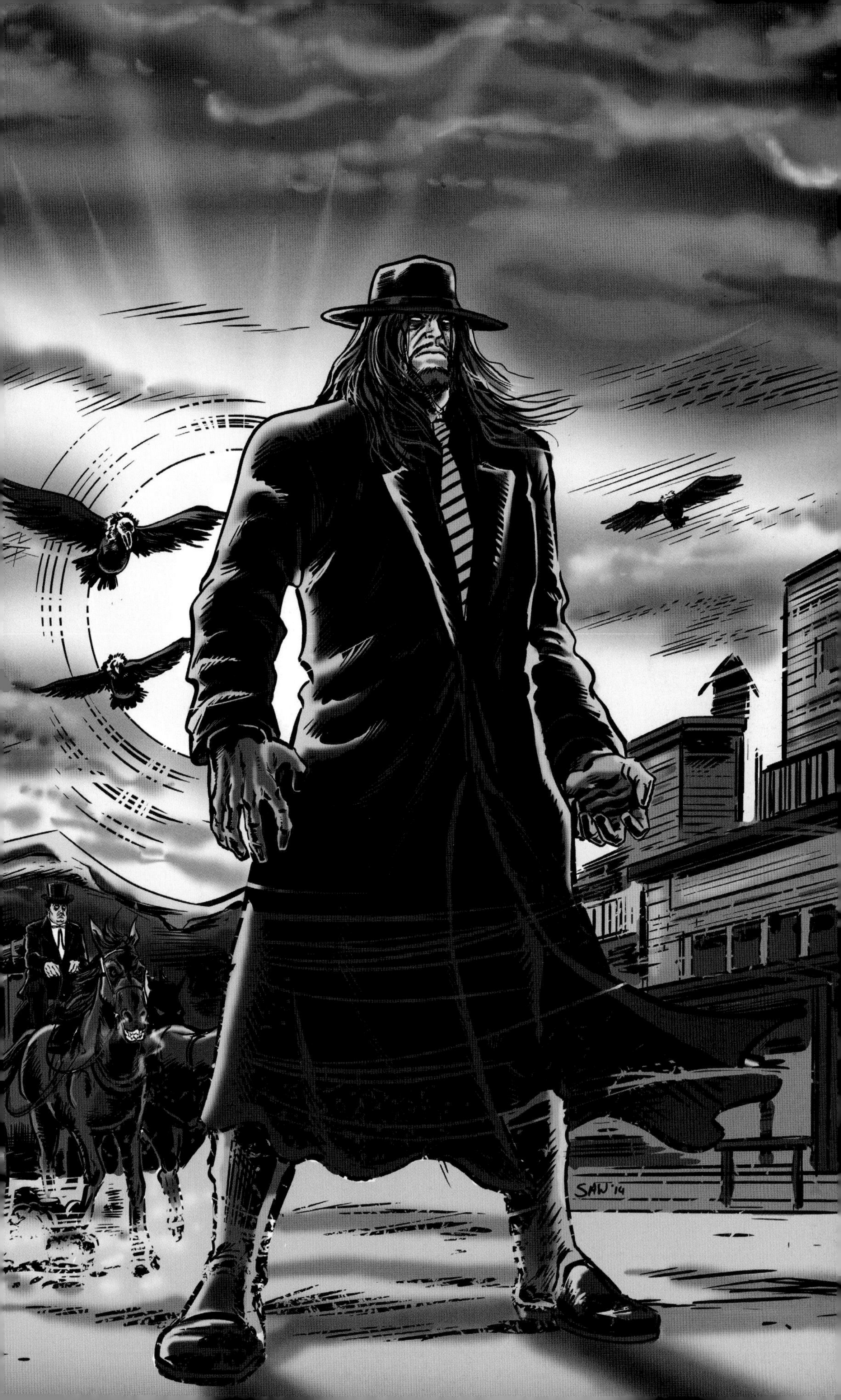
SAW '14

PART TWO "GIANTS"

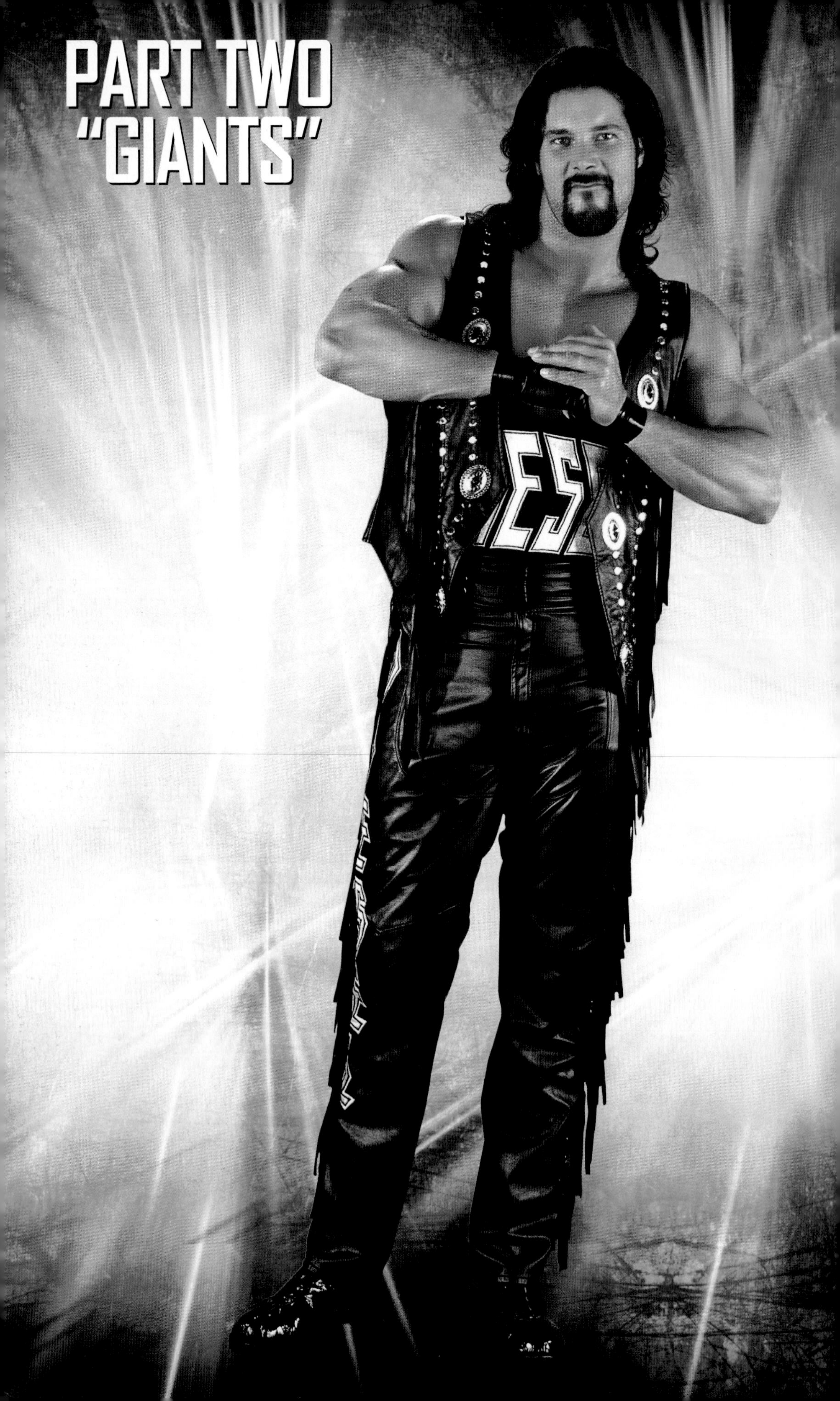

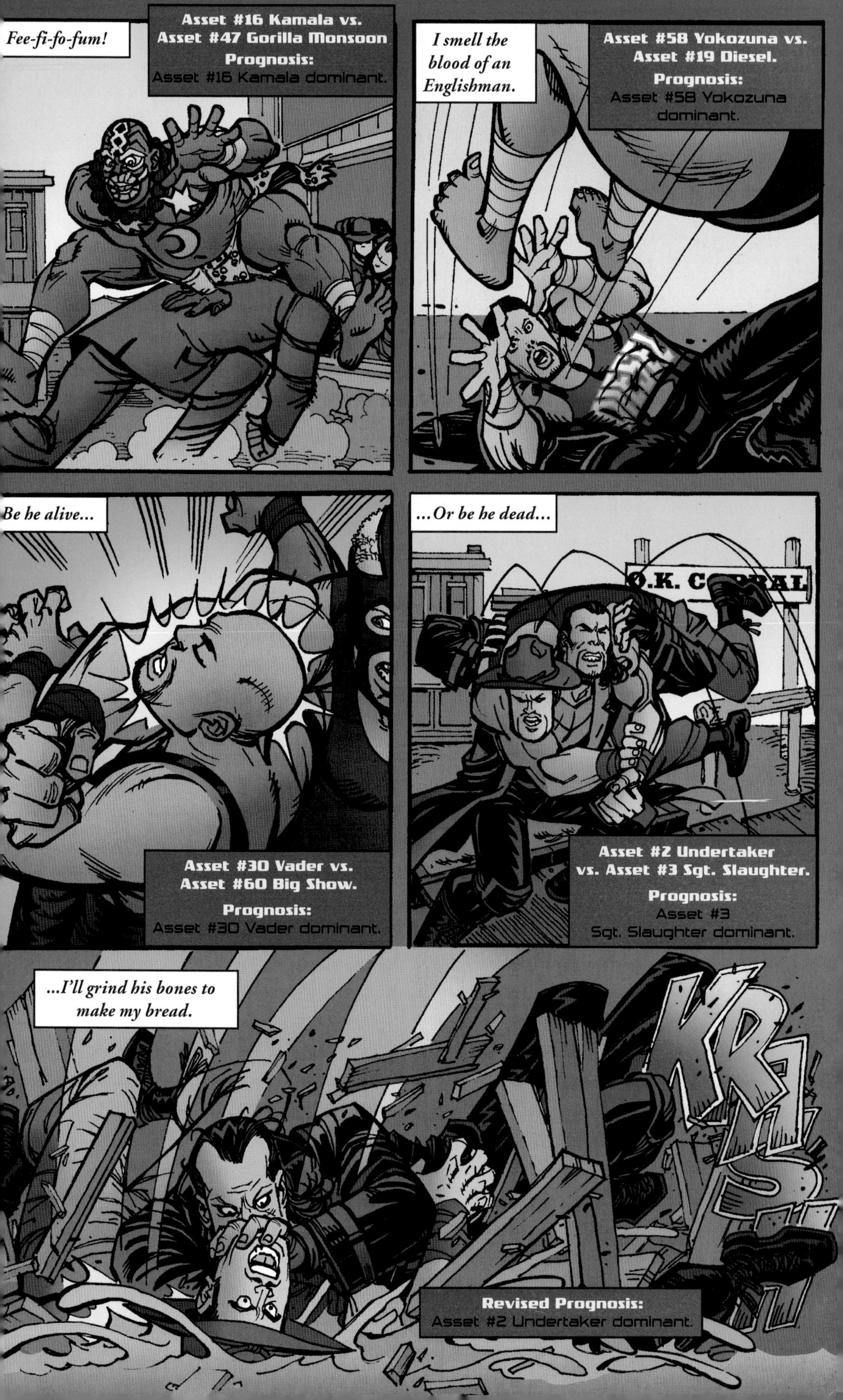
Fee-fi-fo-fum!
Asset #16 Kamala vs. Asset #47 Gorilla Monsoon
Prognosis:
Asset #16 Kamala dominant.
I smell the blood of an Englishman.
Asset #58 Yokozuna vs. Asset #19 Diesel.
Prognosis:
Asset #58 Yokozuna dominant.
Be he alive...
Asset #30 Vader vs. Asset #60 Big Show.
Prognosis:
Asset #30 Vader dominant.
...Or be he dead...
Asset #2 Undertaker vs. Asset #3 Sgt. Slaughter.
Prognosis:
Asset #3 Sgt. Slaughter dominant.
...I'll grind his bones to make my bread.
KRASH
Revised Prognosis:
Asset #2 Undertaker dominant.

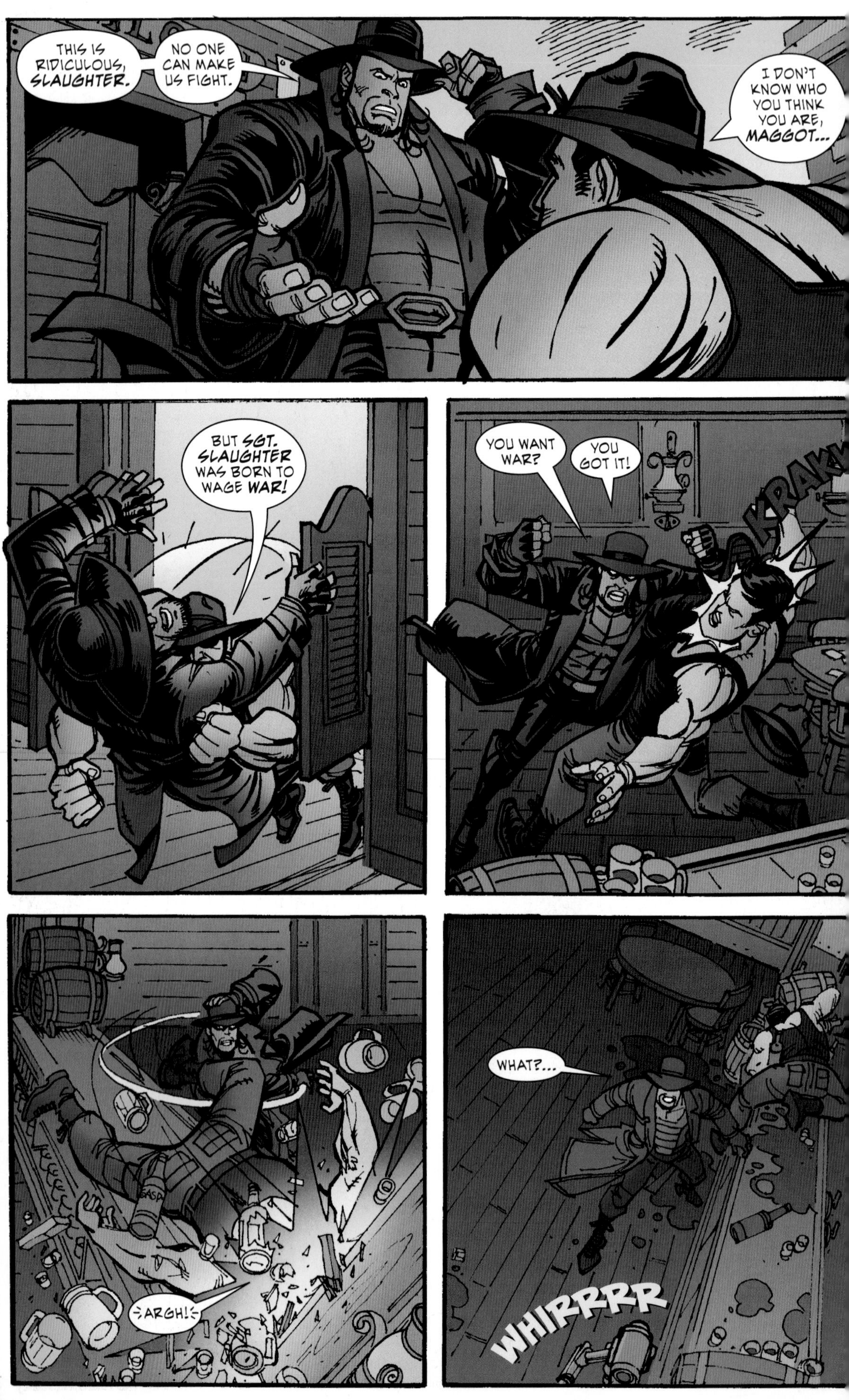

THIS IS RIDICULOUS, SLAUGHTER.
NO ONE CAN MAKE US FIGHT.
I DON'T KNOW WHO YOU THINK YOU ARE, MAGGOT...
BUT SGT. SLAUGHTER WAS BORN TO WAGE WAR!
YOU WANT WAR?
YOU GOT IT!
KRAK
ARGH!
WHAT?...
WHIRRRR

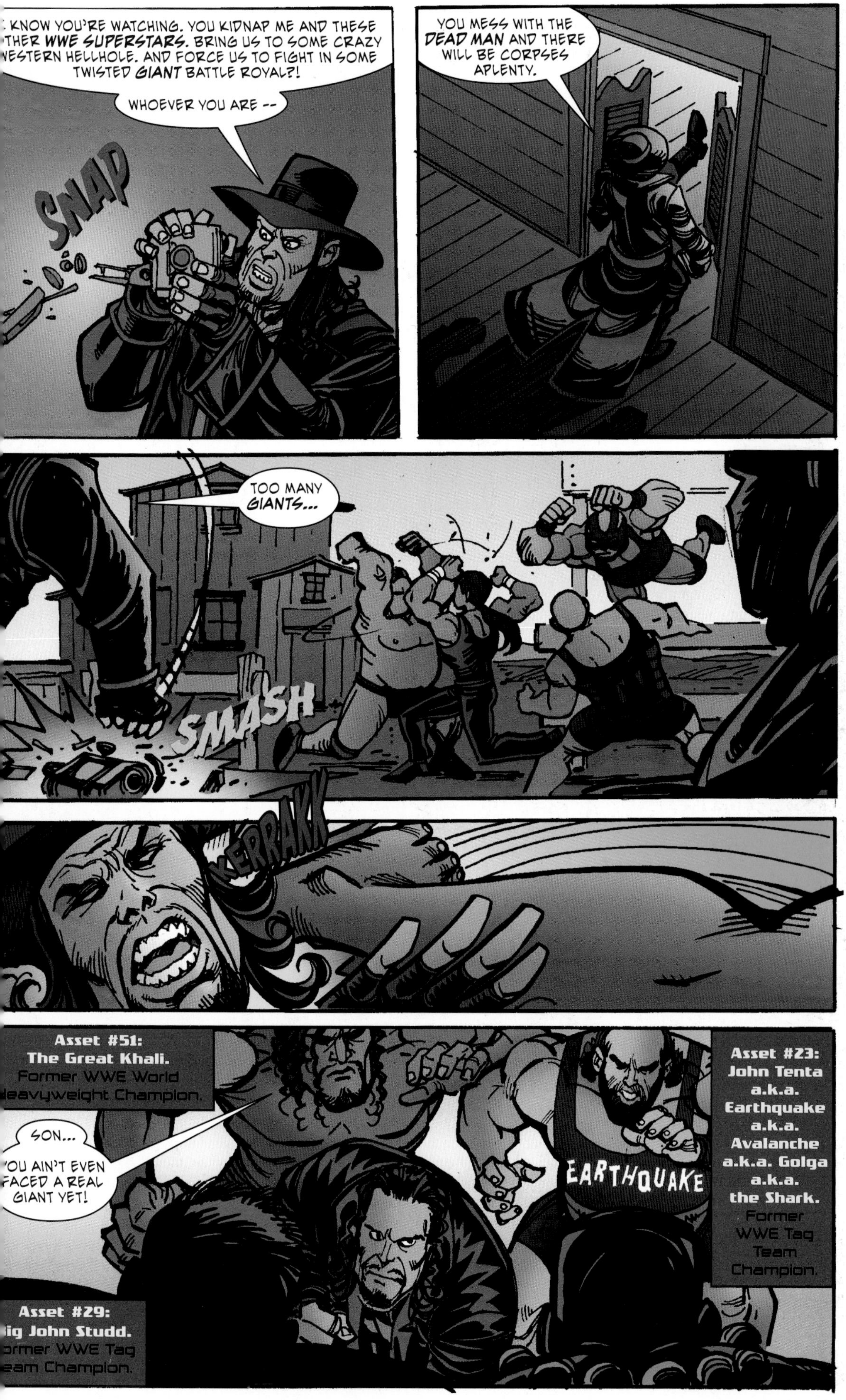

KNOW YOU'RE WATCHING. YOU KIDNAP ME AND THESE THER WWE SUPERSTARS. BRING US TO SOME CRAZY WESTERN HELLHOLE. AND FORCE US TO FIGHT IN SOME TWISTED GIANT BATTLE ROYAL?!
WHOEVER YOU ARE --
SNAP
YOU MESS WITH THE DEAD MAN AND THERE WILL BE CORPSES APLENTY.
TOO MANY GIANTS...
SMASH
KERRAKK
Asset #51: The Great Khali. Former WWE World Heavyweight Champion.
SON...
YOU AIN'T EVEN FACED A REAL GIANT YET!
Asset #23: John Tenta a.k.a. Earthquake a.k.a. Avalanche a.k.a. Golga a.k.a. the Shark. Former WWE Tag Team Champion.
EARTHQUAKE
Asset #29: Big John Studd. Former WWE Tag Team Champion.

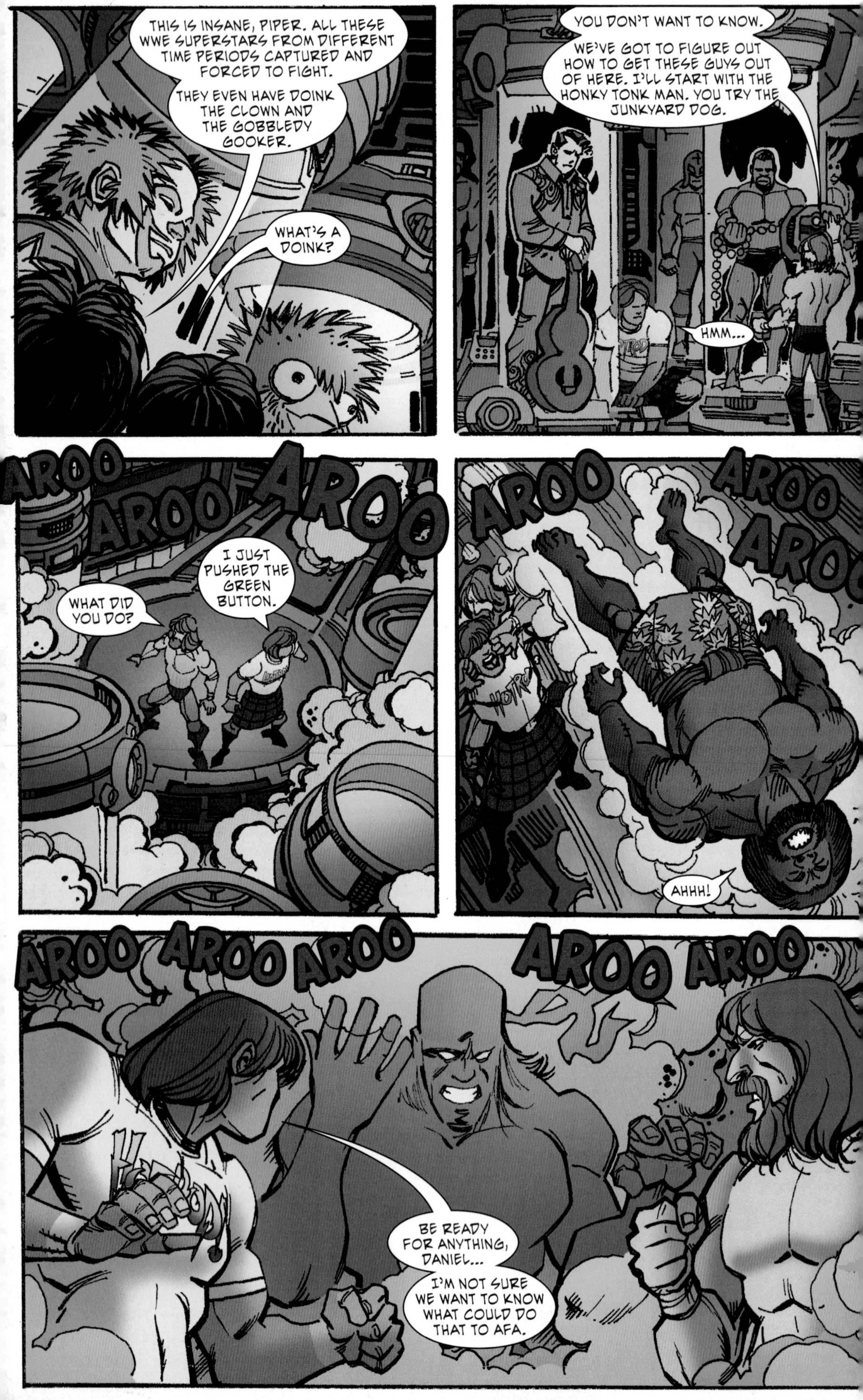
THIS IS INSANE, PIPER. ALL THESE WWE SUPERSTARS FROM DIFFERENT TIME PERIODS CAPTURED AND FORCED TO FIGHT.
THEY EVEN HAVE DOINK THE CLOWN AND THE GOBBLEDY GOOKER.
WHAT'S A DOINK?
YOU DON'T WANT TO KNOW.
WE'VE GOT TO FIGURE OUT HOW TO GET THESE GUYS OUT OF HERE. I'LL START WITH THE HONKY TONK MAN. YOU TRY THE JUNKYARD DOG.
HMM...
AROO AROO AROO
WHAT DID YOU DO?
I JUST PUSHED THE GREEN BUTTON.
AROO AROO AROO
AHHH!
AROO AROO AROO AROO AROO
BE READY FOR ANYTHING, DANIEL...
I'M NOT SURE WE WANT TO KNOW WHAT COULD DO THAT TO AFA.

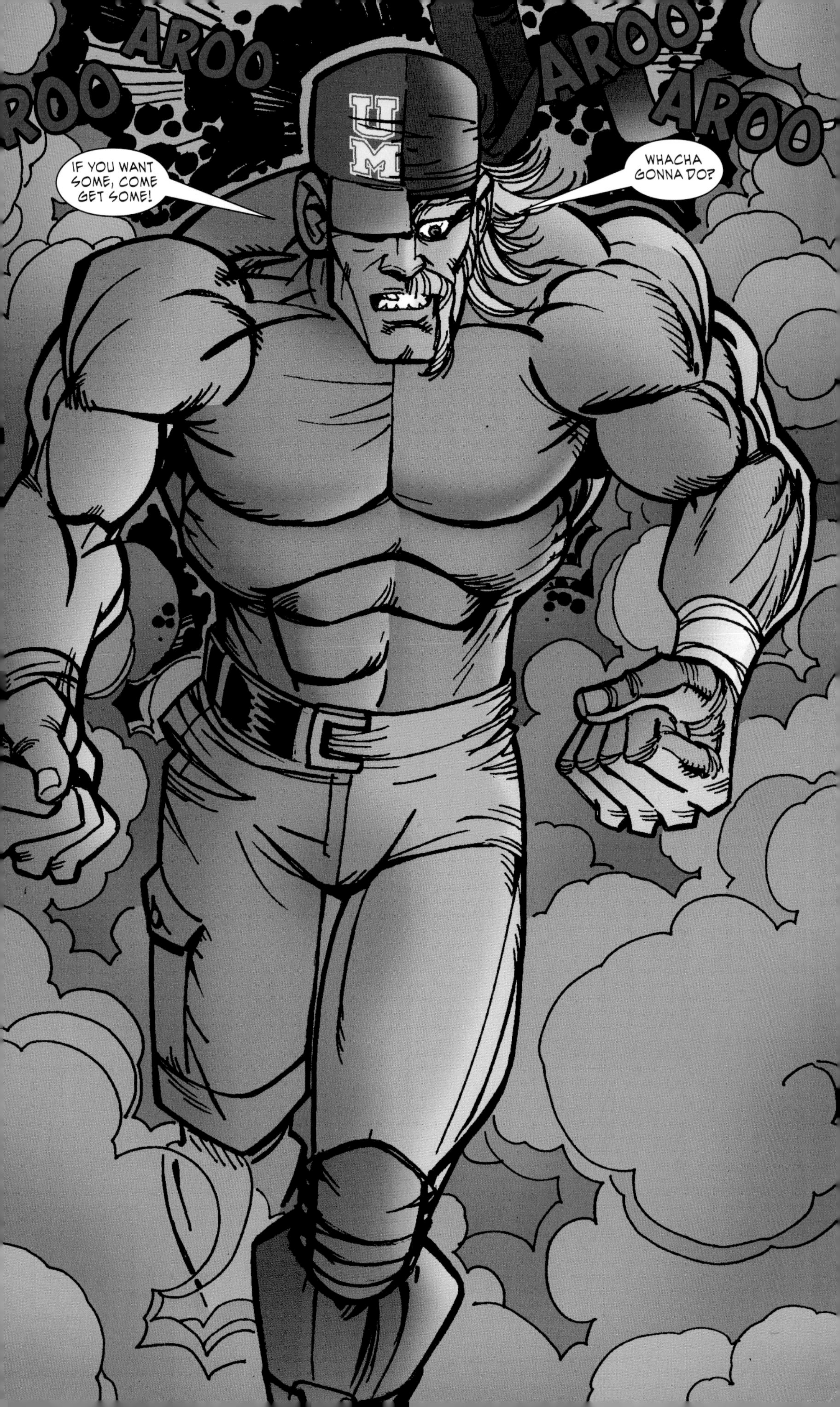
AROO AROO
AROO AROO
IF YOU WANT SOME, COME GET SOME!
WHACHA GONNA DO?

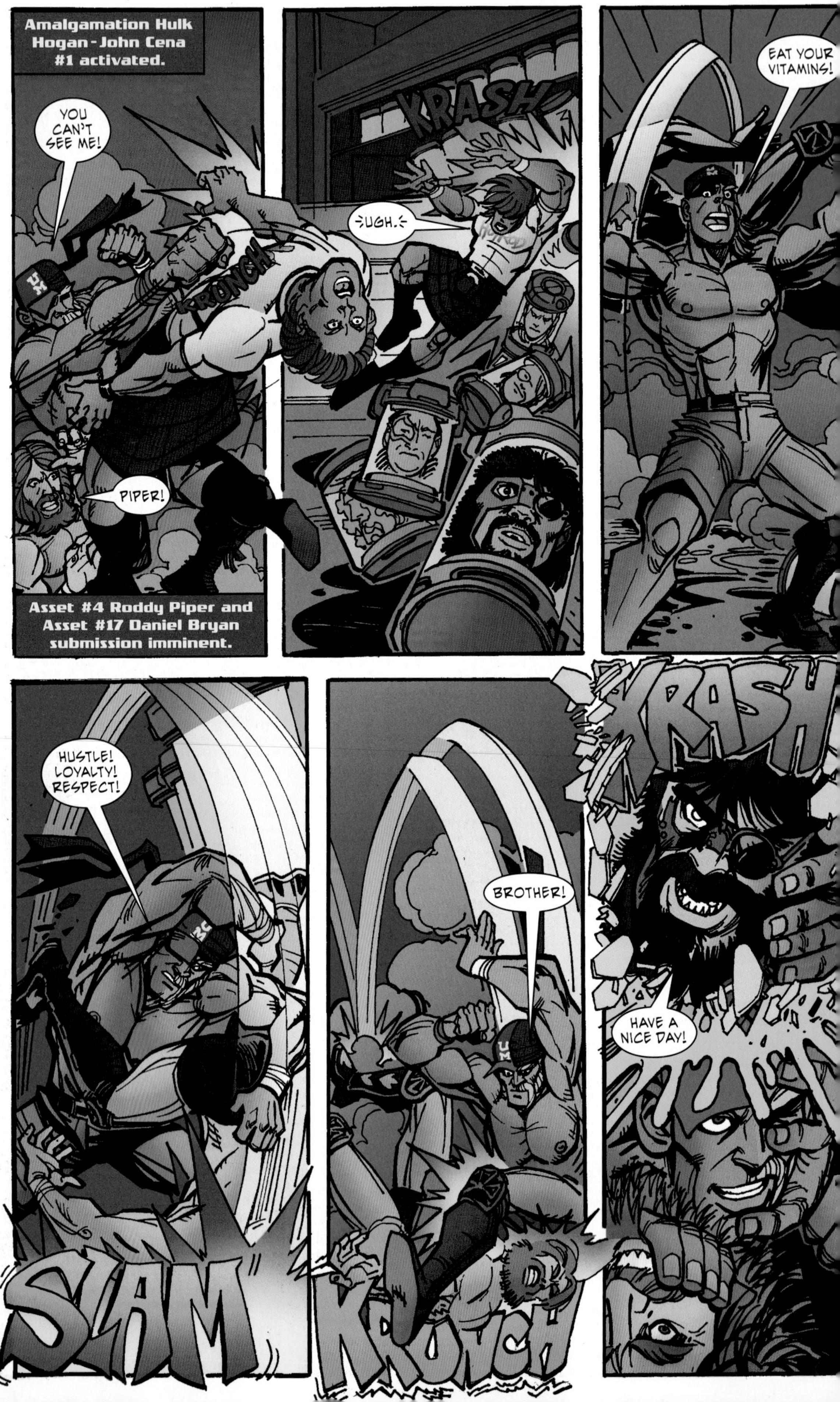

Amalgamation Hulk Hogan - John Cena #1 activated.
YOU CAN'T SEE ME!
KRUNCH
PIPER!
Asset #4 Roddy Piper and Asset #17 Daniel Bryan submission imminent.
KRASH
-UGH.-
EAT YOUR VITAMINS!
HUSTLE! LOYALTY! RESPECT!
SLAM
BROTHER!
KRUNCH
KRASH
HAVE A NICE DAY!

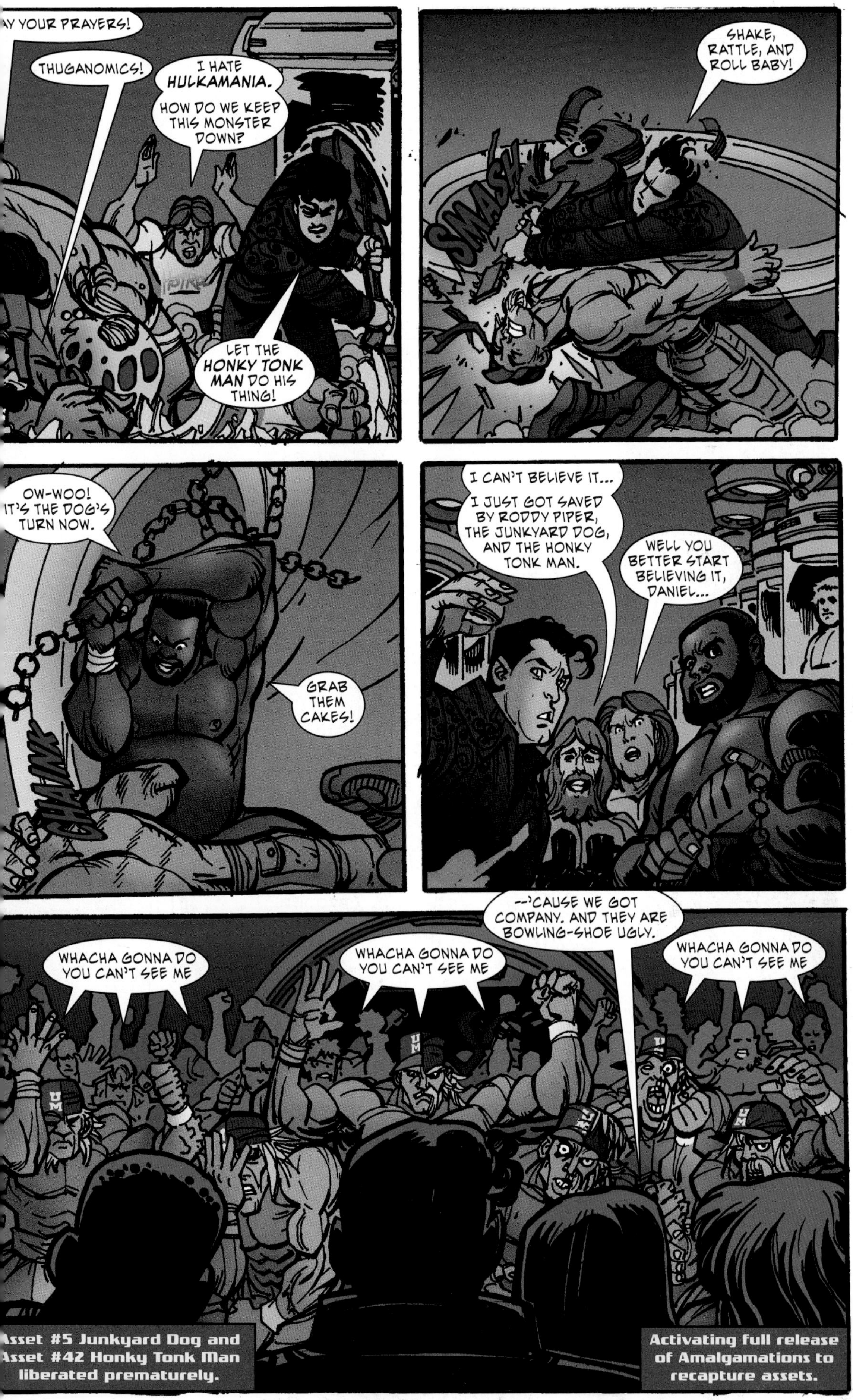
AY YOUR PRAYERS!
THUGANOMICS!
I HATE HULKAMANIA.
HOW DO WE KEEP THIS MONSTER DOWN?
LET THE HONKY TONK MAN DO HIS THING!
SHAKE, RATTLE, AND ROLL BABY!
SMASH
OW-WOO! IT'S THE DOG'S TURN NOW.
GRAB THEM CAKES!
I CAN'T BELIEVE IT...
I JUST GOT SAVED BY RODDY PIPER, THE JUNKYARD DOG, AND THE HONKY TONK MAN.
WELL YOU BETTER START BELIEVING IT, DANIEL...
--'CAUSE WE GOT COMPANY. AND THEY ARE BOWLING-SHOE UGLY.
WHACHA GONNA DO YOU CAN'T SEE ME
WHACHA GONNA DO YOU CAN'T SEE ME
WHACHA GONNA DO YOU CAN'T SEE ME
Asset #5 Junkyard Dog and Asset #42 Honky Tonk Man liberated prematurely.
Activating full release of Amalgamations to recapture assets.

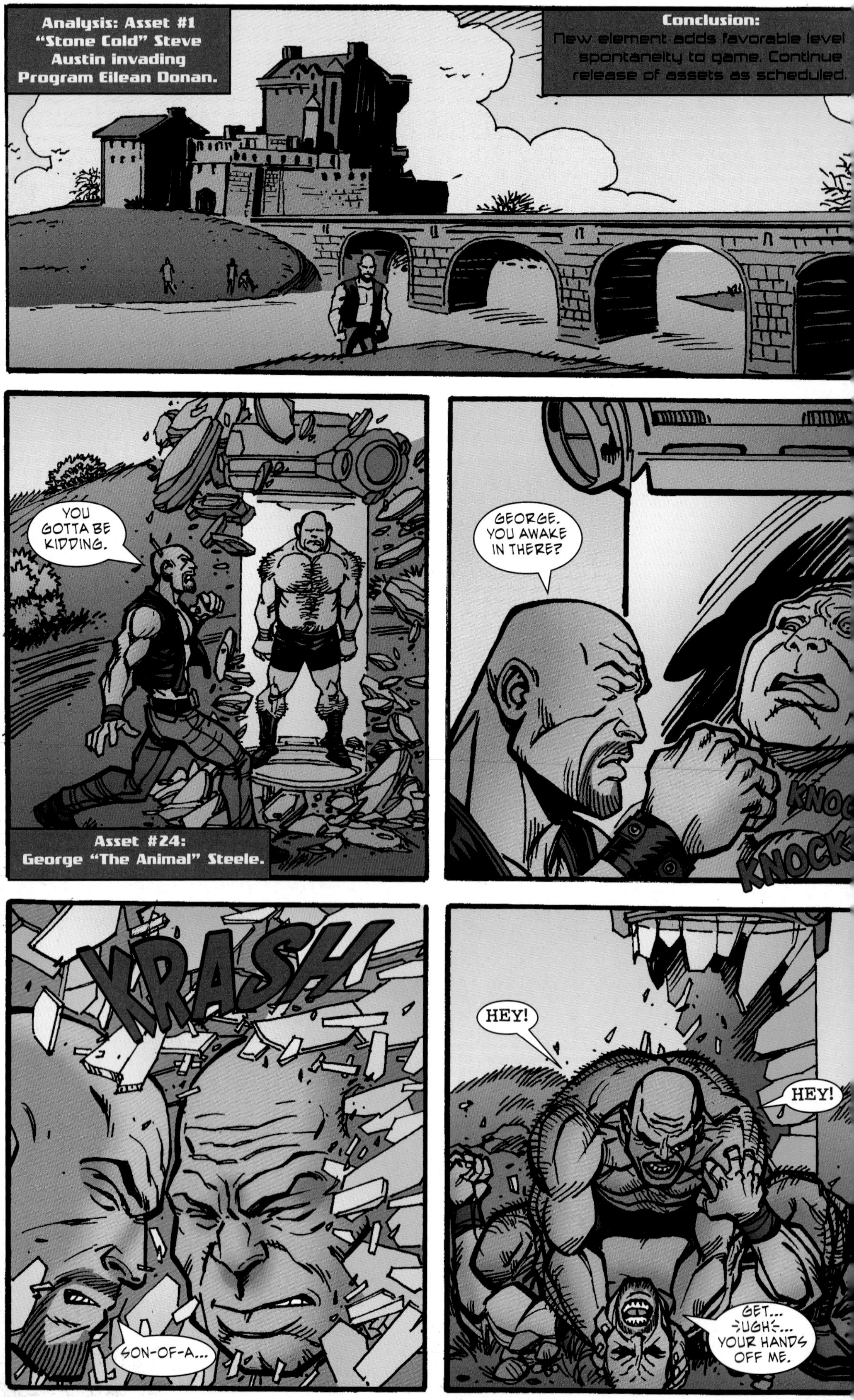
Analysis: Asset #1 "Stone Cold" Steve Austin invading Program Eilean Donan.
Conclusion:
New element adds favorable level spontaneity to game. Continue release of assets as scheduled.
YOU GOTTA BE KIDDING.
Asset #24: George "The Animal" Steele.
GEORGE. YOU AWAKE IN THERE?
KNOCK
KNOCK
KRASH
SON-OF-A...
HEY!
HEY!
GET... UGH... YOUR HANDS OFF ME.

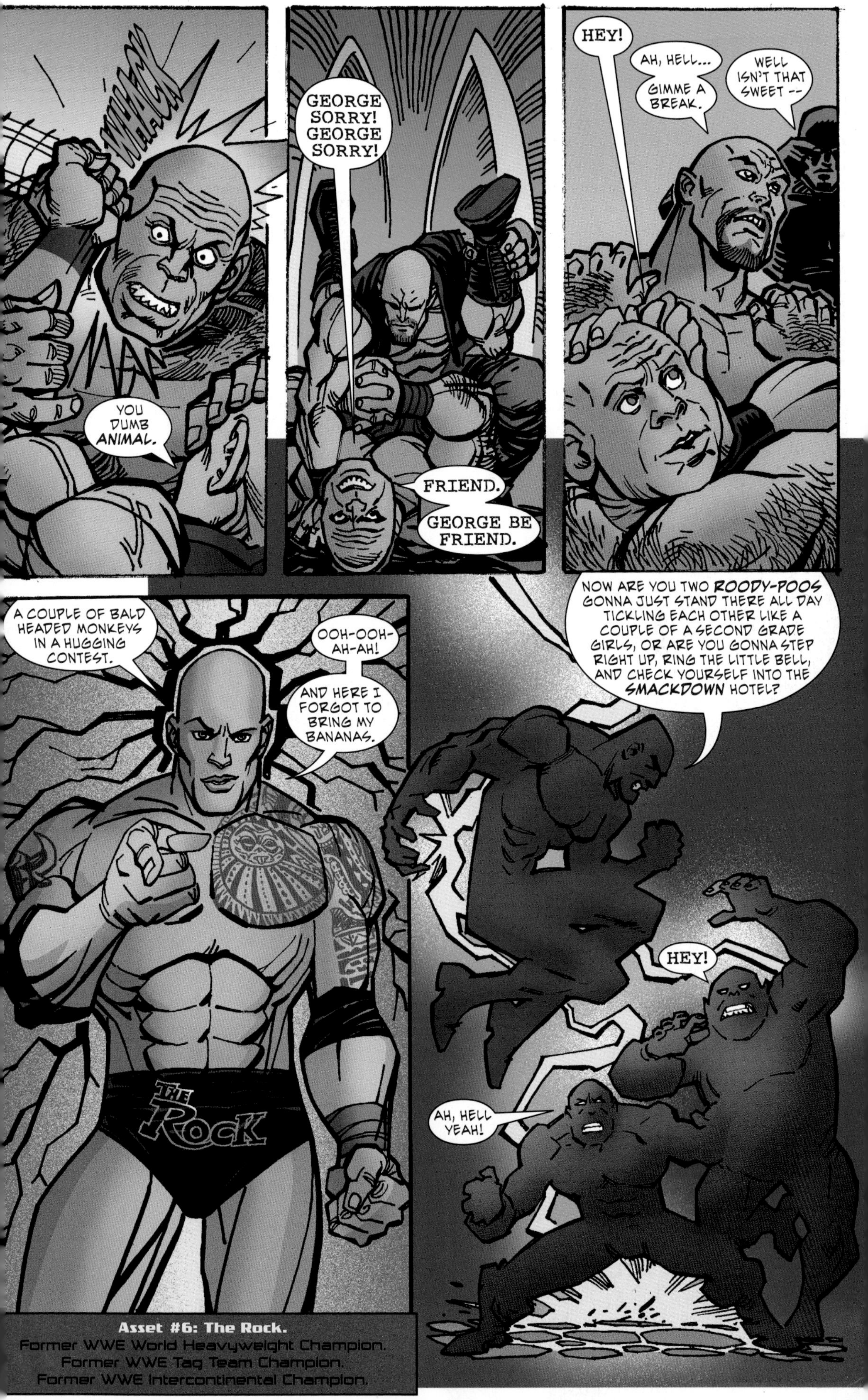
WHACK
YOU DUMB ANIMAL.
GEORGE SORRY! GEORGE SORRY!
FRIEND.
GEORGE BE FRIEND.
HEY!
AH, HELL...
GIMME A BREAK.
WELL ISN'T THAT SWEET --
A COUPLE OF BALD HEADED MONKEYS IN A HUGGING CONTEST.
OOH-OOH-AH-AH!
AND HERE I FORGOT TO BRING MY BANANAS.
NOW ARE YOU TWO ROODY-POOS GONNA JUST STAND THERE ALL DAY TICKLING EACH OTHER LIKE A COUPLE OF A SECOND GRADE GIRLS, OR ARE YOU GONNA STEP RIGHT UP, RING THE LITTLE BELL, AND CHECK YOURSELF INTO THE SMACKDOWN HOTEL?
THE ROCK
HEY!
AH, HELL YEAH!
Asset #6: The Rock.
Former WWE World Heavyweight Champion.
Former WWE Tag Team Champion.
Former WWE Intercontinental Champion.

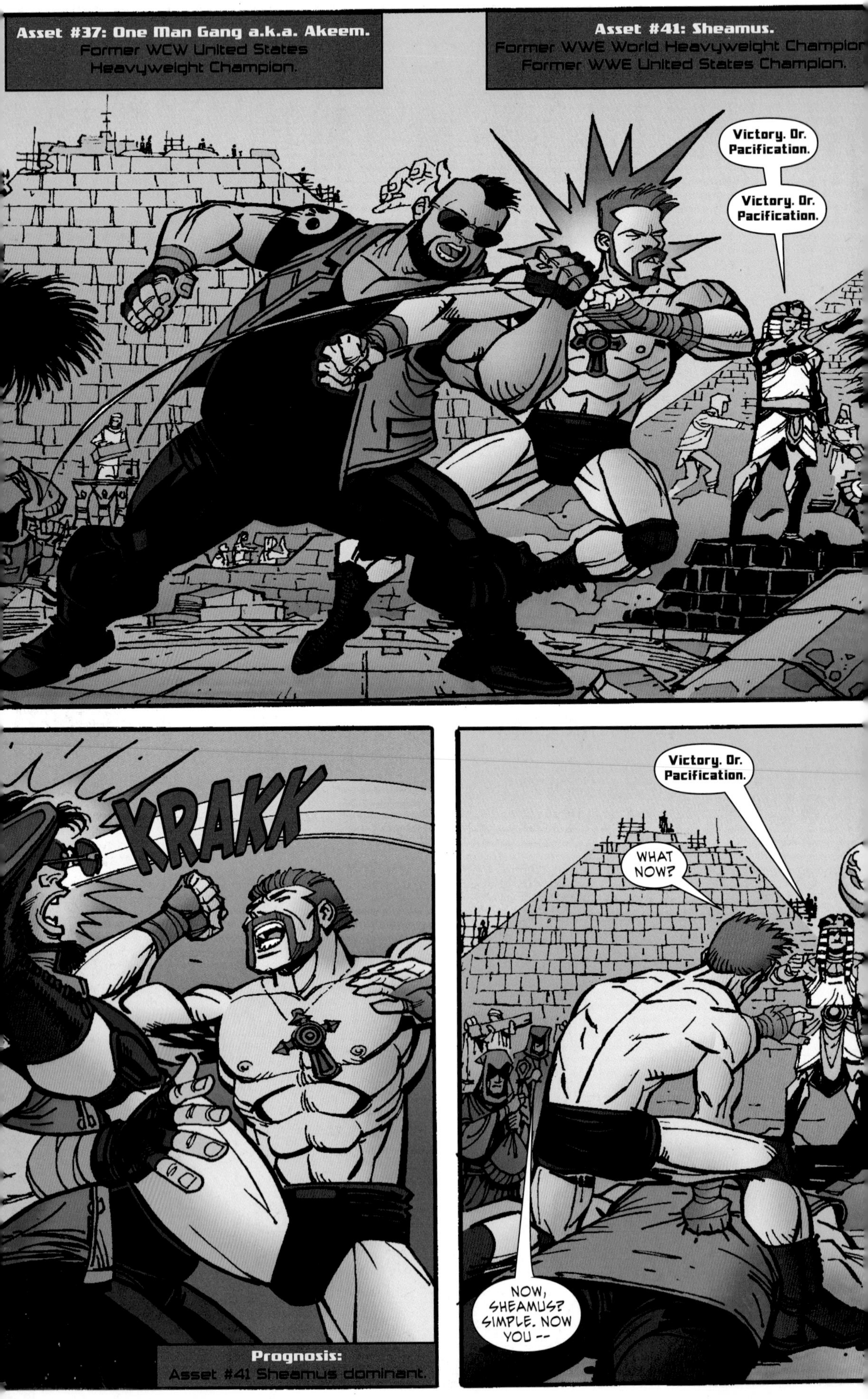
Asset #37: One Man Gang a.k.a. Akeem.
Former WCW United States Heavyweight Champion.
Asset #41: Sheamus.
Former WWE World Heavyweight Champion
Former WWE United States Champion.
Victory. Or. Pacification.
Victory. Or. Pacification.
KRAKK
Prognosis:
Asset #41 Sheamus dominant.
Victory. Or. Pacification.
WHAT NOW?
NOW, SHEAMUS? SIMPLE. NOW YOU --

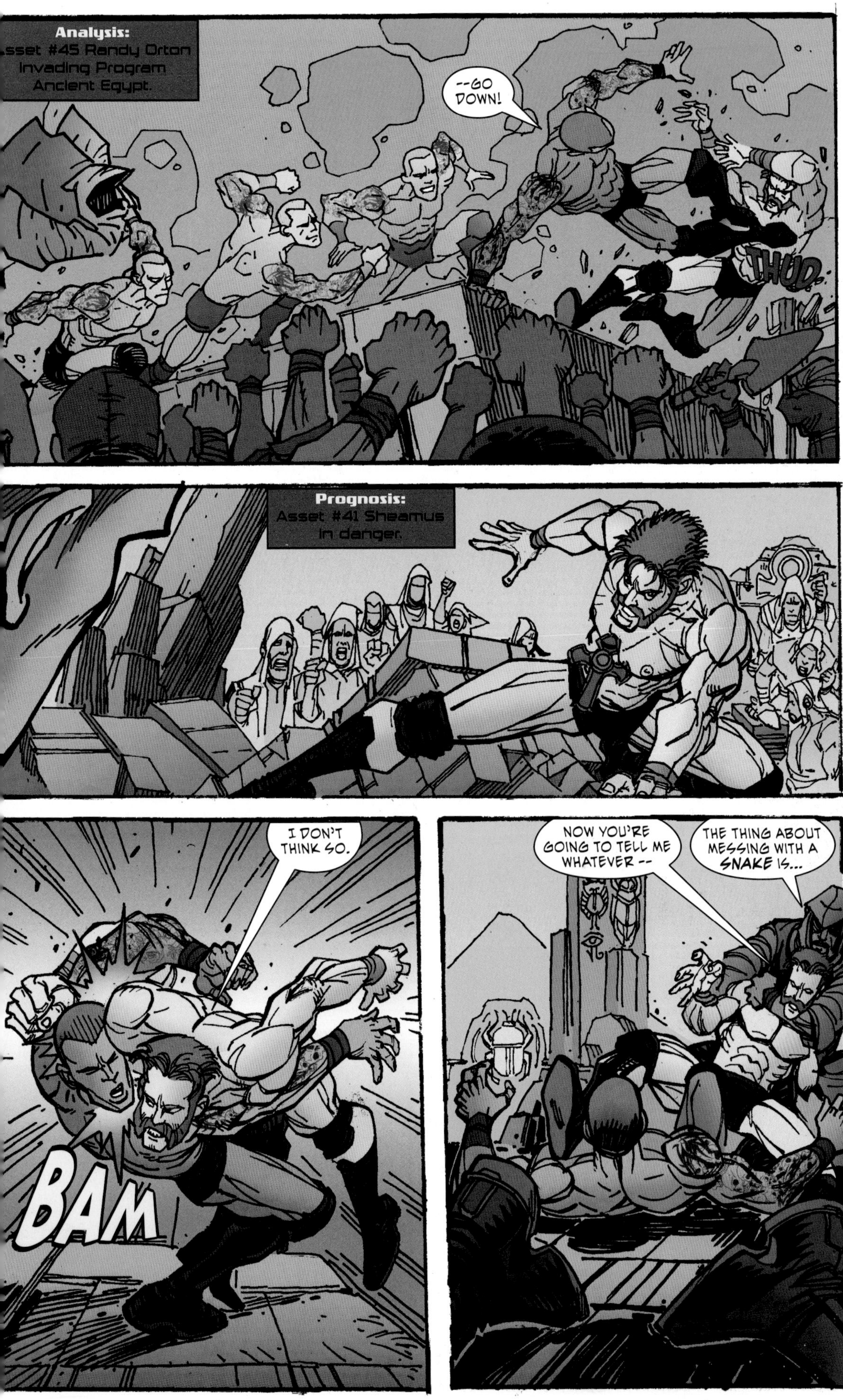
Analysis:
Asset #45 Randy Orton
Invading Program
Ancient Egypt.
--GO DOWN!
THUD
Prognosis:
Asset #41 Sheamus
in danger.
I DON'T THINK SO.
BAM
NOW YOU'RE GOING TO TELL ME WHATEVER --
THE THING ABOUT MESSING WITH A SNAKE IS...

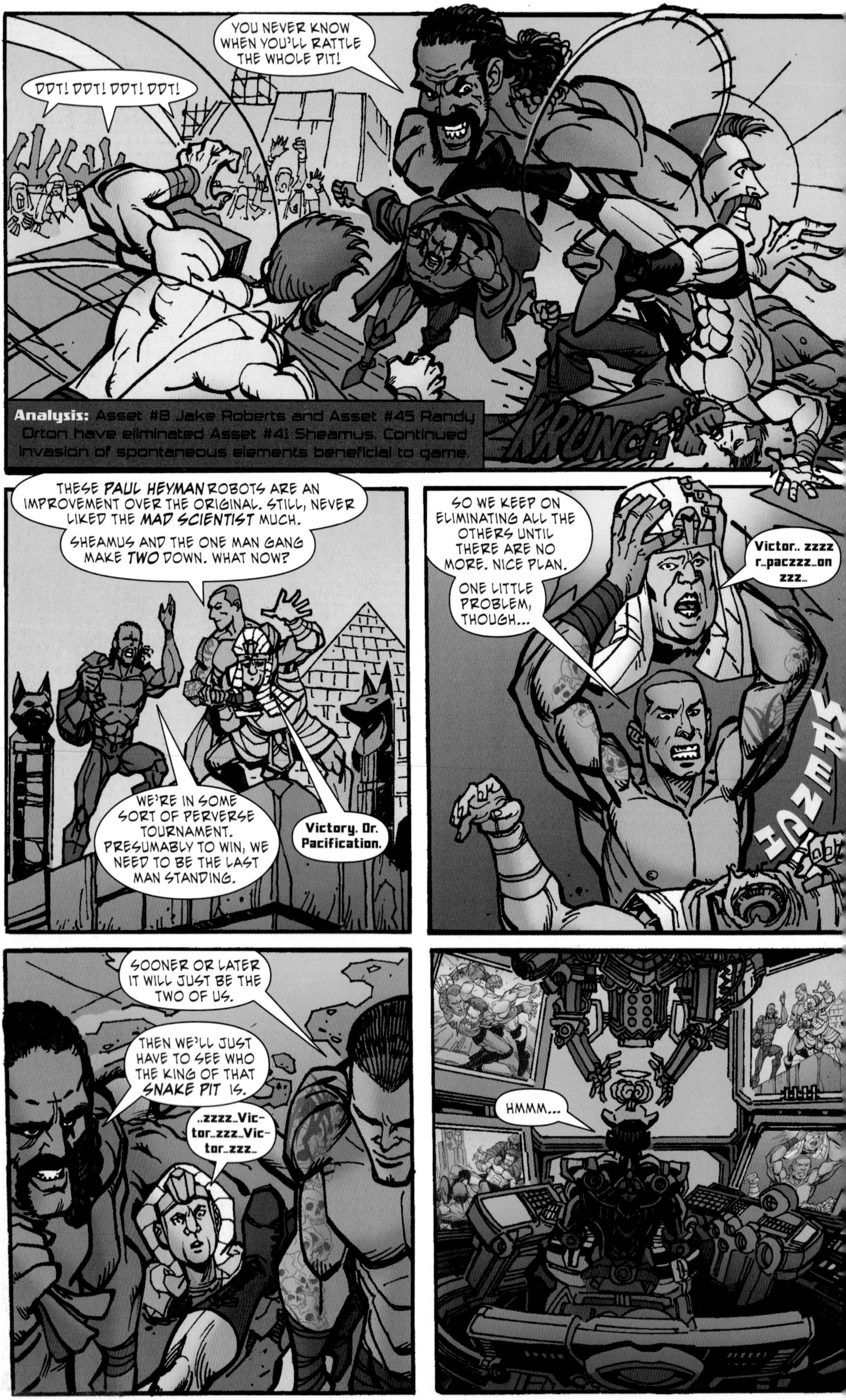
DDT! DDT! DDT! DDT!
YOU NEVER KNOW WHEN YOU'LL RATTLE THE WHOLE PIT!
Analysis: Asset #8 Jake Roberts and Asset #45 Randy Orton have eliminated Asset #41 Sheamus. Continued invasion of spontaneous elements beneficial to game.
KRUNCH
THESE PAUL HEYMAN ROBOTS ARE AN IMPROVEMENT OVER THE ORIGINAL. STILL, NEVER LIKED THE MAD SCIENTIST MUCH.
SHEAMUS AND THE ONE MAN GANG MAKE TWO DOWN. WHAT NOW?
WE'RE IN SOME SORT OF PERVERSE TOURNAMENT. PRESUMABLY TO WIN, WE NEED TO BE THE LAST MAN STANDING.
Victory. Or. Pacification.
SO WE KEEP ON ELIMINATING ALL THE OTHERS UNTIL THERE ARE NO MORE. NICE PLAN.
ONE LITTLE PROBLEM, THOUGH...
Victor.. zzzz r..paczzz...on zzz...
SOONER OR LATER IT WILL JUST BE THE TWO OF US.
THEN WE'LL JUST HAVE TO SEE WHO THE KING OF THAT SNAKE PIT IS.
..zzzz..Vic-tor..zzz..Vic-tor..zzz..
HMMM...

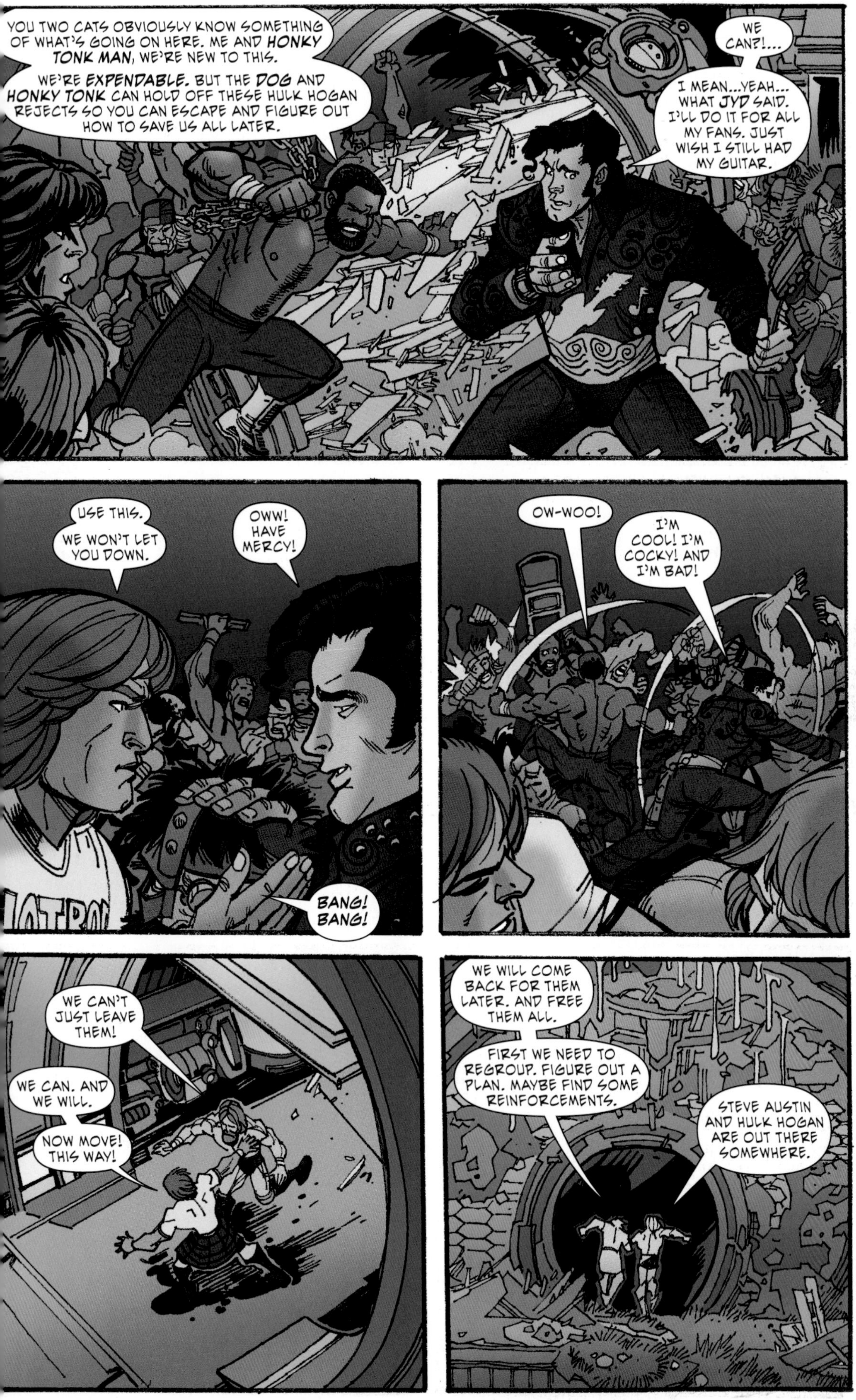
YOU TWO CATS OBVIOUSLY KNOW SOMETHING OF WHAT'S GOING ON HERE. ME AND HONKY TONK MAN, WE'RE NEW TO THIS.
WE'RE EXPENDABLE. BUT THE DOG AND HONKY TONK CAN HOLD OFF THESE HULK HOGAN REJECTS SO YOU CAN ESCAPE AND FIGURE OUT HOW TO SAVE US ALL LATER.
WE CAN?!...
I MEAN...YEAH... WHAT JYD SAID. I'LL DO IT FOR ALL MY FANS. JUST WISH I STILL HAD MY GUITAR.
USE THIS.
WE WON'T LET YOU DOWN.
OWW! HAVE MERCY!
BANG! BANG!
OW-WOO!
I'M COOL! I'M COCKY! AND I'M BAD!
WE CAN'T JUST LEAVE THEM!
WE CAN. AND WE WILL.
NOW MOVE! THIS WAY!
WE WILL COME BACK FOR THEM LATER. AND FREE THEM ALL.
FIRST WE NEED TO REGROUP. FIGURE OUT A PLAN. MAYBE FIND SOME REINFORCEMENTS.
STEVE AUSTIN AND HULK HOGAN ARE OUT THERE SOMEWHERE.

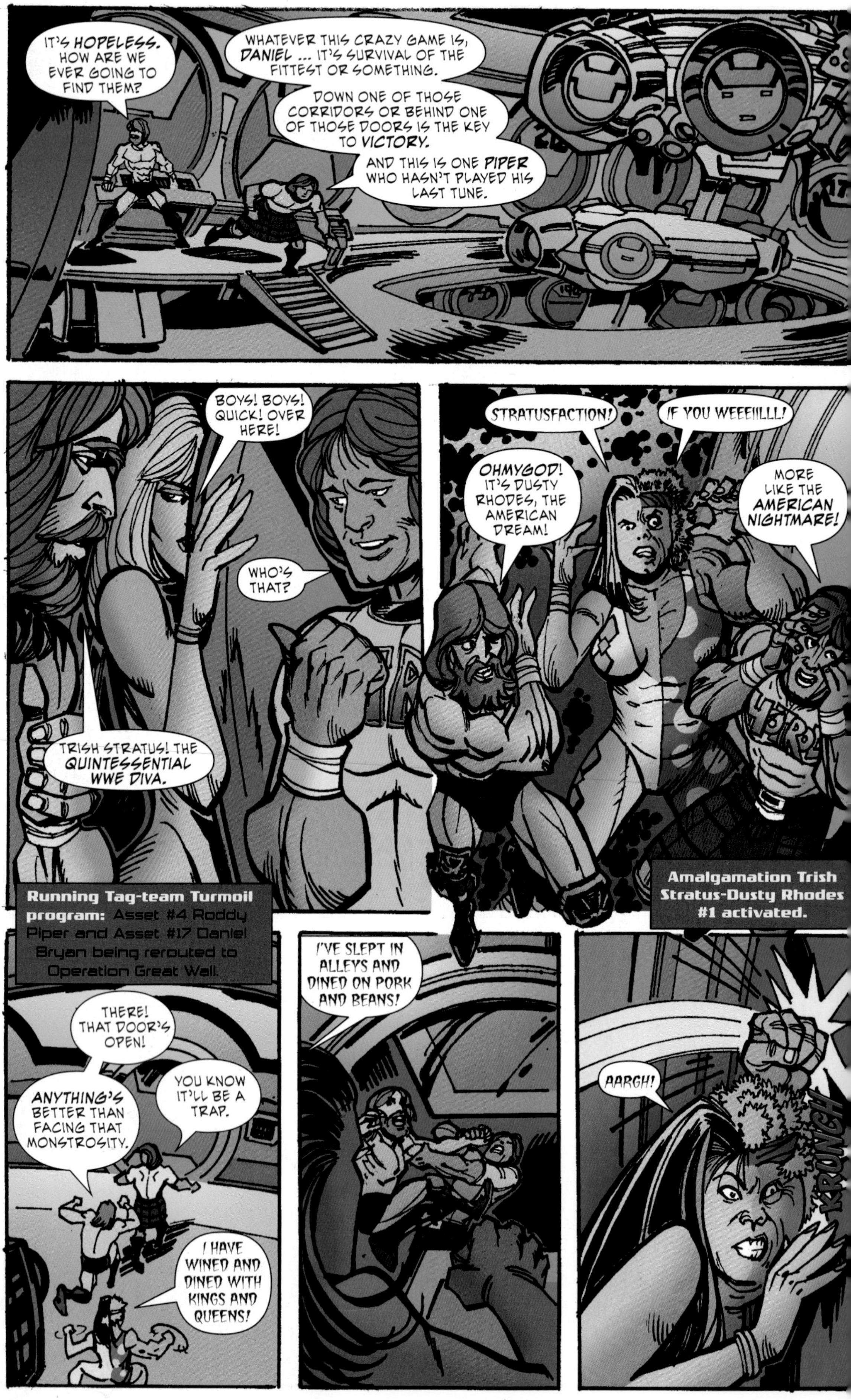
IT'S HOPELESS. HOW ARE WE EVER GOING TO FIND THEM?
WHATEVER THIS CRAZY GAME IS, DANIEL ... IT'S SURVIVAL OF THE FITTEST OR SOMETHING.
DOWN ONE OF THOSE CORRIDORS OR BEHIND ONE OF THOSE DOORS IS THE KEY TO VICTORY.
AND THIS IS ONE PIPER WHO HASN'T PLAYED HIS LAST TUNE.
BOYS! BOYS! QUICK! OVER HERE!
WHO'S THAT?
TRISH STRATUS! THE QUINTESSENTIAL WWE DIVA.
Running Tag-team Turmoil program: Asset #4 Roddy Piper and Asset #17 Daniel Bryan being rerouted to Operation Great Wall.
STRATUSFACTION!
IF YOU WEEEIILLL!
OHMYGOD! IT'S DUSTY RHODES, THE AMERICAN DREAM!
MORE LIKE THE AMERICAN NIGHTMARE!
Amalgamation Trish Stratus-Dusty Rhodes #1 activated.
THERE! THAT DOOR'S OPEN!
ANYTHING'S BETTER THAN FACING THAT MONSTROSITY.
YOU KNOW IT'LL BE A TRAP.
I HAVE WINED AND DINED WITH KINGS AND QUEENS!
I'VE SLEPT IN ALLEYS AND DINED ON PORK AND BEANS!
AARGH!
KRUNCH

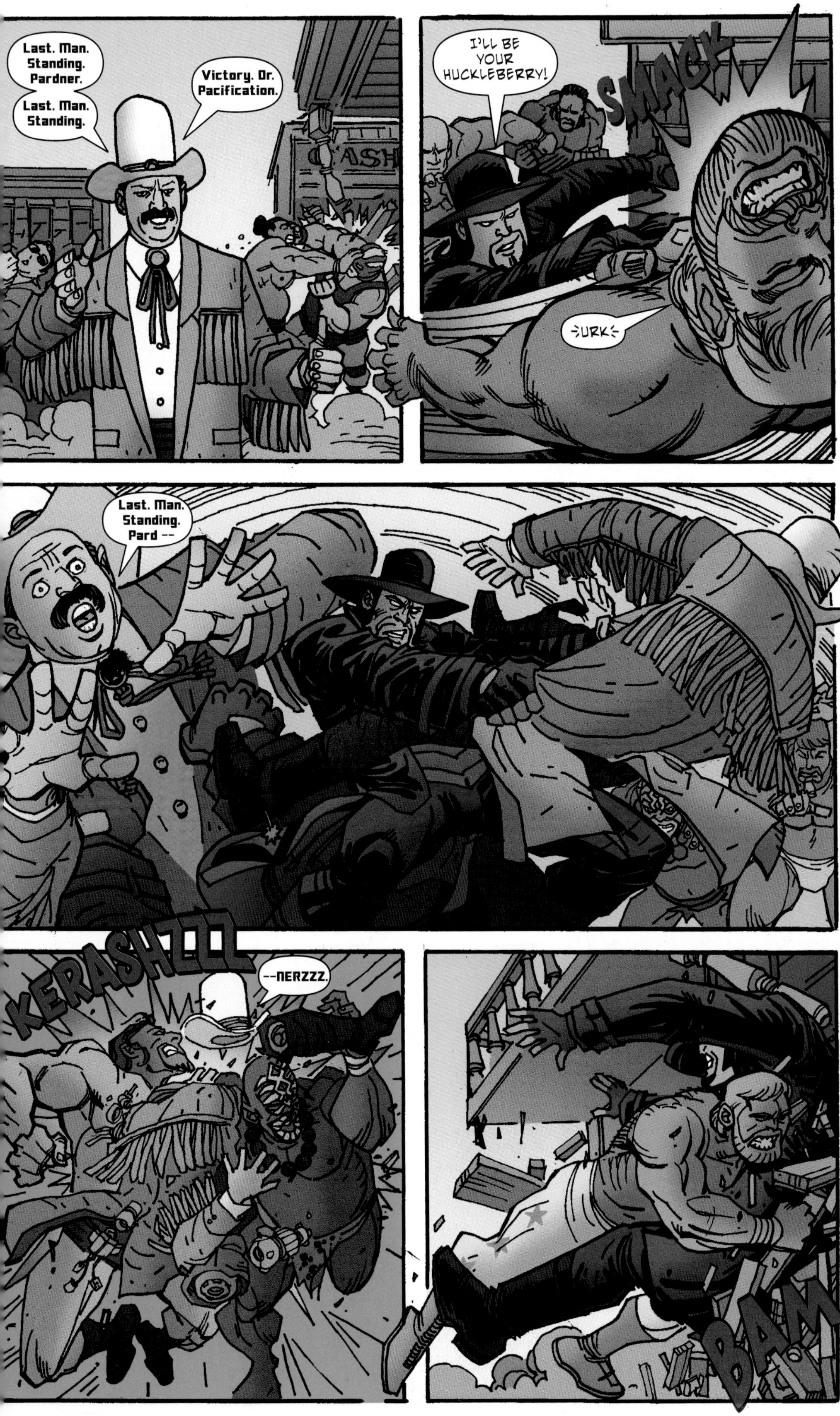
Last. Man. Standing. Pardner.
Last. Man. Standing.
Victory. Or. Pacification.
I'LL BE YOUR HUCKLEBERRY!
SMACK
URK
Last. Man. Standing. Pard --
KERASHZZZ
--NERZZZ.
BAM

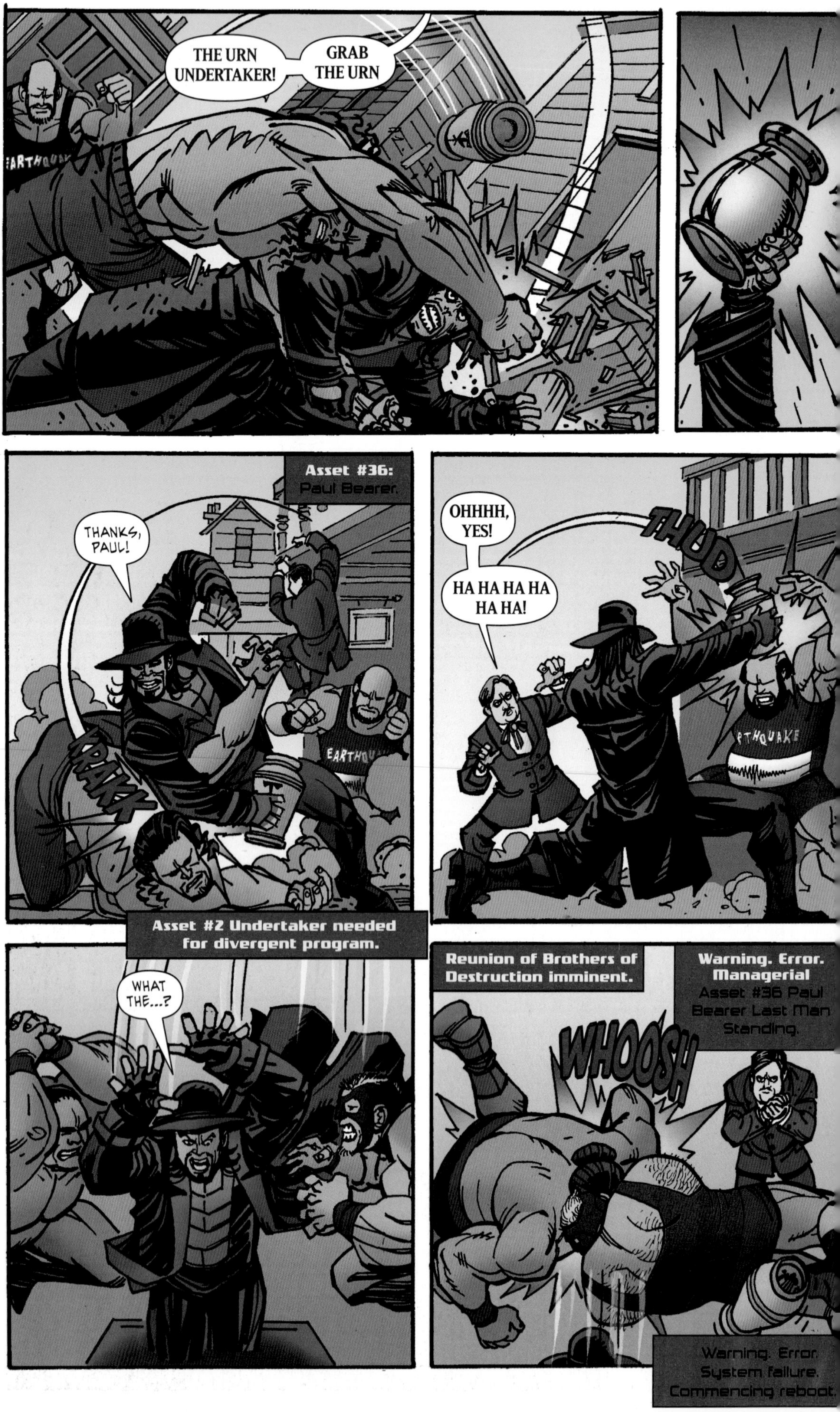
THE URN UNDERTAKER!
GRAB THE URN
EARTHQUAKE
Asset #36: Paul Bearer.
THANKS, PAUL!
KRAKK
EARTHQUAKE
OHHHH, YES!
HA HA HA HA HA HA!
THUD
Asset #2 Undertaker needed for divergent program.
WHAT THE...?
Reunion of Brothers of Destruction imminent.
Warning. Error. Managerial Asset #36 Paul Bearer Last Man Standing.
WHOOSH
Warning. Error. System failure. Commencing reboot.

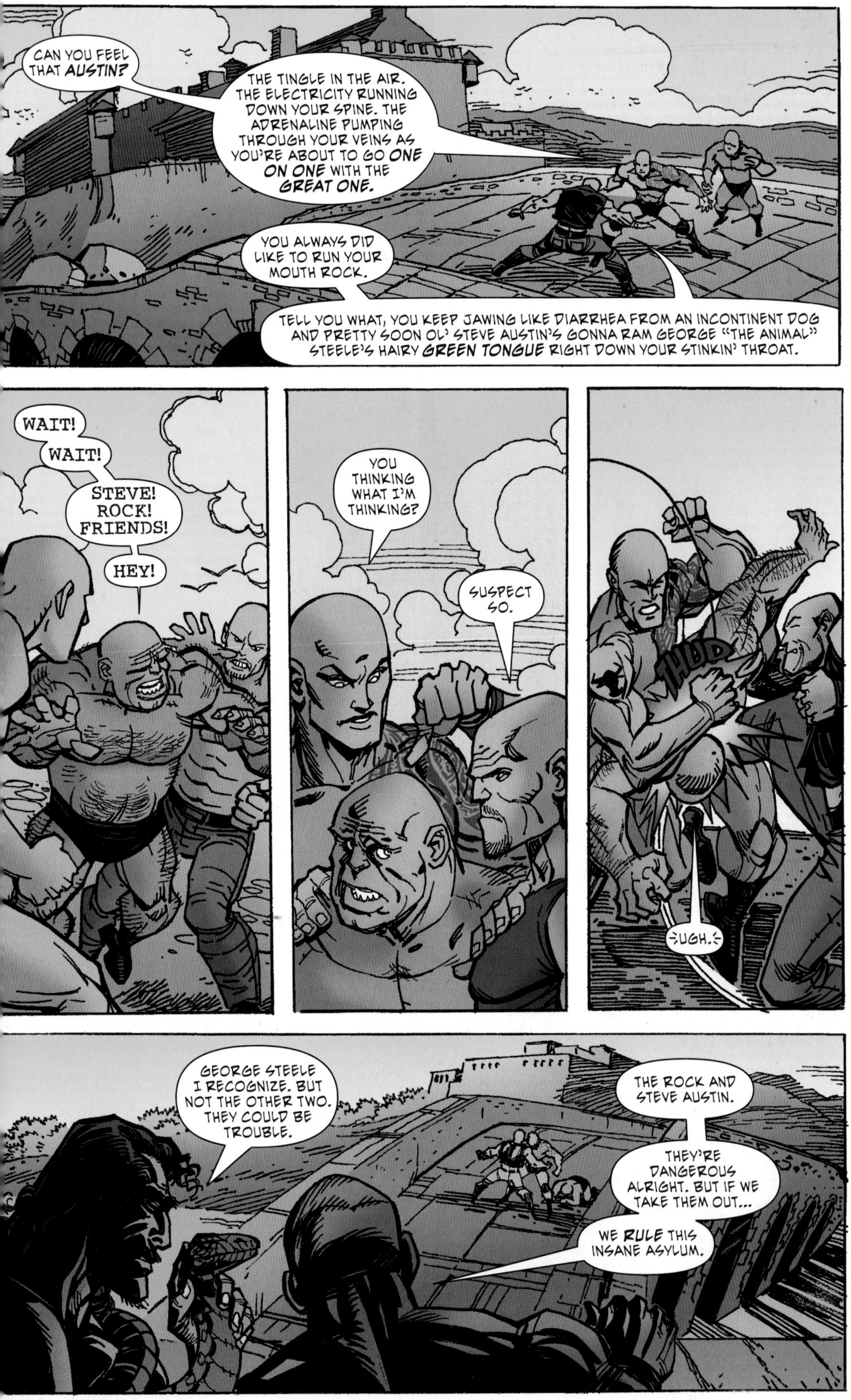

CAN YOU FEEL THAT AUSTIN?
THE TINGLE IN THE AIR. THE ELECTRICITY RUNNING DOWN YOUR SPINE. THE ADRENALINE PUMPING THROUGH YOUR VEINS AS YOU'RE ABOUT TO GO ONE ON ONE WITH THE GREAT ONE.
YOU ALWAYS DID LIKE TO RUN YOUR MOUTH ROCK.
TELL YOU WHAT, YOU KEEP JAWING LIKE DIARRHEA FROM AN INCONTINENT DOG AND PRETTY SOON OL' STEVE AUSTIN'S GONNA RAM GEORGE "THE ANIMAL" STEELE'S HAIRY GREEN TONGUE RIGHT DOWN YOUR STINKIN' THROAT.
WAIT!
WAIT!
STEVE! ROCK! FRIENDS!
HEY!
YOU THINKING WHAT I'M THINKING?
SUSPECT SO.
THUD
UGH.
GEORGE STEELE I RECOGNIZE. BUT NOT THE OTHER TWO. THEY COULD BE TROUBLE.
THE ROCK AND STEVE AUSTIN.
THEY'RE DANGEROUS ALRIGHT. BUT IF WE TAKE THEM OUT...
WE RULE THIS INSANE ASYLUM.

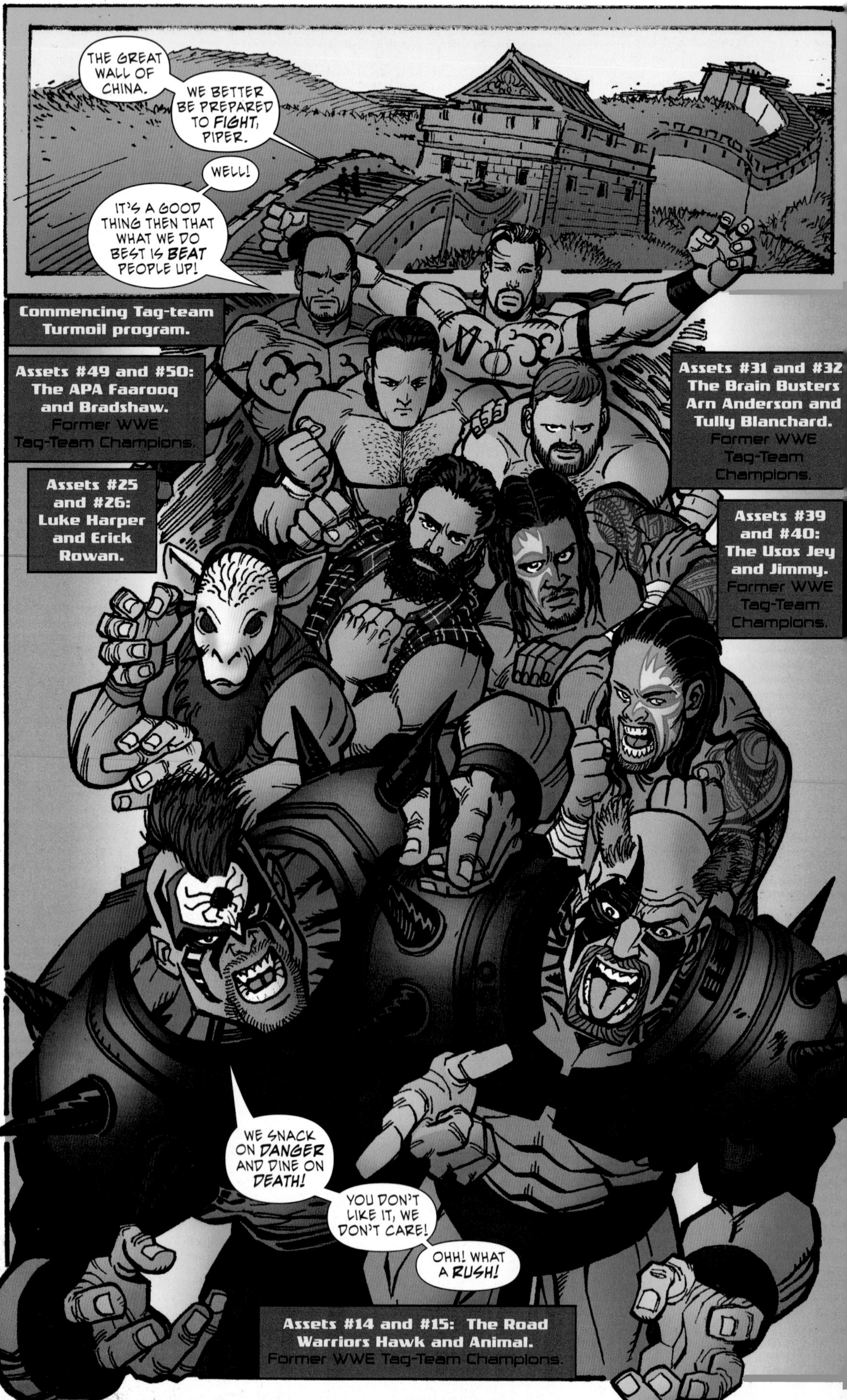
THE GREAT WALL OF CHINA.
WE BETTER BE PREPARED TO FIGHT, PIPER.
WELL!
IT'S A GOOD THING THEN THAT WHAT WE DO BEST IS BEAT PEOPLE UP!
Commencing Tag-team Turmoil program.
Assets #49 and #50: The APA Faarooq and Bradshaw. Former WWE Tag-Team Champions.
Assets #31 and #32 The Brain Busters Arn Anderson and Tully Blanchard. Former WWE Tag-Team Champions.
Assets #25 and #26: Luke Harper and Erick Rowan.
Assets #39 and #40: The Usos Jey and Jimmy. Former WWE Tag-Team Champions.
WE SNACK ON DANGER AND DINE ON DEATH!
YOU DON'T LIKE IT, WE DON'T CARE!
OHH! WHAT A RUSH!
Assets #14 and #15: The Road Warriors Hawk and Animal. Former WWE Tag-Team Champions.

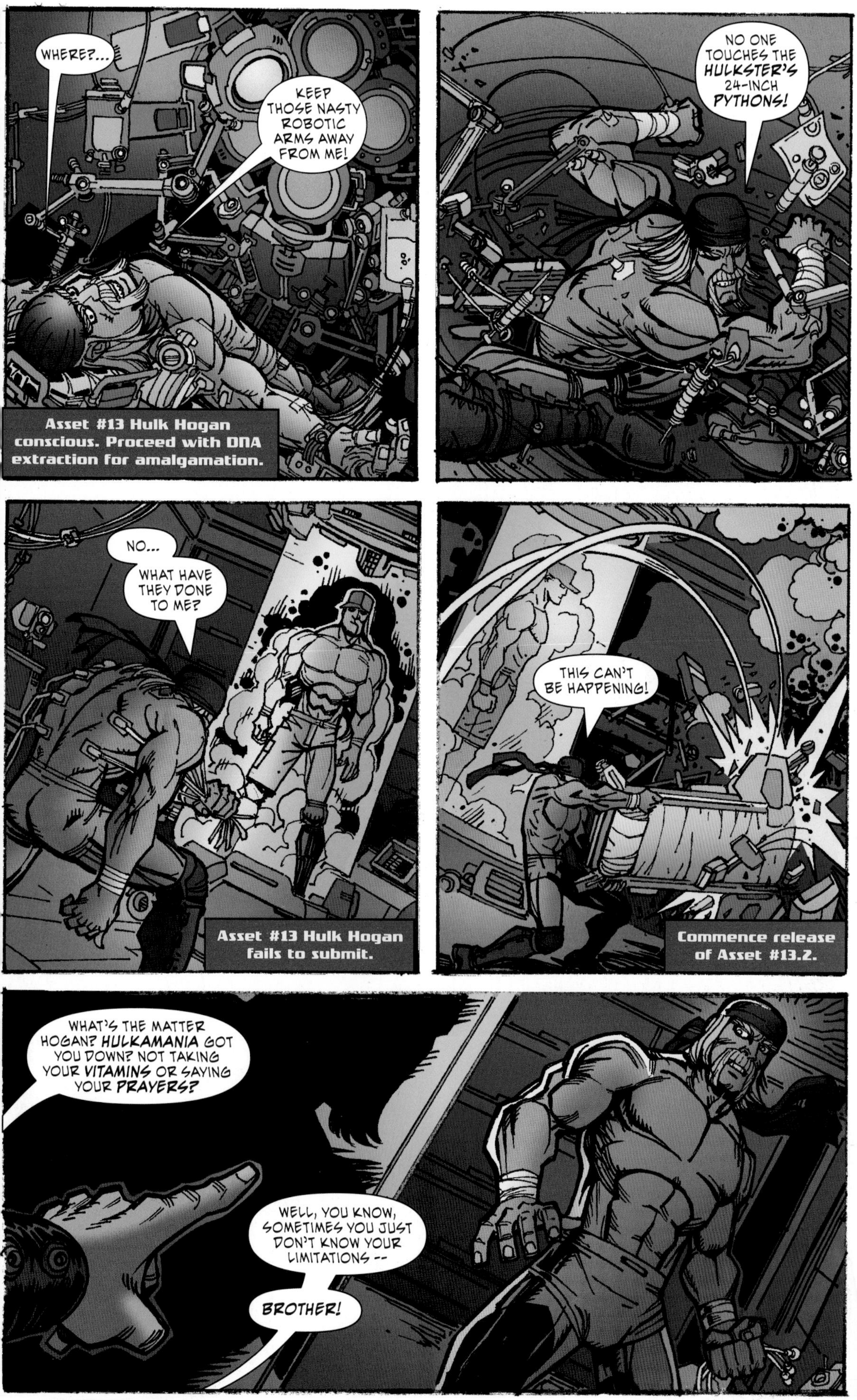
WHERE?...
KEEP THOSE NASTY ROBOTIC ARMS AWAY FROM ME!
Asset #13 Hulk Hogan conscious. Proceed with DNA extraction for amalgamation.
NO ONE TOUCHES THE HULKSTER'S 24-INCH PYTHONS!
NO...
WHAT HAVE THEY DONE TO ME?
Asset #13 Hulk Hogan fails to submit.
THIS CAN'T BE HAPPENING!
Commence release of Asset #13.2.
WHAT'S THE MATTER HOGAN? HULKAMANIA GOT YOU DOWN? NOT TAKING YOUR VITAMINS OR SAYING YOUR PRAYERS?
WELL, YOU KNOW, SOMETIMES YOU JUST DON'T KNOW YOUR LIMITATIONS --
BROTHER!

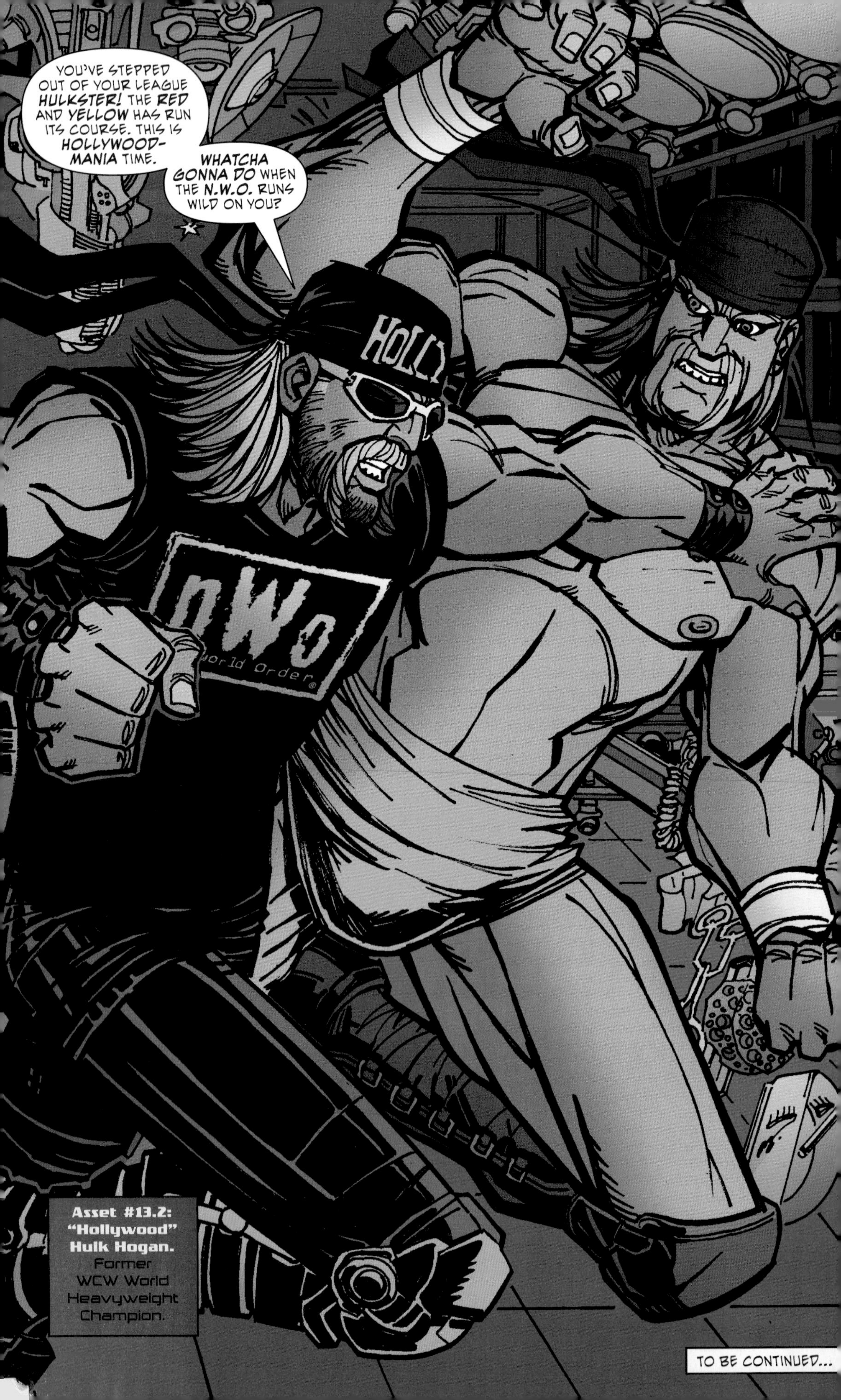

YOU'VE STEPPED OUT OF YOUR LEAGUE HULKSTER! THE RED AND YELLOW HAS RUN ITS COURSE. THIS IS HOLLYWOOD-MANIA TIME.
WHATCHA GONNA DO WHEN THE N.W.O. RUNS WILD ON YOU?
Asset #13.2: "Hollywood" Hulk Hogan. Former WCW World Heavyweight Champion.
TO BE CONTINUED...

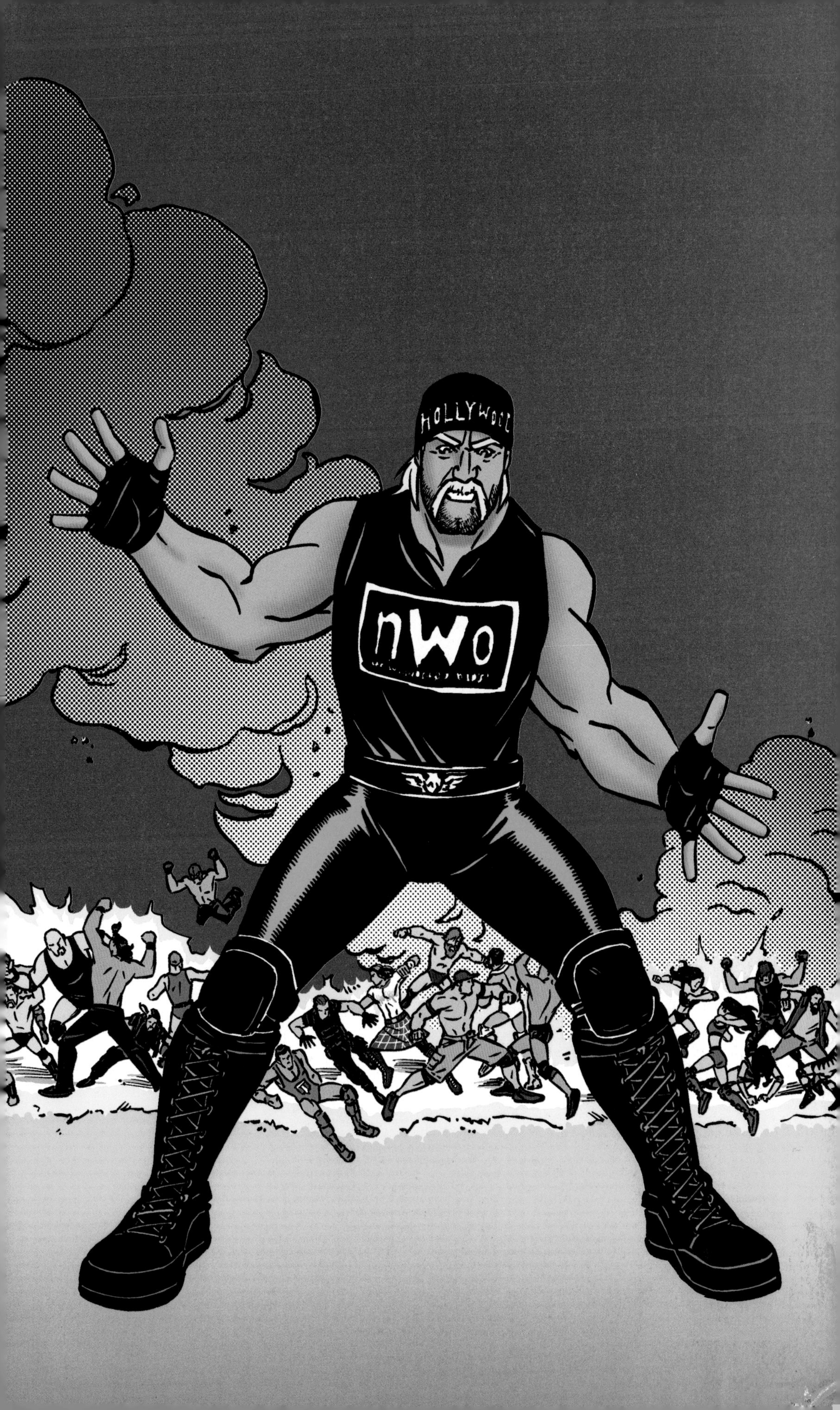
nWo

PART THREE
"WHAT A RUSH!"

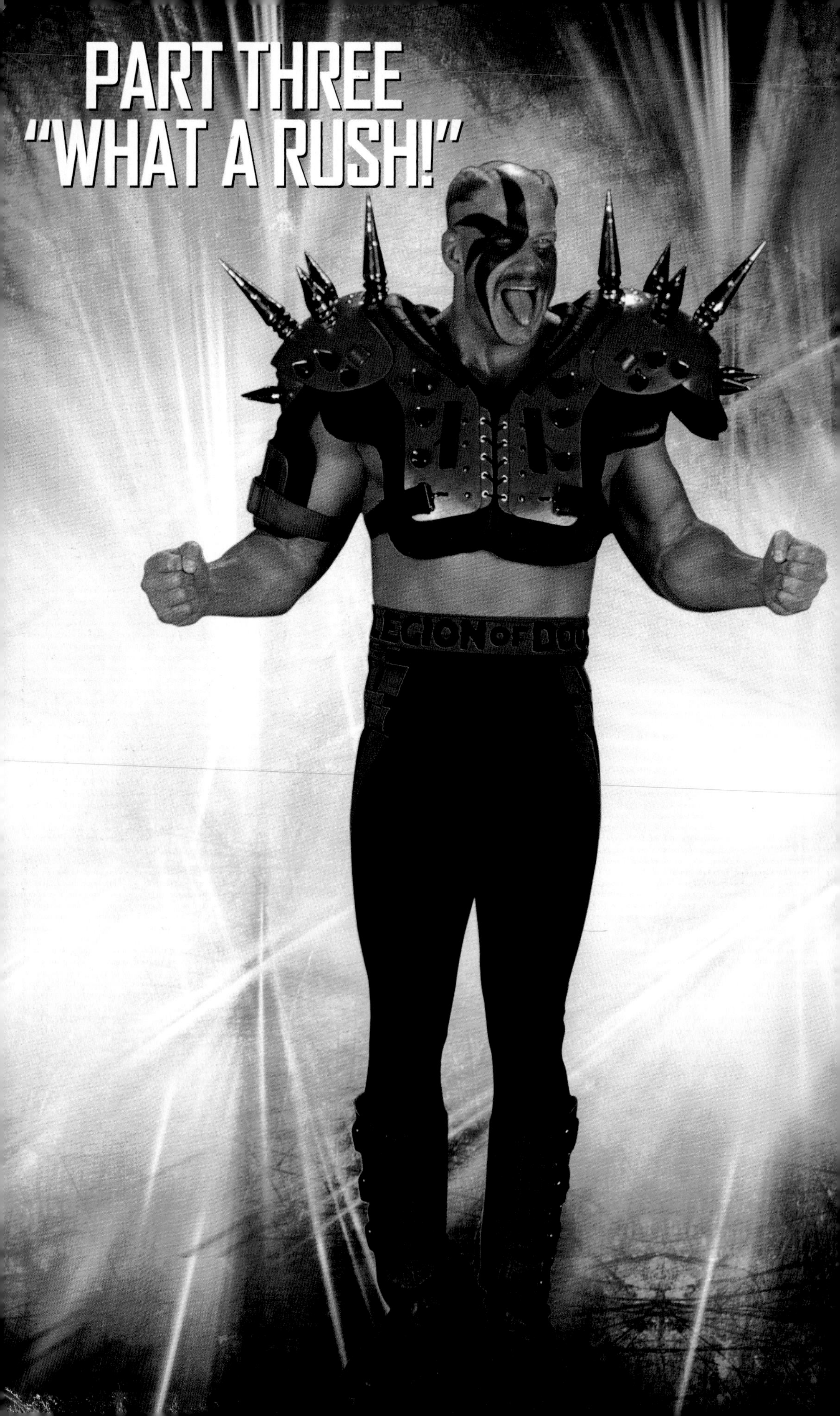

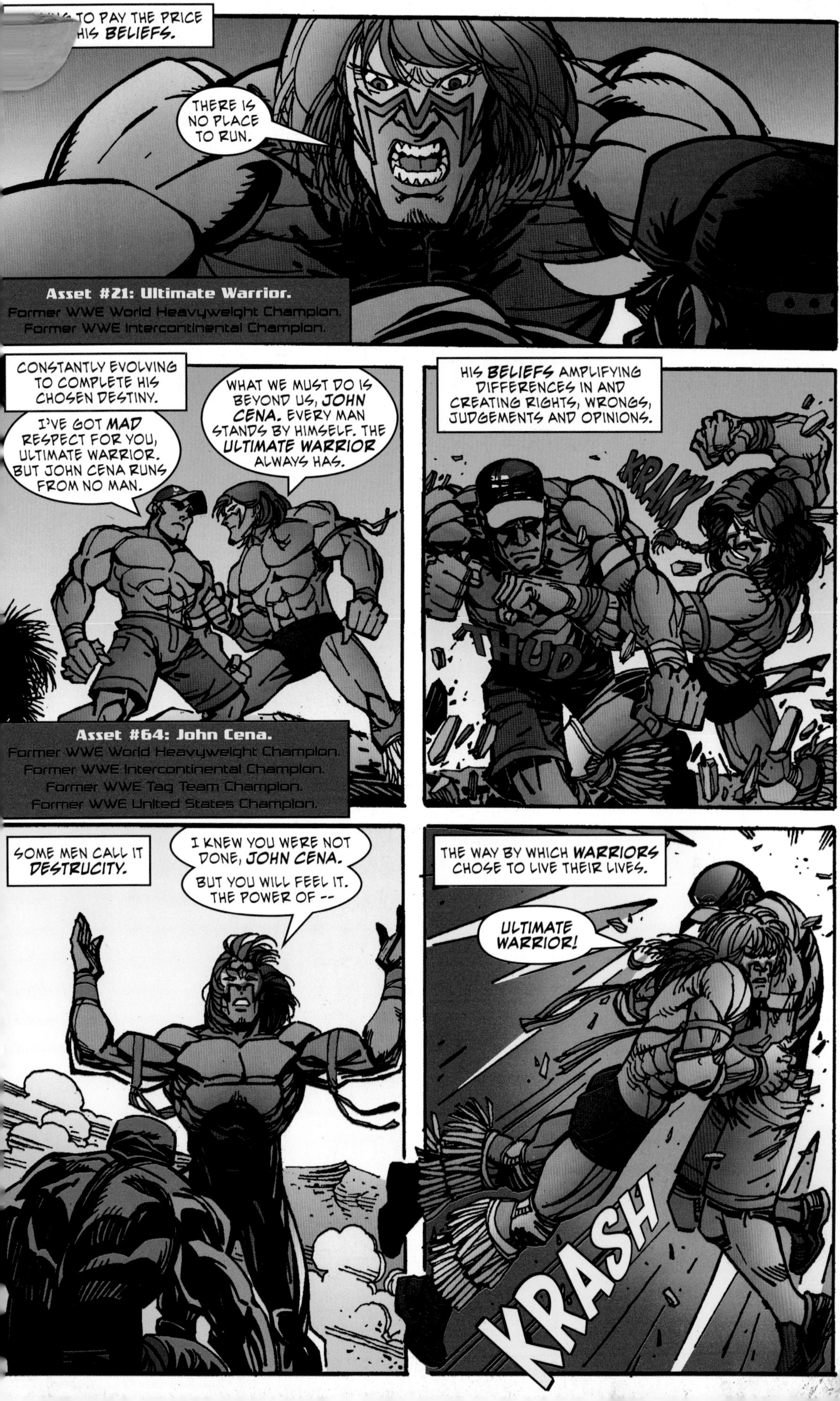

TO PAY THE PRICE HIS BELIEFS.
THERE IS NO PLACE TO RUN.
Asset #21: Ultimate Warrior.
Former WWE World Heavyweight Champion.
Former WWE Intercontinental Champion.
CONSTANTLY EVOLVING TO COMPLETE HIS CHOSEN DESTINY.
I'VE GOT MAD RESPECT FOR YOU, ULTIMATE WARRIOR. BUT JOHN CENA RUNS FROM NO MAN.
WHAT WE MUST DO IS BEYOND US, JOHN CENA. EVERY MAN STANDS BY HIMSELF. THE ULTIMATE WARRIOR ALWAYS HAS.
Asset #64: John Cena.
Former WWE World Heavyweight Champion.
Former WWE Intercontinental Champion.
Former WWE Tag Team Champion.
Former WWE United States Champion.
HIS BELIEFS AMPLIFYING DIFFERENCES IN AND CREATING RIGHTS, WRONGS, JUDGEMENTS AND OPINIONS.
KRAKK
THUD
SOME MEN CALL IT DESTRUCITY.
I KNEW YOU WERE NOT DONE, JOHN CENA.
BUT YOU WILL FEEL IT. THE POWER OF --
THE WAY BY WHICH WARRIORS CHOSE TO LIVE THEIR LIVES.
ULTIMATE WARRIOR!
KRASH

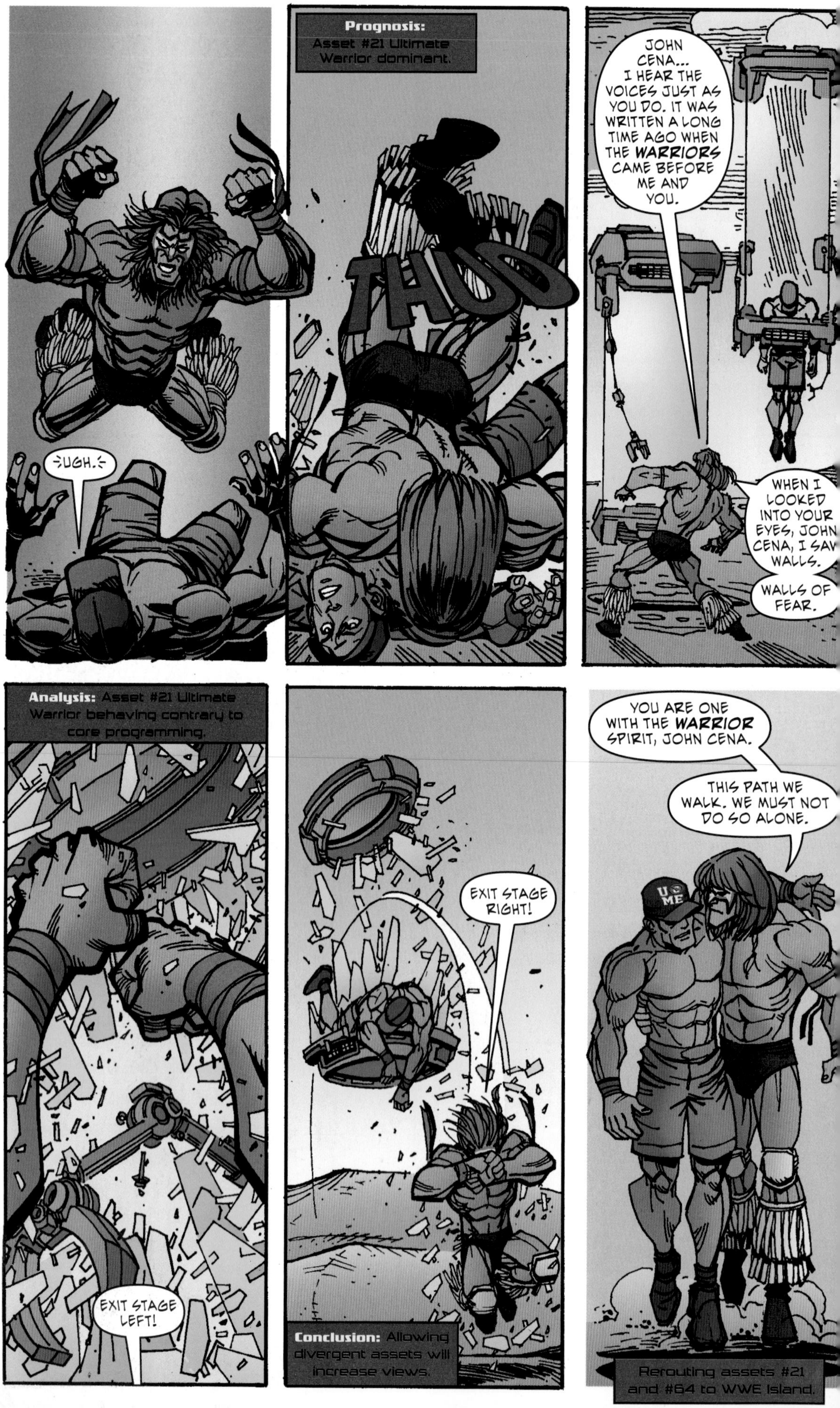
UGH.
Prognosis:
Asset #21 Ultimate Warrior dominant.
THUD
JOHN CENA... I HEAR THE VOICES JUST AS YOU DO. IT WAS WRITTEN A LONG TIME AGO WHEN THE WARRIORS CAME BEFORE ME AND YOU.
WHEN I LOOKED INTO YOUR EYES, JOHN CENA, I SAW WALLS.
WALLS OF FEAR.
Analysis: Asset #21 Ultimate Warrior behaving contrary to core programming.
EXIT STAGE LEFT!
EXIT STAGE RIGHT!
Conclusion: Allowing divergent assets will increase views.
YOU ARE ONE WITH THE WARRIOR SPIRIT, JOHN CENA.
THIS PATH WE WALK. WE MUST NOT DO SO ALONE.
UME
Rerouting assets #21 and #64 to WWE Island.

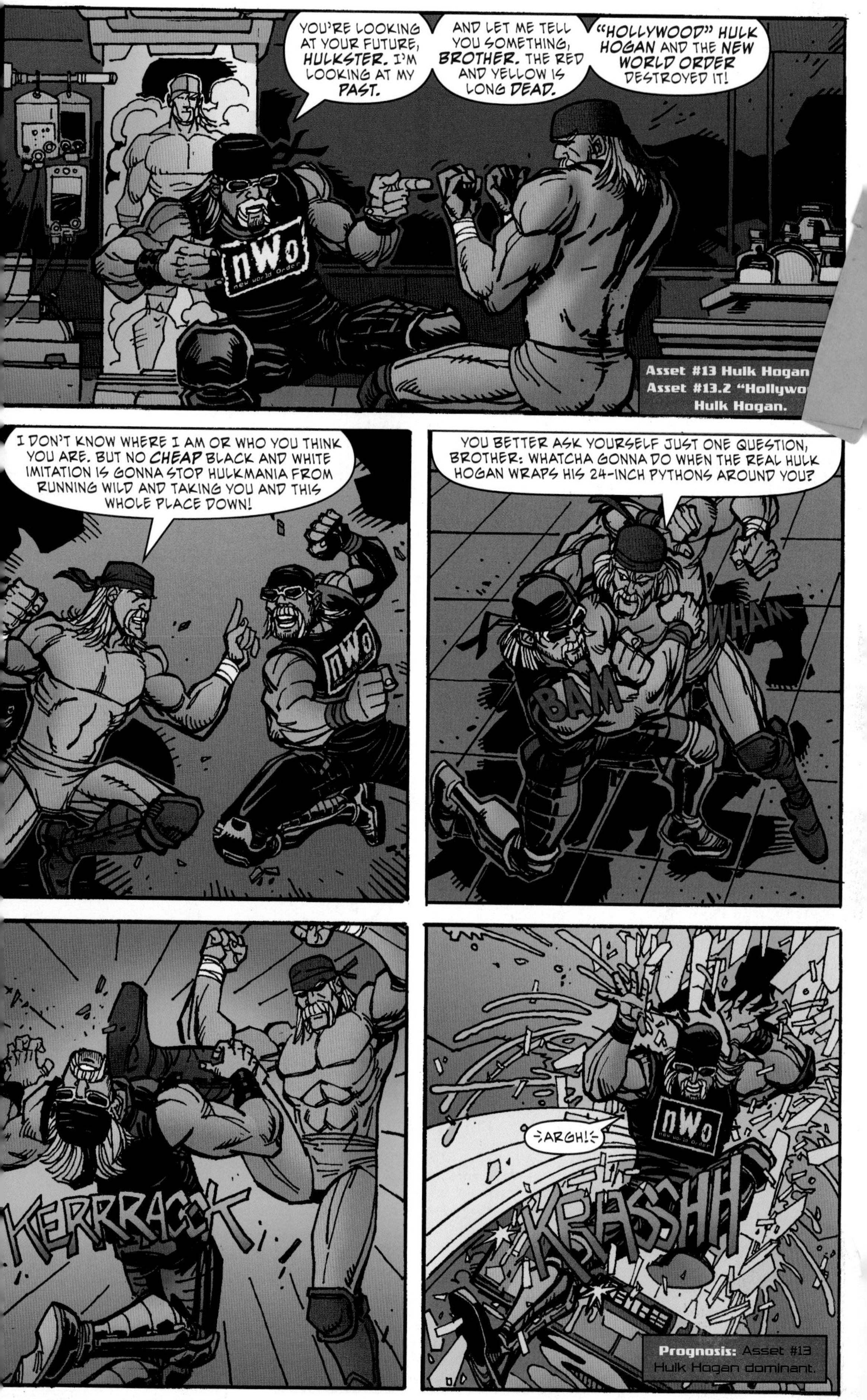

YOU'RE LOOKING AT YOUR FUTURE, HULKSTER. I'M LOOKING AT MY PAST.
AND LET ME TELL YOU SOMETHING, BROTHER. THE RED AND YELLOW IS LONG DEAD.
"HOLLYWOOD" HULK HOGAN AND THE NEW WORLD ORDER DESTROYED IT!
Asset #13 Hulk Hogan
Asset #13.2 "Hollywo
Hulk Hogan.
I DON'T KNOW WHERE I AM OR WHO YOU THINK YOU ARE. BUT NO CHEAP BLACK AND WHITE IMITATION IS GONNA STOP HULKMANIA FROM RUNNING WILD AND TAKING YOU AND THIS WHOLE PLACE DOWN!
nWo
YOU BETTER ASK YOURSELF JUST ONE QUESTION, BROTHER: WHATCHA GONNA DO WHEN THE REAL HULK HOGAN WRAPS HIS 24-INCH PYTHONS AROUND YOU?
WHAM
BAM
KERRRACCK
ARGH!
KRASHH
Prognosis: Asset #13 Hulk Hogan dominant.

WHATEVER THIS MADHOUSE IS, I WANT SOME ANSWERS.

EVEN IF I HAVE TO BEAT IT OUT OF YOU!

YOU JUST DON'T GET IT, HULKSTER.

TELL HIM, BIG MAN!

WHEN YOU'RE N.W.O., YOU'RE N.W.O. FOR LIFE

WHAT?

THE BAND IS BACK TOGETHER!

Asset #19.2: N.W.O. Kevin Nash.

KRUNCH

FINISH OFF THIS LOSER, NASH!

WITH PLEASURE.

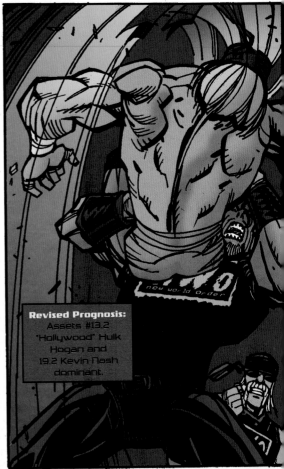

Revised Prognosis: Assets #13.2 "Hollywood" Hulk Hogan and 19.2 Kevin Nash dominant.

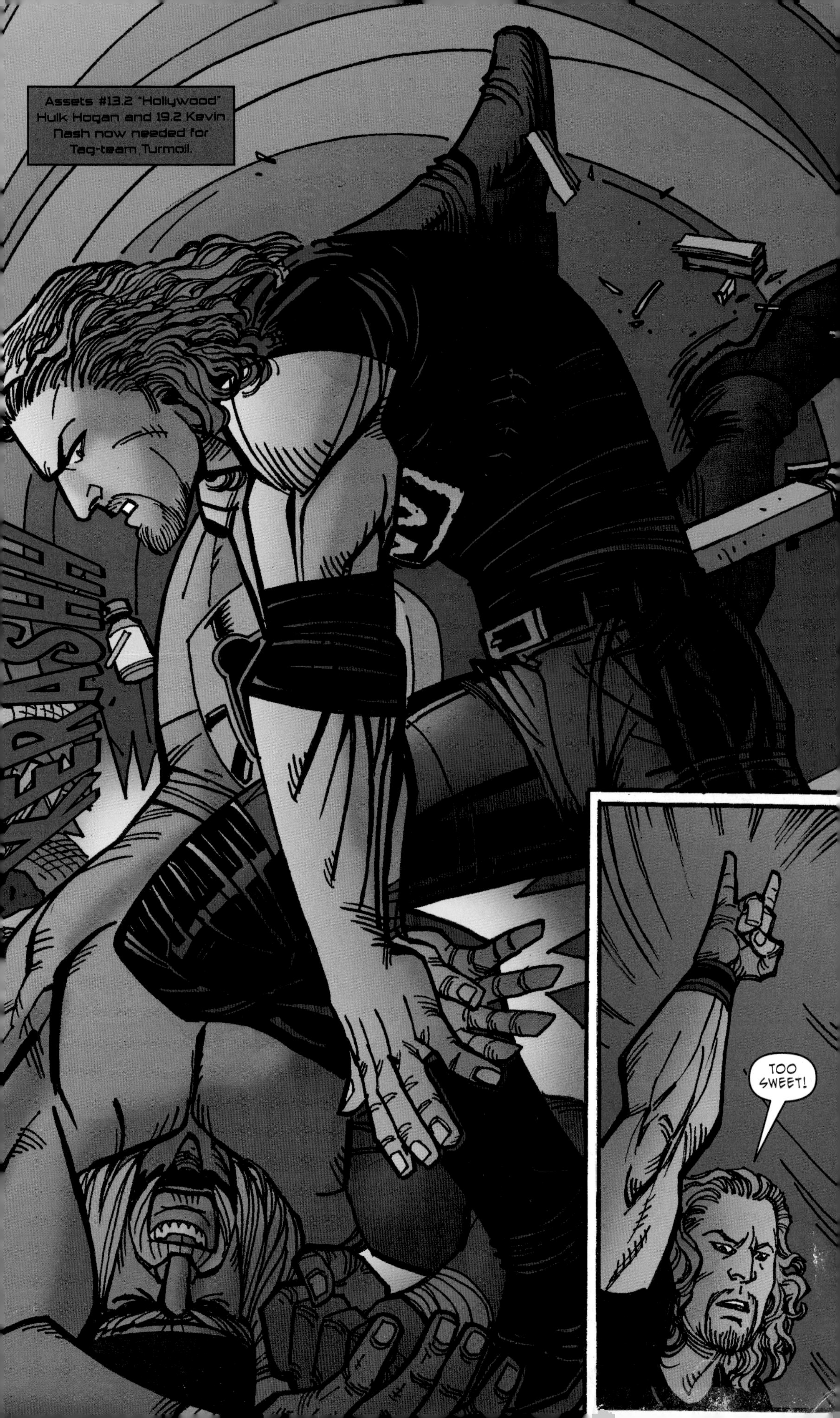
Assets #13.2 "Hollywood" Hulk Hogan and 19.2 Kevin Nash now needed for Tag-team Turmoil.
TOO SWEET!

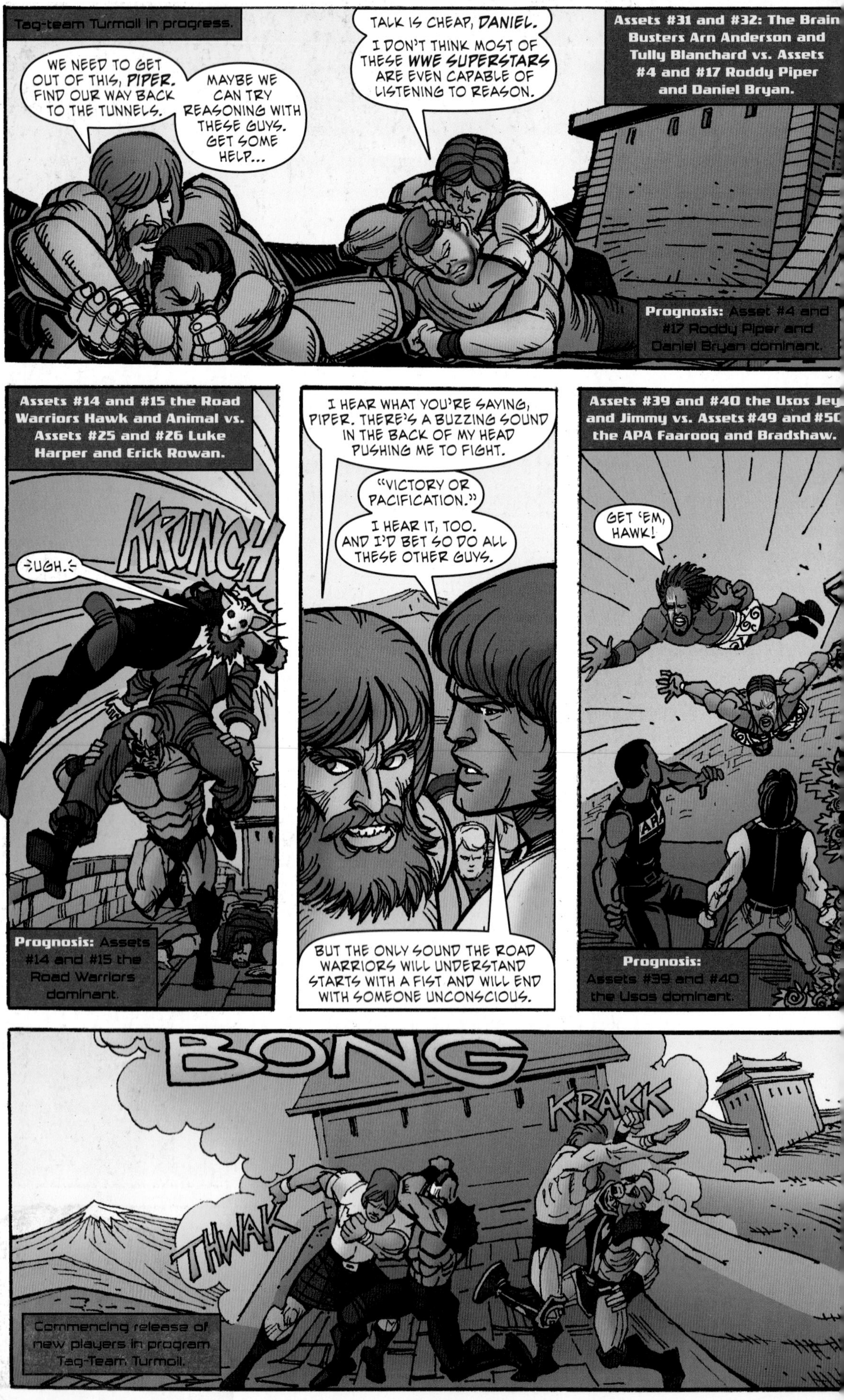
Tag-team Turmoil in progress.
WE NEED TO GET OUT OF THIS, PIPER. FIND OUR WAY BACK TO THE TUNNELS.
MAYBE WE CAN TRY REASONING WITH THESE GUYS. GET SOME HELP...
TALK IS CHEAP, DANIEL.
I DON'T THINK MOST OF THESE WWE SUPERSTARS ARE EVEN CAPABLE OF LISTENING TO REASON.
Assets #31 and #32: The Brain Busters Arn Anderson and Tully Blanchard vs. Assets #4 and #17 Roddy Piper and Daniel Bryan.
Prognosis: Asset #4 and #17 Roddy Piper and Daniel Bryan dominant.
Assets #14 and #15 the Road Warriors Hawk and Animal vs. Assets #25 and #26 Luke Harper and Erick Rowan.
KRUNCH
UGH.
Prognosis: Assets #14 and #15 the Road Warriors dominant.
I HEAR WHAT YOU'RE SAYING, PIPER. THERE'S A BUZZING SOUND IN THE BACK OF MY HEAD PUSHING ME TO FIGHT.
"VICTORY OR PACIFICATION."
I HEAR IT, TOO. AND I'D BET SO DO ALL THESE OTHER GUYS.
BUT THE ONLY SOUND THE ROAD WARRIORS WILL UNDERSTAND STARTS WITH A FIST AND WILL END WITH SOMEONE UNCONSCIOUS.
Assets #39 and #40 the Usos Jey and Jimmy vs. Assets #49 and #50 the APA Faarooq and Bradshaw.
GET 'EM, HAWK!
Prognosis: Assets #39 and #40 the Usos dominant.
BONG
KRAKK
THWAK
Commencing release of new players in program Tag-Team Turmoil.

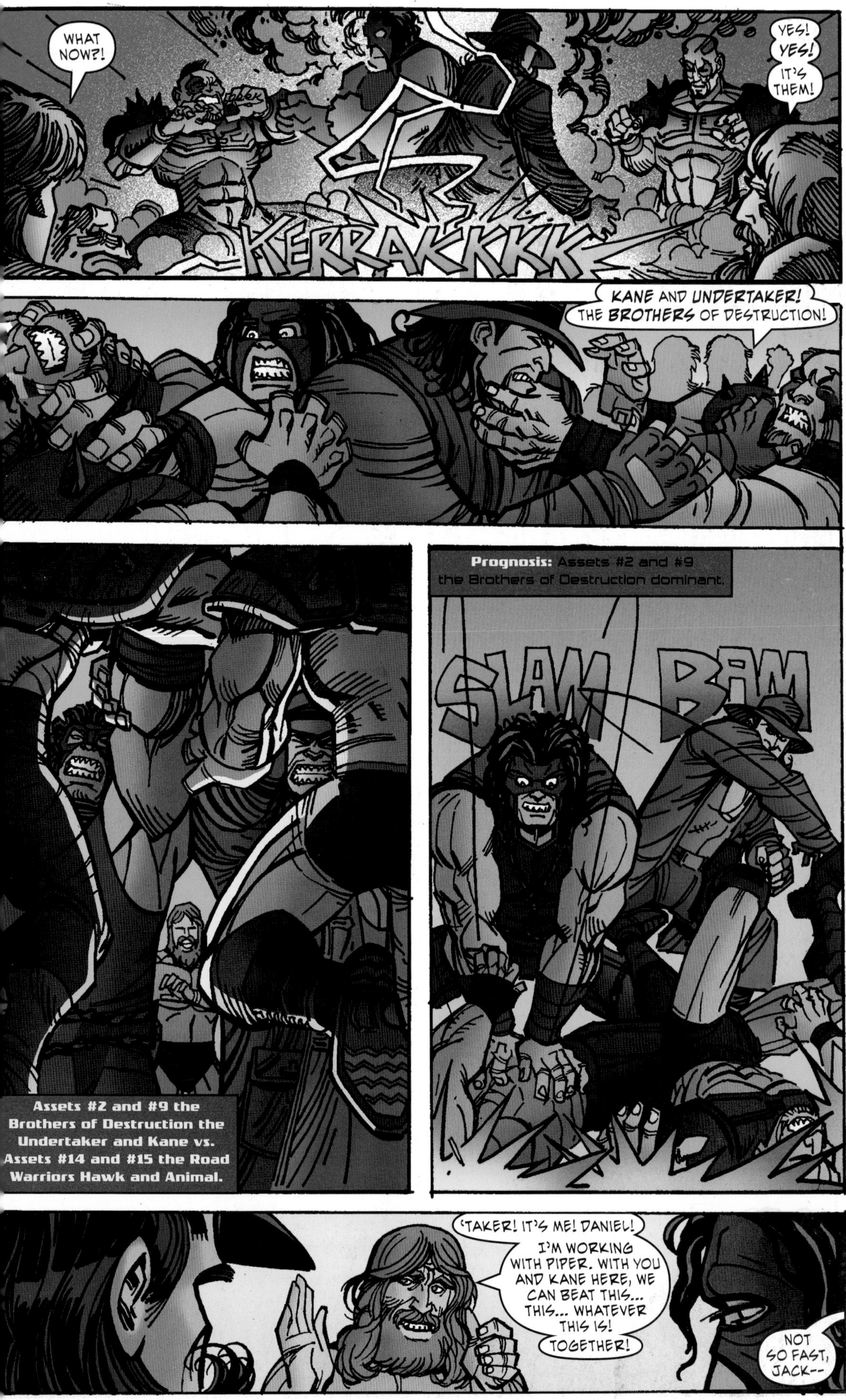

WHAT NOW?!
YES! YES! IT'S THEM!
KERRAKKKK
KANE AND UNDERTAKER! THE BROTHERS OF DESTRUCTION!
Assets #2 and #9 the Brothers of Destruction the Undertaker and Kane vs. Assets #14 and #15 the Road Warriors Hawk and Animal.
Prognosis: Assets #2 and #9 the Brothers of Destruction dominant.
SLAM
BAM
'TAKER! IT'S ME! DANIEL!
I'M WORKING WITH PIPER. WITH YOU AND KANE HERE, WE CAN BEAT THIS... THIS... WHATEVER THIS IS!
TOGETHER!
NOT SO FAST, JACK--

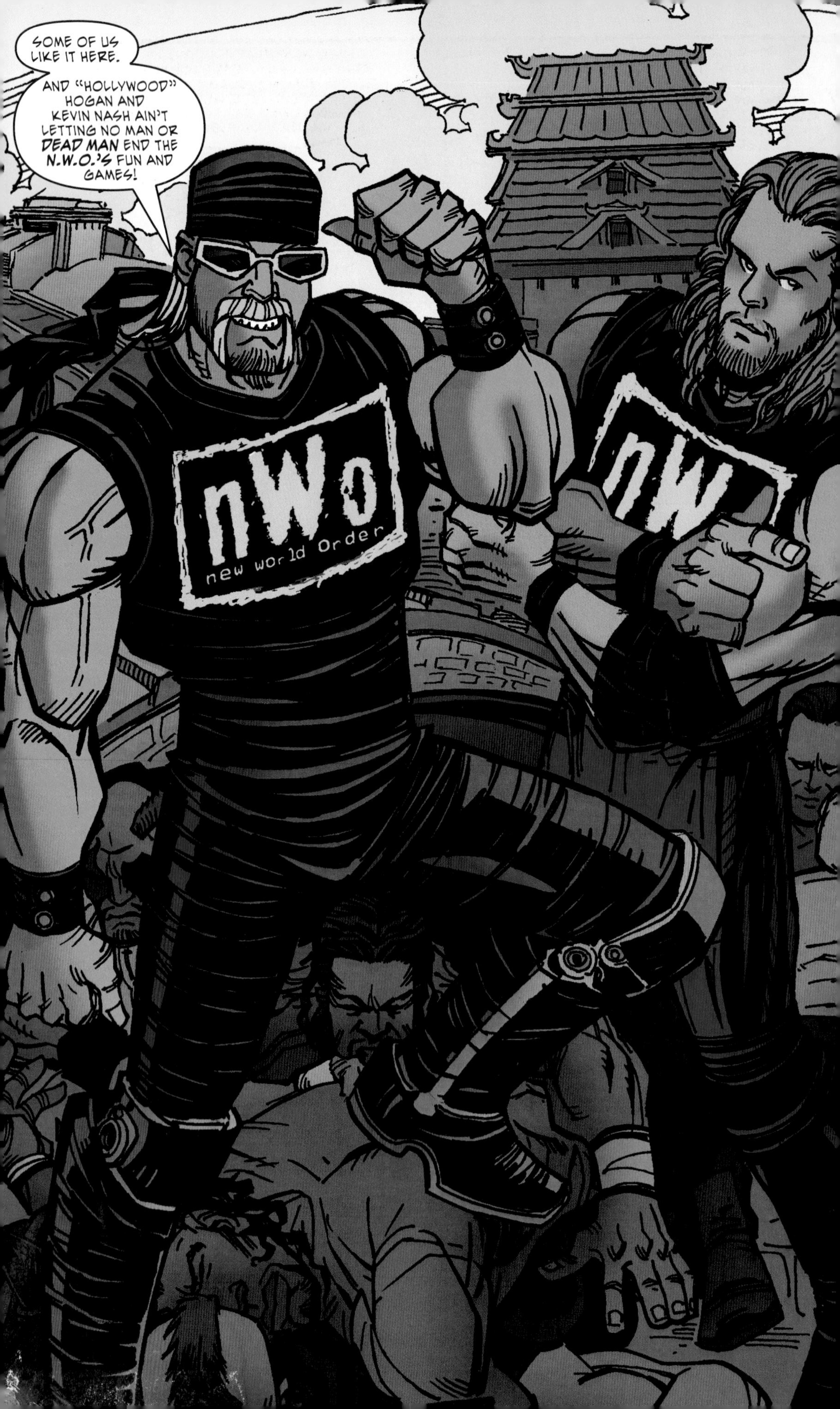
SOME OF US LIKE IT HERE.
AND "HOLLYWOOD" HOGAN AND KEVIN NASH AIN'T LETTING NO MAN OR DEAD MAN END THE N.W.O.'S FUN AND GAMES!
nWo new world Order
nWo

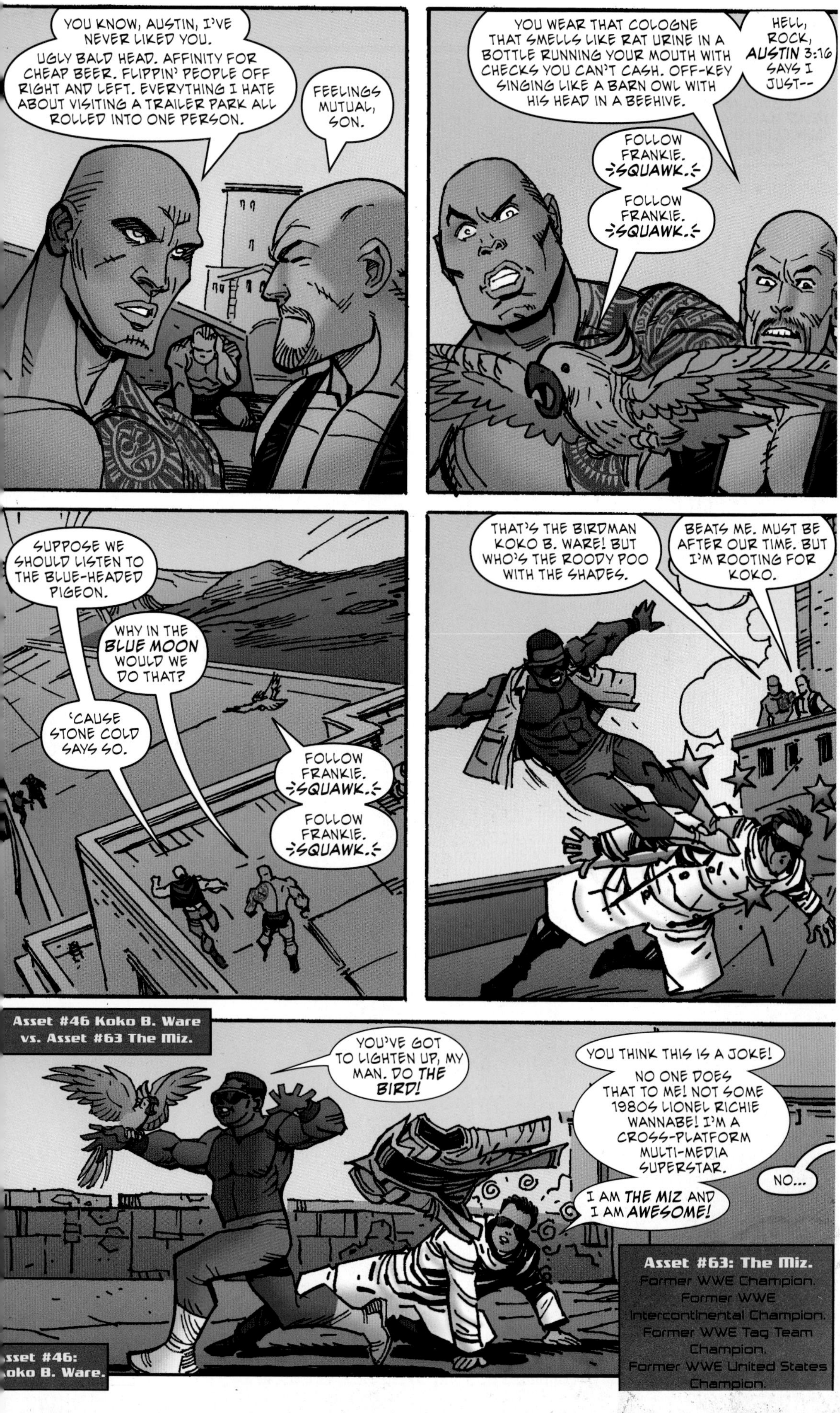
YOU KNOW, AUSTIN, I'VE NEVER LIKED YOU.
UGLY BALD HEAD. AFFINITY FOR CHEAP BEER. FLIPPIN' PEOPLE OFF RIGHT AND LEFT. EVERYTHING I HATE ABOUT VISITING A TRAILER PARK ALL ROLLED INTO ONE PERSON.
FEELINGS MUTUAL, SON.
YOU WEAR THAT COLOGNE THAT SMELLS LIKE RAT URINE IN A BOTTLE RUNNING YOUR MOUTH WITH CHECKS YOU CAN'T CASH. OFF-KEY SINGING LIKE A BARN OWL WITH HIS HEAD IN A BEEHIVE.
HELL, ROCK, AUSTIN 3:16 SAYS I JUST--
FOLLOW FRANKIE. SQUAWK.
FOLLOW FRANKIE. SQUAWK.
SUPPOSE WE SHOULD LISTEN TO THE BLUE-HEADED PIGEON.
WHY IN THE BLUE MOON WOULD WE DO THAT?
'CAUSE STONE COLD SAYS SO.
FOLLOW FRANKIE. SQUAWK.
FOLLOW FRANKIE. SQUAWK.
THAT'S THE BIRDMAN KOKO B. WARE! BUT WHO'S THE ROODY POO WITH THE SHADES.
BEATS ME. MUST BE AFTER OUR TIME. BUT I'M ROOTING FOR KOKO.
Asset #46 Koko B. Ware vs. Asset #63 The Miz.
YOU'VE GOT TO LIGHTEN UP, MY MAN. DO THE BIRD!
YOU THINK THIS IS A JOKE!
NO ONE DOES THAT TO ME! NOT SOME 1980S LIONEL RICHIE WANNABE! I'M A CROSS-PLATFORM MULTI-MEDIA SUPERSTAR.
I AM THE MIZ AND I AM AWESOME!
NO...
Asset #63: The Miz. Former WWE Champion. Former WWE Intercontinental Champion. Former WWE Tag Team Champion. Former WWE United States Champion.
sset #46: oko B. Ware.

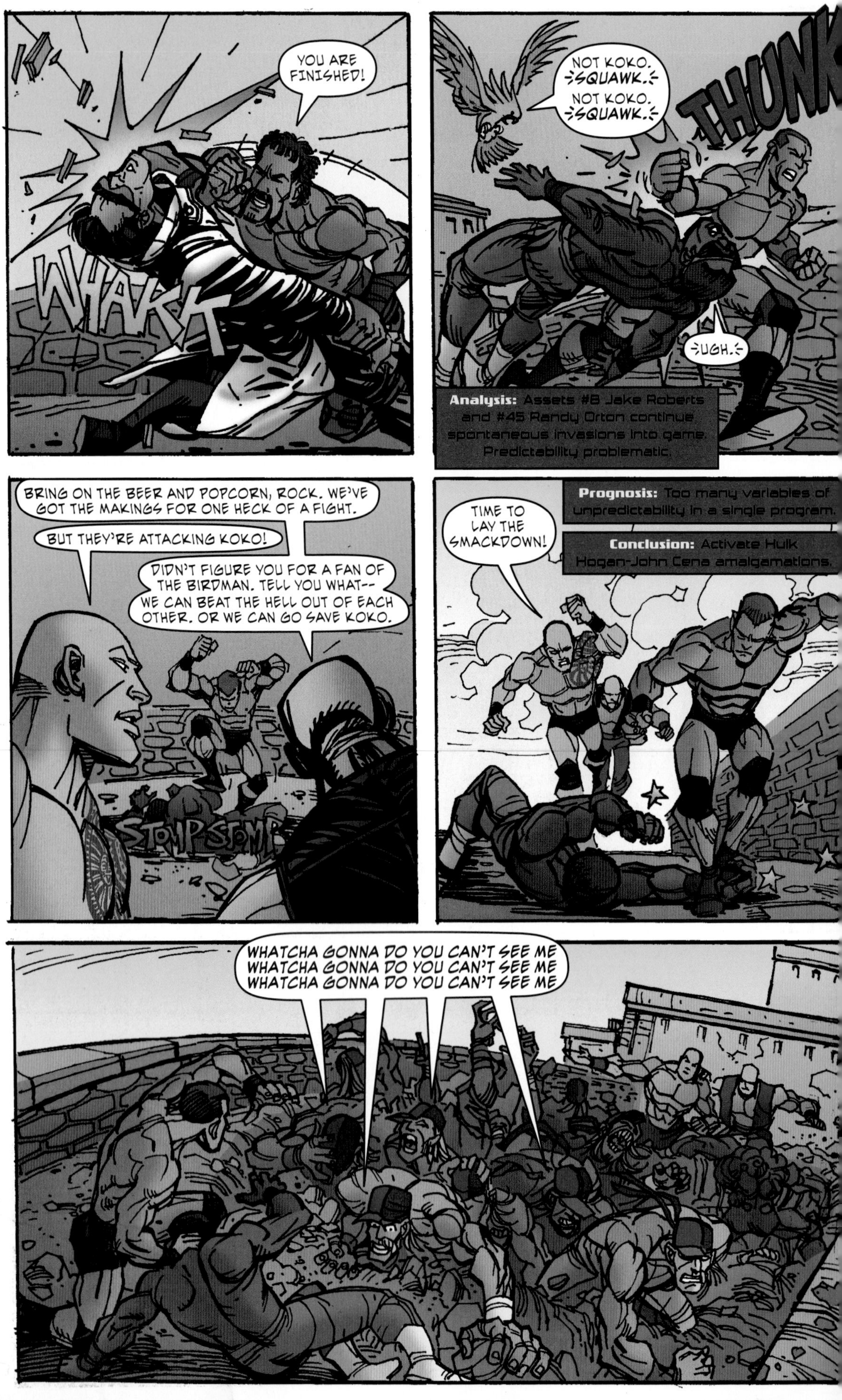
YOU ARE FINISHED!
WHAKK
NOT KOKO. SQUAWK. NOT KOKO. SQUAWK.
THUNK
UGH.
Analysis: Assets #8 Jake Roberts and #45 Randy Orton continue spontaneous invasions into game. Predictability problematic.
BRING ON THE BEER AND POPCORN, ROCK. WE'VE GOT THE MAKINGS FOR ONE HECK OF A FIGHT.
BUT THEY'RE ATTACKING KOKO!
DIDN'T FIGURE YOU FOR A FAN OF THE BIRDMAN. TELL YOU WHAT-- WE CAN BEAT THE HELL OUT OF EACH OTHER. OR WE CAN GO SAVE KOKO.
STOMP STOMP
Prognosis: Too many variables of unpredictability in a single program.
Conclusion: Activate Hulk Hogan-John Cena amalgamations.
TIME TO LAY THE SMACKDOWN!
WHATCHA GONNA DO YOU CAN'T SEE ME
WHATCHA GONNA DO YOU CAN'T SEE ME
WHATCHA GONNA DO YOU CAN'T SEE ME

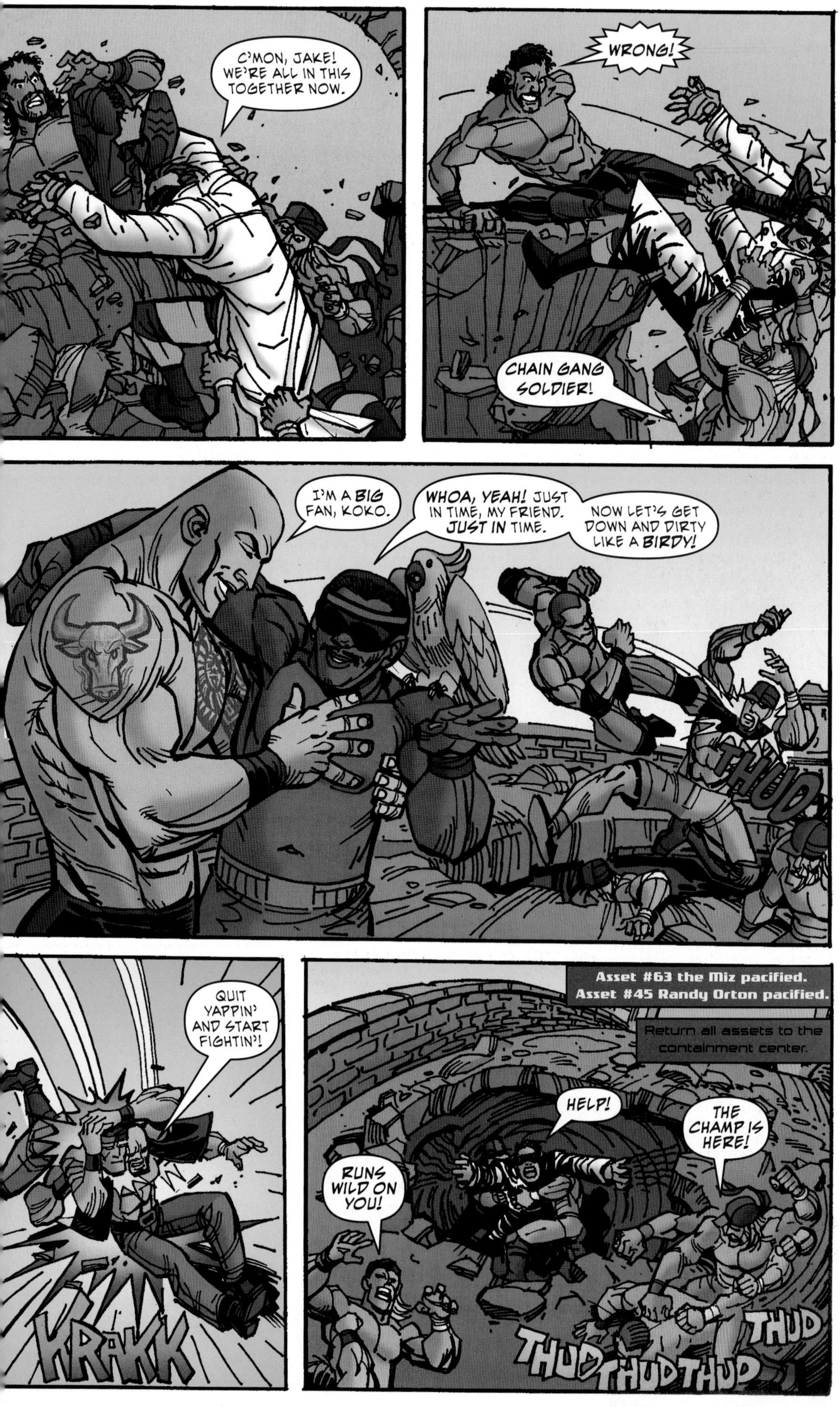
C'MON, JAKE! WE'RE ALL IN THIS TOGETHER NOW.
WRONG!
CHAIN GANG SOLDIER!
I'M A BIG FAN, KOKO.
WHOA, YEAH! JUST IN TIME, MY FRIEND. JUST IN TIME.
NOW LET'S GET DOWN AND DIRTY LIKE A BIRDY!
THUD
QUIT YAPPIN' AND START FIGHTIN'!
KRAKK
Asset #63 the Miz pacified.
Asset #45 Randy Orton pacified.
Return all assets to the containment center.
HELP!
THE CHAMP IS HERE!
RUNS WILD ON YOU!
THUD THUD THUD THUD

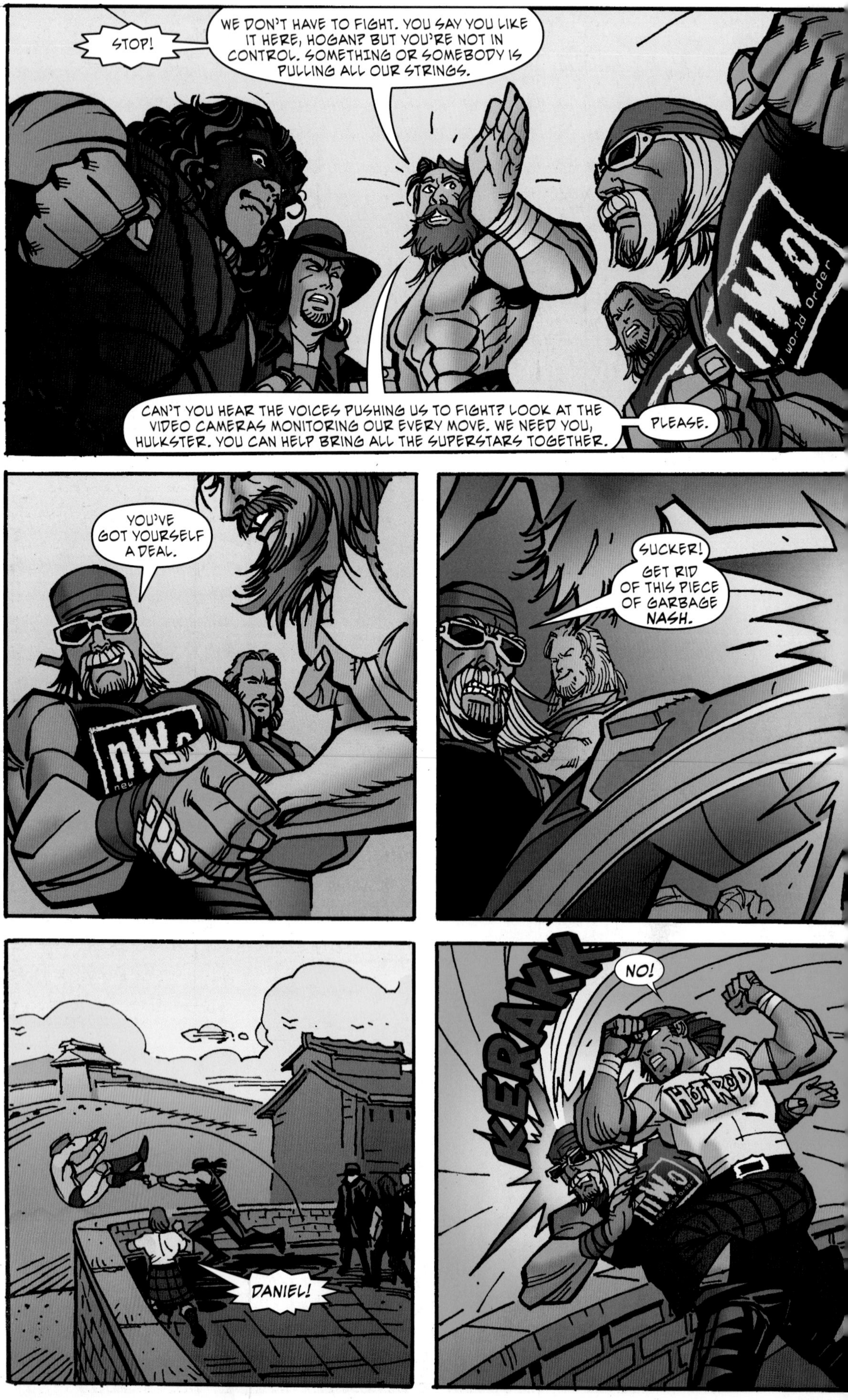
STOP!
WE DON'T HAVE TO FIGHT. YOU SAY YOU LIKE IT HERE, HOGAN? BUT YOU'RE NOT IN CONTROL. SOMETHING OR SOMEBODY IS PULLING ALL OUR STRINGS.
CAN'T YOU HEAR THE VOICES PUSHING US TO FIGHT? LOOK AT THE VIDEO CAMERAS MONITORING OUR EVERY MOVE. WE NEED YOU, HULKSTER. YOU CAN HELP BRING ALL THE SUPERSTARS TOGETHER.
PLEASE.
YOU'VE GOT YOURSELF A DEAL.
SUCKER! GET RID OF THIS PIECE OF GARBAGE NASH.
DANIEL!
KERAKK
NO!

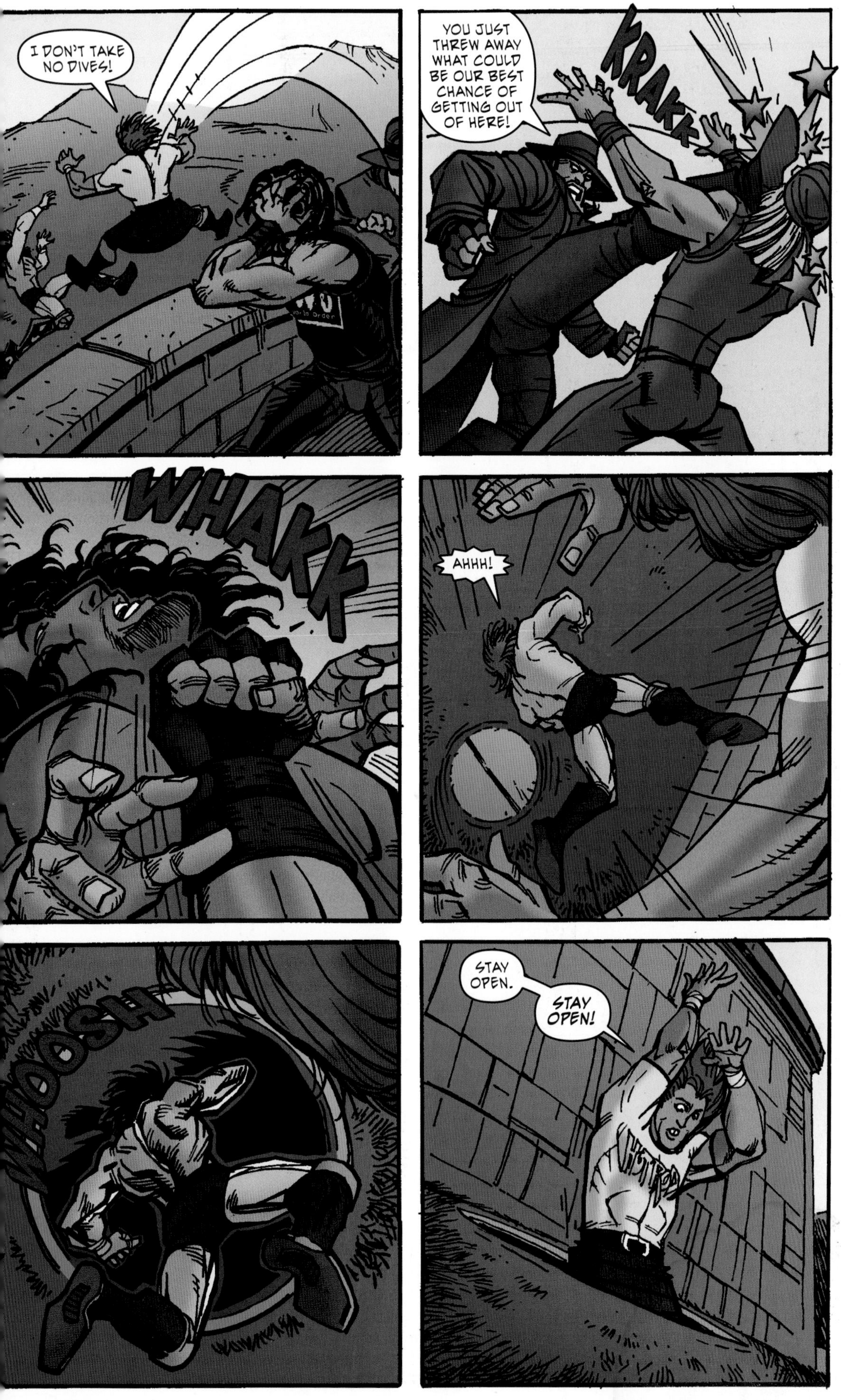
I DON'T TAKE NO DIVES!
YOU JUST THREW AWAY WHAT COULD BE OUR BEST CHANCE OF GETTING OUT OF HERE!
KRAKK
WHAKK
AHHH!
WHOOSH
STAY OPEN.
STAY OPEN!

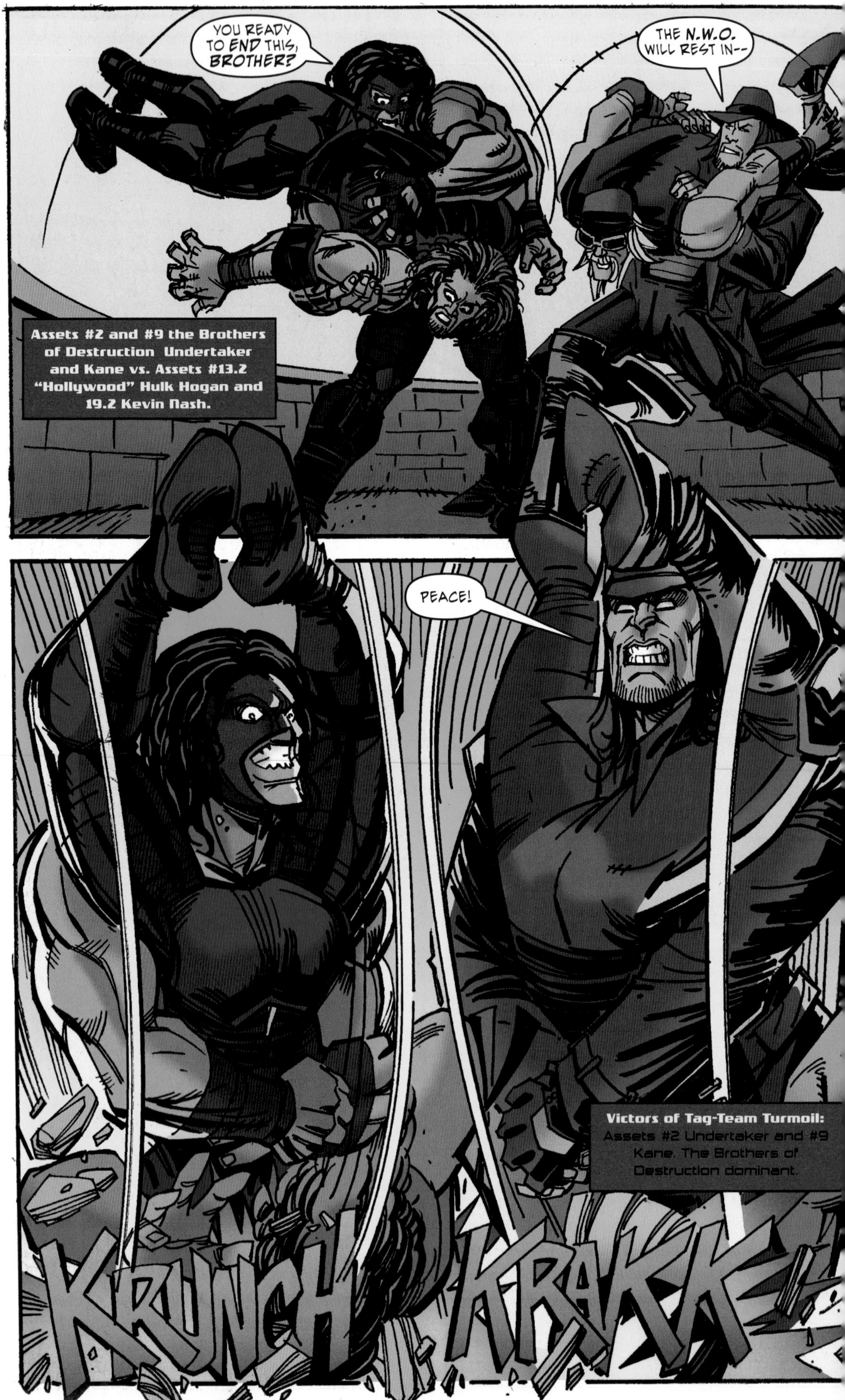
YOU READY TO END THIS, BROTHER?
THE N.W.O. WILL REST IN--
Assets #2 and #9 the Brothers of Destruction Undertaker and Kane vs. Assets #13.2 "Hollywood" Hulk Hogan and 19.2 Kevin Nash.
PEACE!
Victors of Tag-Team Turmoil: Assets #2 Undertaker and #9 Kane. The Brothers of Destruction dominant.
KRUNCH
KRAKK

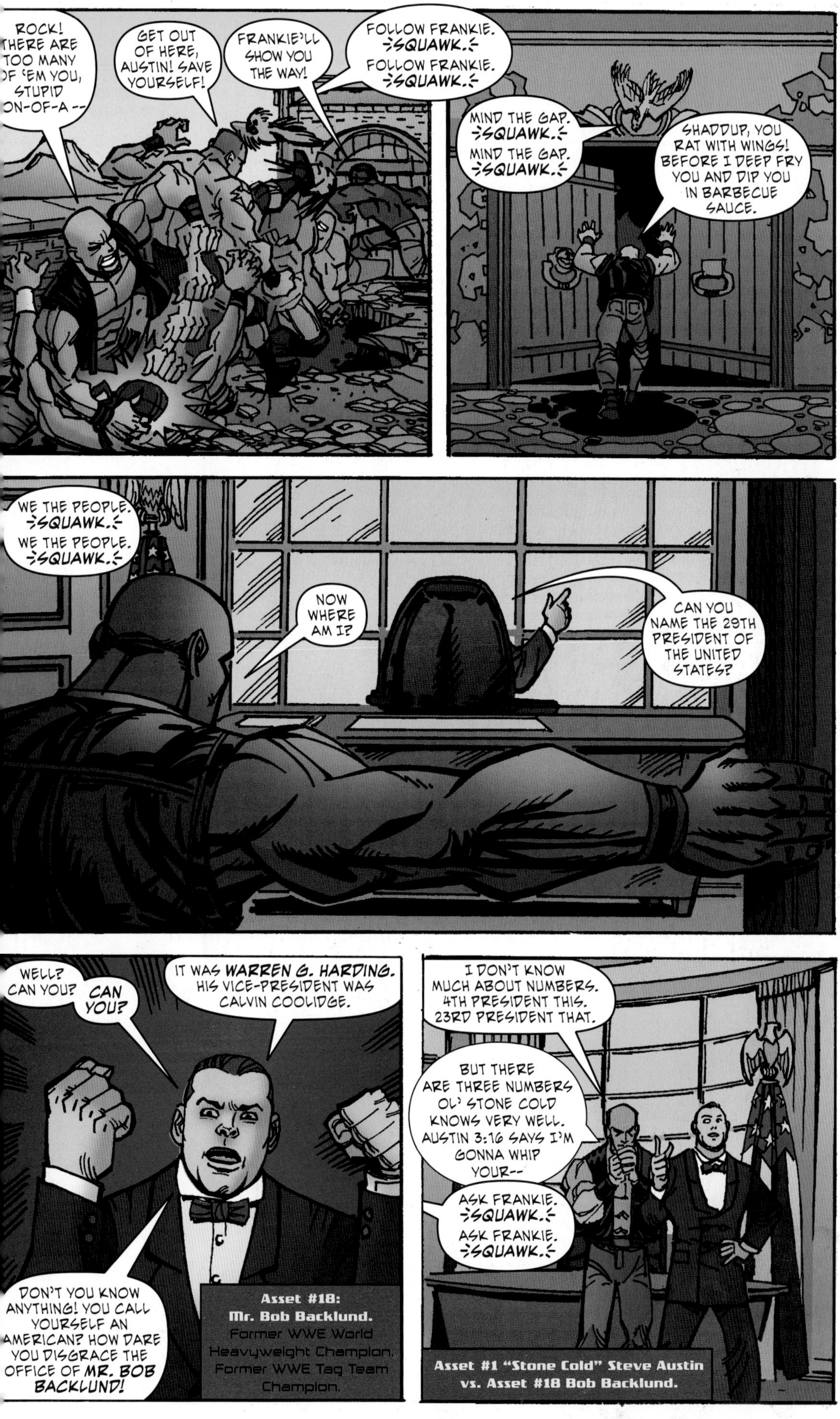

ROCK! THERE ARE TOO MANY OF 'EM YOU, STUPID SON-OF-A --
GET OUT OF HERE, AUSTIN! SAVE YOURSELF!
FRANKIE'LL SHOW YOU THE WAY!
FOLLOW FRANKIE. SQUAWK. FOLLOW FRANKIE. SQUAWK.
MIND THE GAP. SQUAWK. MIND THE GAP. SQUAWK.
SHADDUP, YOU RAT WITH WINGS! BEFORE I DEEP FRY YOU AND DIP YOU IN BARBECUE SAUCE.
WE THE PEOPLE. SQUAWK. WE THE PEOPLE. SQUAWK.
NOW WHERE AM I?
CAN YOU NAME THE 29TH PRESIDENT OF THE UNITED STATES?
WELL? CAN YOU? CAN YOU?
IT WAS WARREN G. HARDING. HIS VICE-PRESIDENT WAS CALVIN COOLIDGE.
DON'T YOU KNOW ANYTHING! YOU CALL YOURSELF AN AMERICAN? HOW DARE YOU DISGRACE THE OFFICE OF MR. BOB BACKLUND!
Asset #18: Mr. Bob Backlund. Former WWE World Heavyweight Champion. Former WWE Tag Team Champion.
I DON'T KNOW MUCH ABOUT NUMBERS. 4TH PRESIDENT THIS. 23RD PRESIDENT THAT.
BUT THERE ARE THREE NUMBERS OL' STONE COLD KNOWS VERY WELL. AUSTIN 3:16 SAYS I'M GONNA WHIP YOUR--
ASK FRANKIE. SQUAWK. ASK FRANKIE. SQUAWK.
Asset #1 "Stone Cold" Steve Austin vs. Asset #18 Bob Backlund.

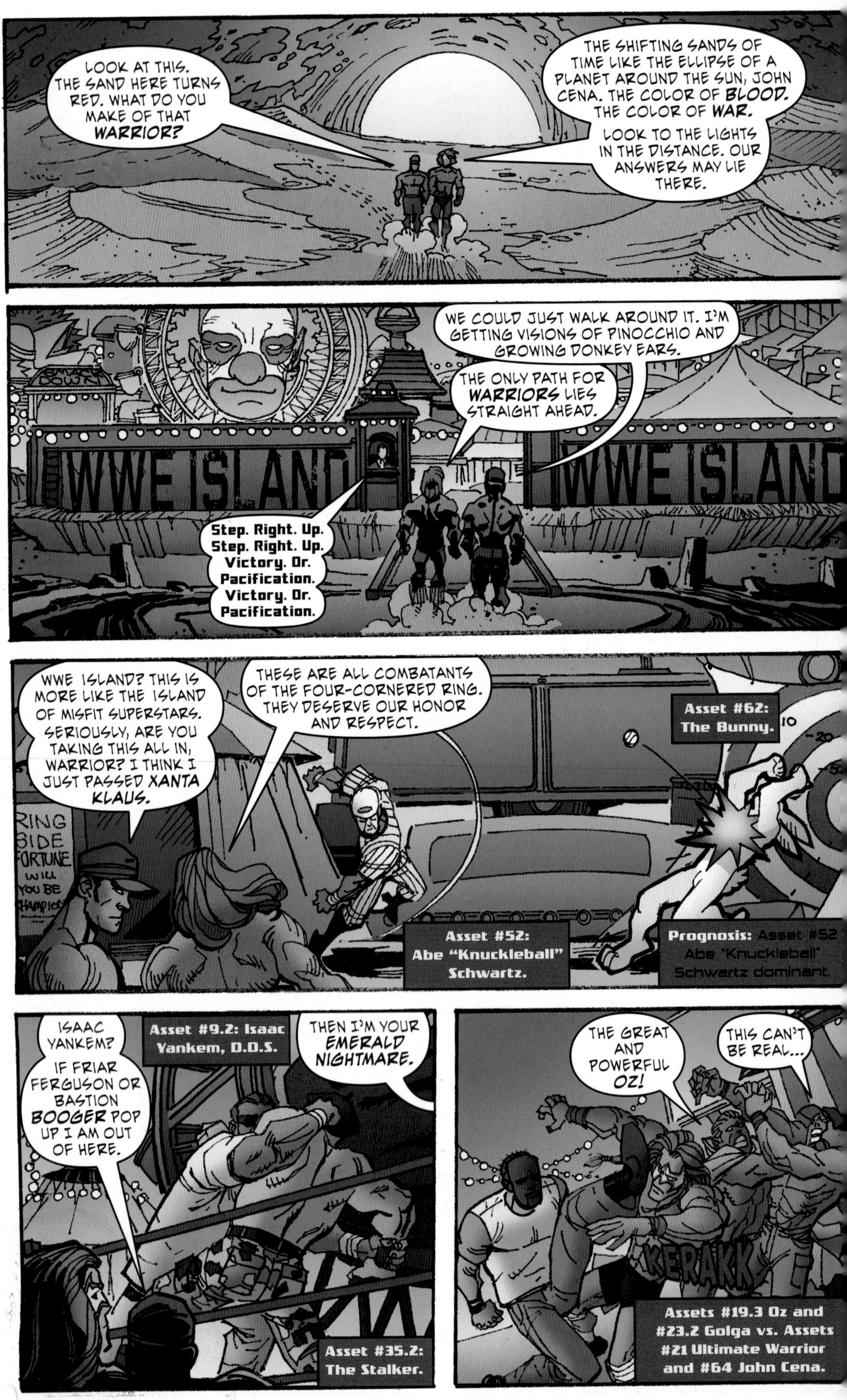
LOOK AT THIS. THE SAND HERE TURNS RED. WHAT DO YOU MAKE OF THAT WARRIOR?
THE SHIFTING SANDS OF TIME LIKE THE ELLIPSE OF A PLANET AROUND THE SUN, JOHN CENA. THE COLOR OF BLOOD. THE COLOR OF WAR.
LOOK TO THE LIGHTS IN THE DISTANCE. OUR ANSWERS MAY LIE THERE.
WE COULD JUST WALK AROUND IT. I'M GETTING VISIONS OF PINOCCHIO AND GROWING DONKEY EARS.
THE ONLY PATH FOR WARRIORS LIES STRAIGHT AHEAD.
WWE ISLAND
WWE ISLAND
Step. Right. Up. Step. Right. Up. Victory. Or. Pacification. Victory. Or. Pacification.
WWE ISLAND? THIS IS MORE LIKE THE ISLAND OF MISFIT SUPERSTARS. SERIOUSLY, ARE YOU TAKING THIS ALL IN, WARRIOR? I THINK I JUST PASSED XANTA KLAUS.
THESE ARE ALL COMBATANTS OF THE FOUR-CORNERED RING. THEY DESERVE OUR HONOR AND RESPECT.
Asset #62: The Bunny.
RING SIDE FORTUNE WILL YOU BE CHAMPION
Asset #52: Abe "Knuckleball" Schwartz.
Prognosis: Asset #52 Abe "Knuckleball" Schwartz dominant.
ISAAC YANKEM?
IF FRIAR FERGUSON OR BASTION BOOGER POP UP I AM OUT OF HERE.
Asset #9.2: Isaac Yankem, D.D.S.
THEN I'M YOUR EMERALD NIGHTMARE.
Asset #35.2: The Stalker.
THE GREAT AND POWERFUL OZ!
THIS CAN'T BE REAL...
KERAKK
Assets #19.3 Oz and #23.2 Golga vs. Assets #21 Ultimate Warrior and #64 John Cena.

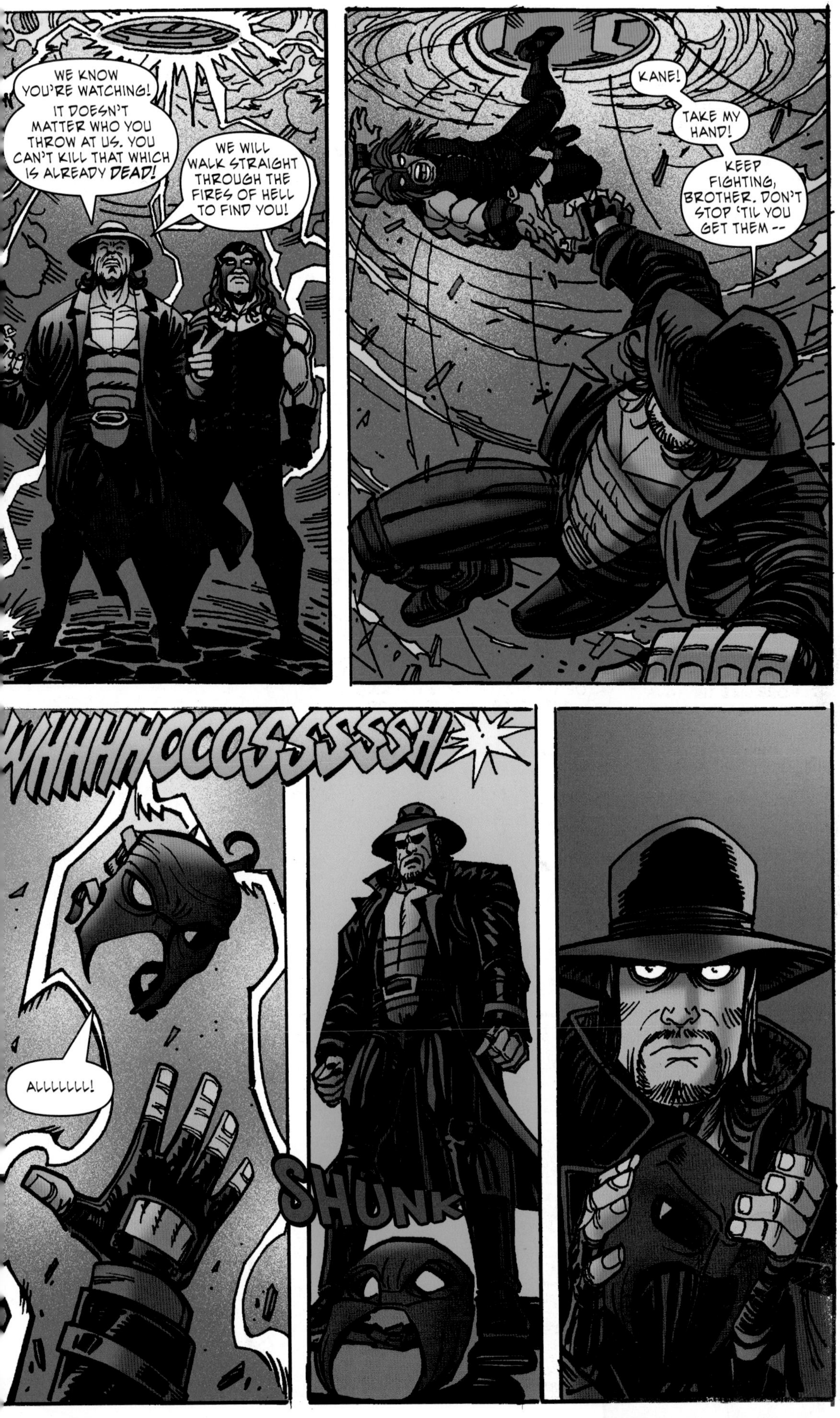
WE KNOW YOU'RE WATCHING! IT DOESN'T MATTER WHO YOU THROW AT US. YOU CAN'T KILL THAT WHICH IS ALREADY DEAD!
WE WILL WALK STRAIGHT THROUGH THE FIRES OF HELL TO FIND YOU!
KANE!
TAKE MY HAND!
KEEP FIGHTING, BROTHER. DON'T STOP 'TIL YOU GET THEM --
WHHHHOOOOSSSSSSH
ALLLLLLLL!
SHUNK

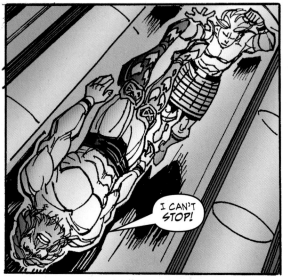

I CAN'T STOP!

≥UMPH.≤

SMACK

BACK WHERE WE STARTED. I DON'T GET IT, PIPER. IF THEY CAN JUST TRANSPORT US ANYWHERE WHY EVEN ALLOW US TO ROAM FREE?

IT'S ALL PART OF SOME SICK GAME.

IT DOESN'T MATTER IF THEY ARE WATCHING OUR EVERY MOVE. WE WILL FIGURE OUT A WAY TO TAKE THEM DOWN.

PIPER!

KERAKK

THE MASTER SAYS YOU'RE BREAKING THE CODES.

YOU'RE NOT PLAYING THE GAME.

YOU'RE LESS THAN PERFECT.

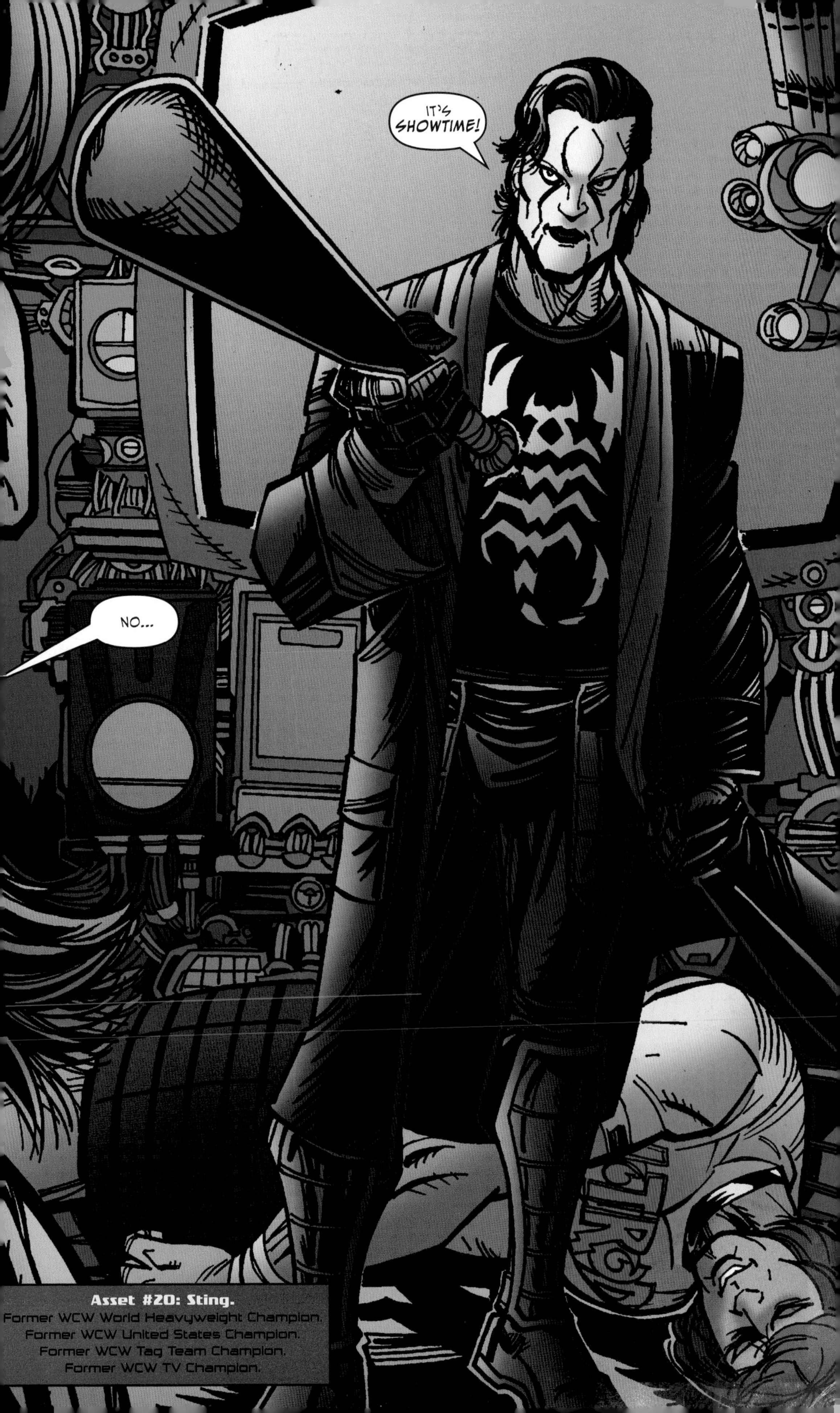
IT'S SHOWTIME!
NO...
Asset #20: Sting.
Former WCW World Heavyweight Champion.
Former WCW United States Champion.
Former WCW Tag Team Champion.
Former WCW TV Champion.

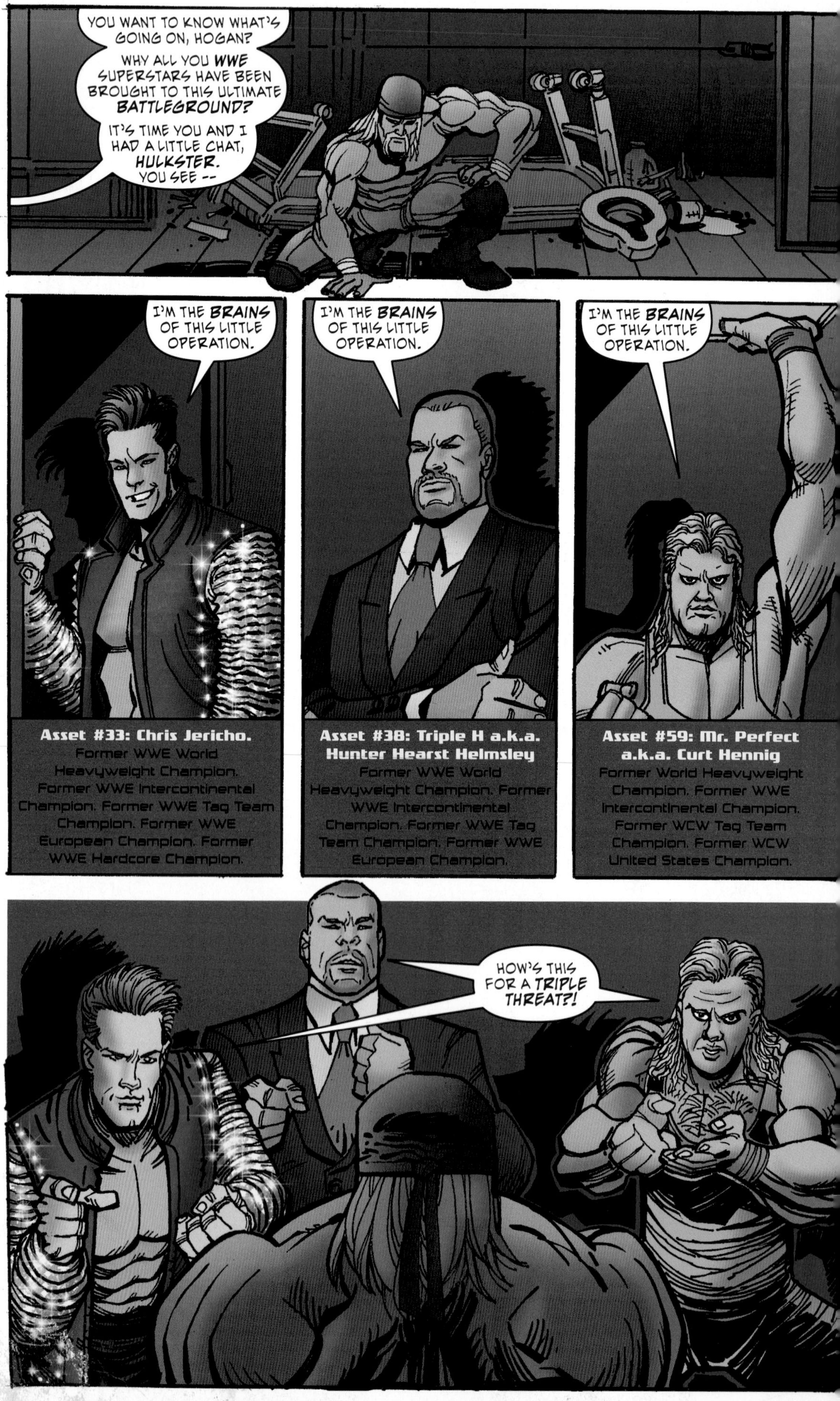
YOU WANT TO KNOW WHAT'S GOING ON, HOGAN?
WHY ALL YOU WWE SUPERSTARS HAVE BEEN BROUGHT TO THIS ULTIMATE BATTLEGROUND?
IT'S TIME YOU AND I HAD A LITTLE CHAT, HULKSTER. YOU SEE --
I'M THE BRAINS OF THIS LITTLE OPERATION.
Asset #33: Chris Jericho. Former WWE World Heavyweight Champion. Former WWE Intercontinental Champion. Former WWE Tag Team Champion. Former WWE European Champion. Former WWE Hardcore Champion.
I'M THE BRAINS OF THIS LITTLE OPERATION.
Asset #38: Triple H a.k.a. Hunter Hearst Helmsley Former WWE World Heavyweight Champion. Former WWE Intercontinental Champion. Former WWE Tag Team Champion. Former WWE European Champion.
I'M THE BRAINS OF THIS LITTLE OPERATION.
Asset #59: Mr. Perfect a.k.a. Curt Hennig Former World Heavyweight Champion. Former WWE Intercontinental Champion. Former WCW Tag Team Champion. Former WCW United States Champion.
HOW'S THIS FOR A TRIPLE THREAT?!

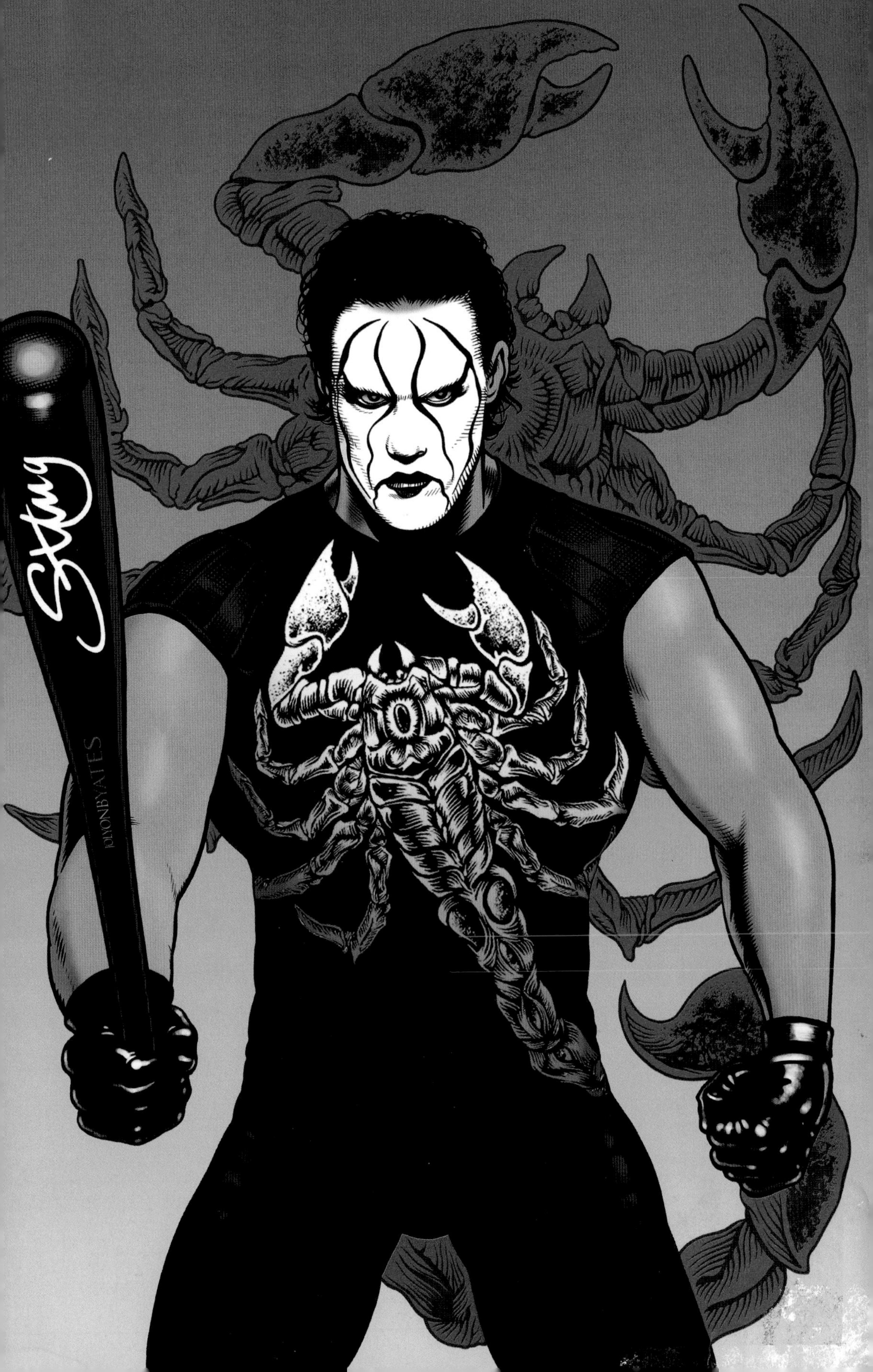
Sting

PART FOUR
"3:16"

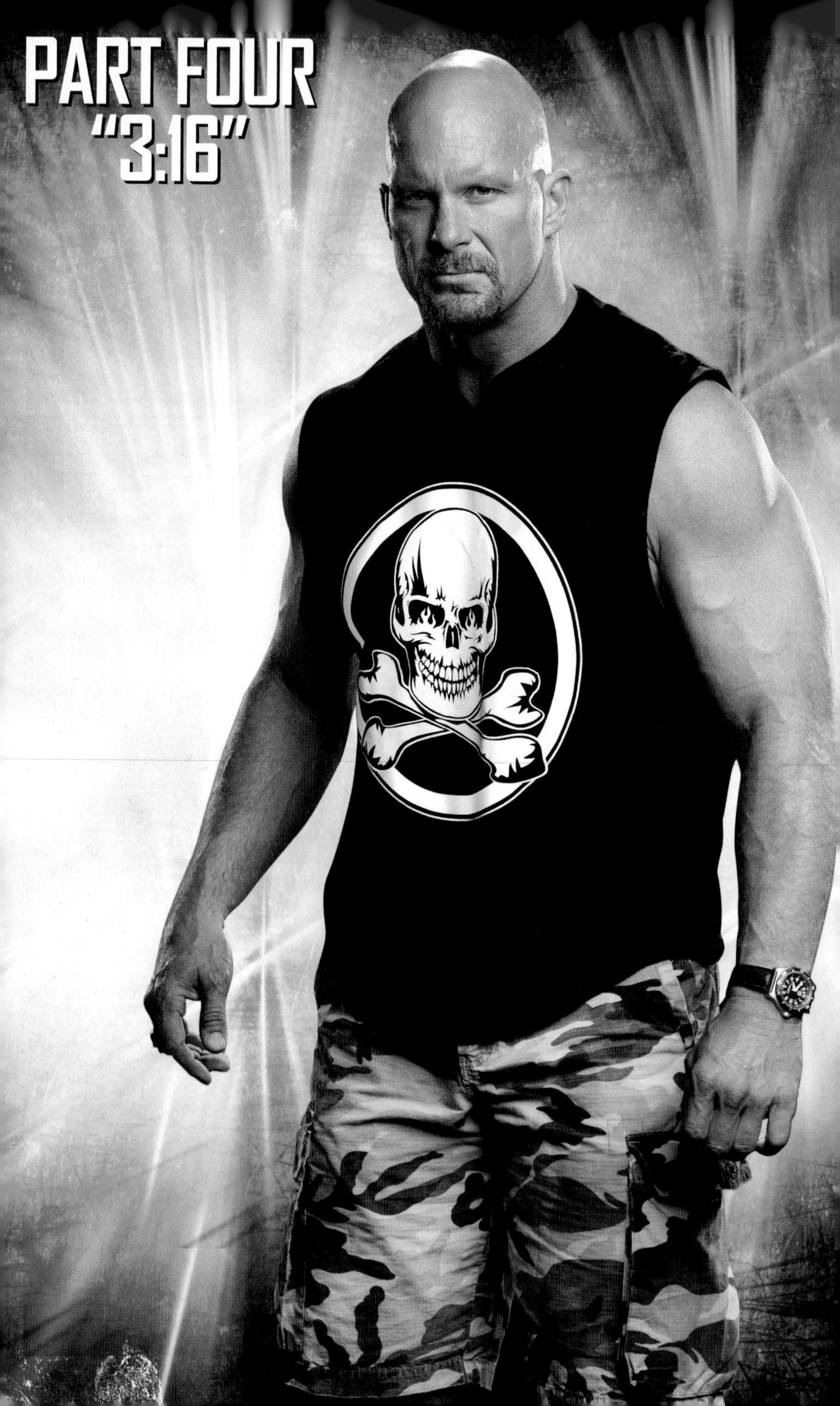

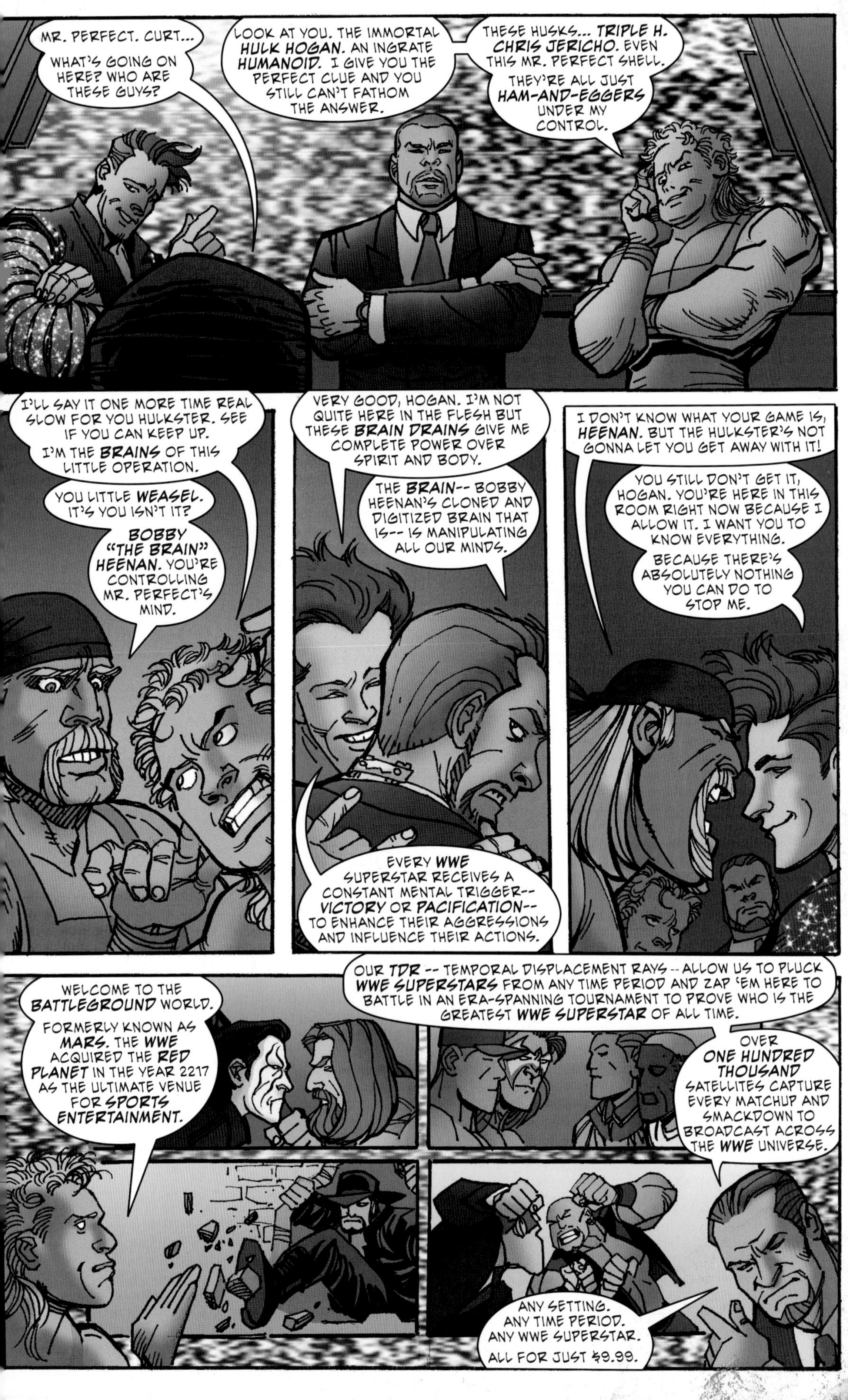
MR. PERFECT. CURT... WHAT'S GOING ON HERE? WHO ARE THESE GUYS?
LOOK AT YOU. THE IMMORTAL HULK HOGAN. AN INGRATE HUMANOID. I GIVE YOU THE PERFECT CLUE AND YOU STILL CAN'T FATHOM THE ANSWER.
THESE HUSKS... TRIPLE H. CHRIS JERICHO. EVEN THIS MR. PERFECT SHELL.
THEY'RE ALL JUST HAM-AND-EGGERS UNDER MY CONTROL.
I'LL SAY IT ONE MORE TIME REAL SLOW FOR YOU HULKSTER. SEE IF YOU CAN KEEP UP.
I'M THE BRAINS OF THIS LITTLE OPERATION.
YOU LITTLE WEASEL. IT'S YOU ISN'T IT?
BOBBY "THE BRAIN" HEENAN. YOU'RE CONTROLLING MR. PERFECT'S MIND.
VERY GOOD, HOGAN. I'M NOT QUITE HERE IN THE FLESH BUT THESE BRAIN DRAINS GIVE ME COMPLETE POWER OVER SPIRIT AND BODY.
THE BRAIN-- BOBBY HEENAN'S CLONED AND DIGITIZED BRAIN THAT IS-- IS MANIPULATING ALL OUR MINDS.
EVERY WWE SUPERSTAR RECEIVES A CONSTANT MENTAL TRIGGER-- VICTORY OR PACIFICATION-- TO ENHANCE THEIR AGGRESSIONS AND INFLUENCE THEIR ACTIONS.
I DON'T KNOW WHAT YOUR GAME IS, HEENAN. BUT THE HULKSTER'S NOT GONNA LET YOU GET AWAY WITH IT!
YOU STILL DON'T GET IT, HOGAN. YOU'RE HERE IN THIS ROOM RIGHT NOW BECAUSE I ALLOW IT. I WANT YOU TO KNOW EVERYTHING.
BECAUSE THERE'S ABSOLUTELY NOTHING YOU CAN DO TO STOP ME.
WELCOME TO THE BATTLEGROUND WORLD.
FORMERLY KNOWN AS MARS. THE WWE ACQUIRED THE RED PLANET IN THE YEAR 2217 AS THE ULTIMATE VENUE FOR SPORTS ENTERTAINMENT.
OUR TDR -- TEMPORAL DISPLACEMENT RAYS -- ALLOW US TO PLUCK WWE SUPERSTARS FROM ANY TIME PERIOD AND ZAP 'EM HERE TO BATTLE IN AN ERA-SPANNING TOURNAMENT TO PROVE WHO IS THE GREATEST WWE SUPERSTAR OF ALL TIME.
OVER ONE HUNDRED THOUSAND SATELLITES CAPTURE EVERY MATCHUP AND SMACKDOWN TO BROADCAST ACROSS THE WWE UNIVERSE.
ANY SETTING. ANY TIME PERIOD. ANY WWE SUPERSTAR.
ALL FOR JUST $9.99.

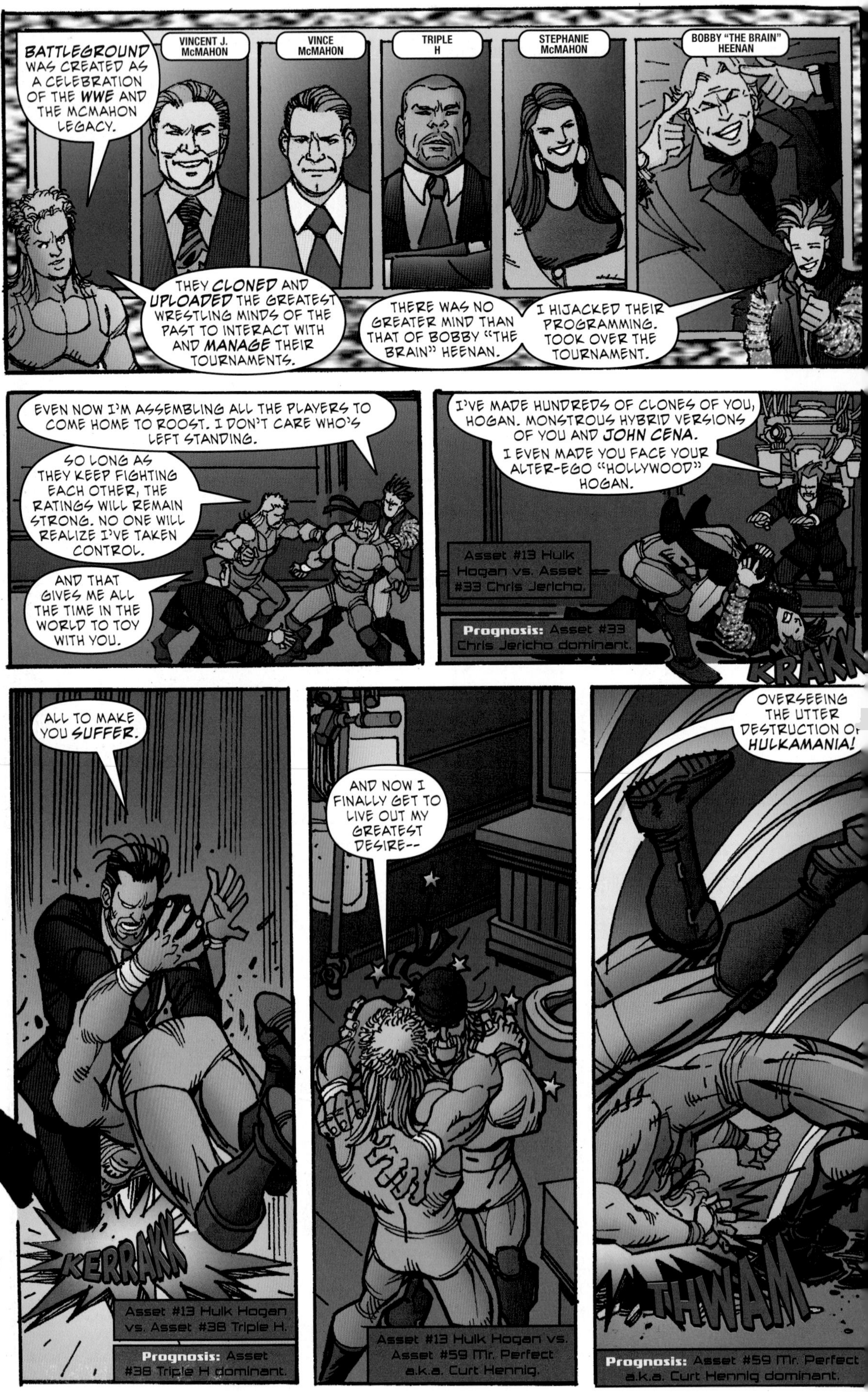

BATTLEGROUND WAS CREATED AS A CELEBRATION OF THE WWE AND THE MCMAHON LEGACY.
VINCENT J. McMAHON
VINCE McMAHON
TRIPLE H
STEPHANIE McMAHON
BOBBY "THE BRAIN" HEENAN
THEY CLONED AND UPLOADED THE GREATEST WRESTLING MINDS OF THE PAST TO INTERACT WITH AND MANAGE THEIR TOURNAMENTS.
THERE WAS NO GREATER MIND THAN THAT OF BOBBY "THE BRAIN" HEENAN.
I HIJACKED THEIR PROGRAMMING. TOOK OVER THE TOURNAMENT.
EVEN NOW I'M ASSEMBLING ALL THE PLAYERS TO COME HOME TO ROOST. I DON'T CARE WHO'S LEFT STANDING.
SO LONG AS THEY KEEP FIGHTING EACH OTHER, THE RATINGS WILL REMAIN STRONG. NO ONE WILL REALIZE I'VE TAKEN CONTROL.
AND THAT GIVES ME ALL THE TIME IN THE WORLD TO TOY WITH YOU.
I'VE MADE HUNDREDS OF CLONES OF YOU, HOGAN. MONSTROUS HYBRID VERSIONS OF YOU AND JOHN CENA.
I EVEN MADE YOU FACE YOUR ALTER-EGO "HOLLYWOOD" HOGAN.
Asset #13 Hulk Hogan vs. Asset #33 Chris Jericho.
Prognosis: Asset #33 Chris Jericho dominant.
KRAKK
ALL TO MAKE YOU SUFFER.
KERRAKK
Asset #13 Hulk Hogan vs. Asset #38 Triple H.
Prognosis: Asset #38 Triple H dominant.
AND NOW I FINALLY GET TO LIVE OUT MY GREATEST DESIRE--
Asset #13 Hulk Hogan vs. Asset #59 Mr. Perfect a.k.a. Curt Hennig.
OVERSEEING THE UTTER DESTRUCTION OF HULKAMANIA!
THWAM
Prognosis: Asset #59 Mr. Perfect a.k.a. Curt Hennig dominant.

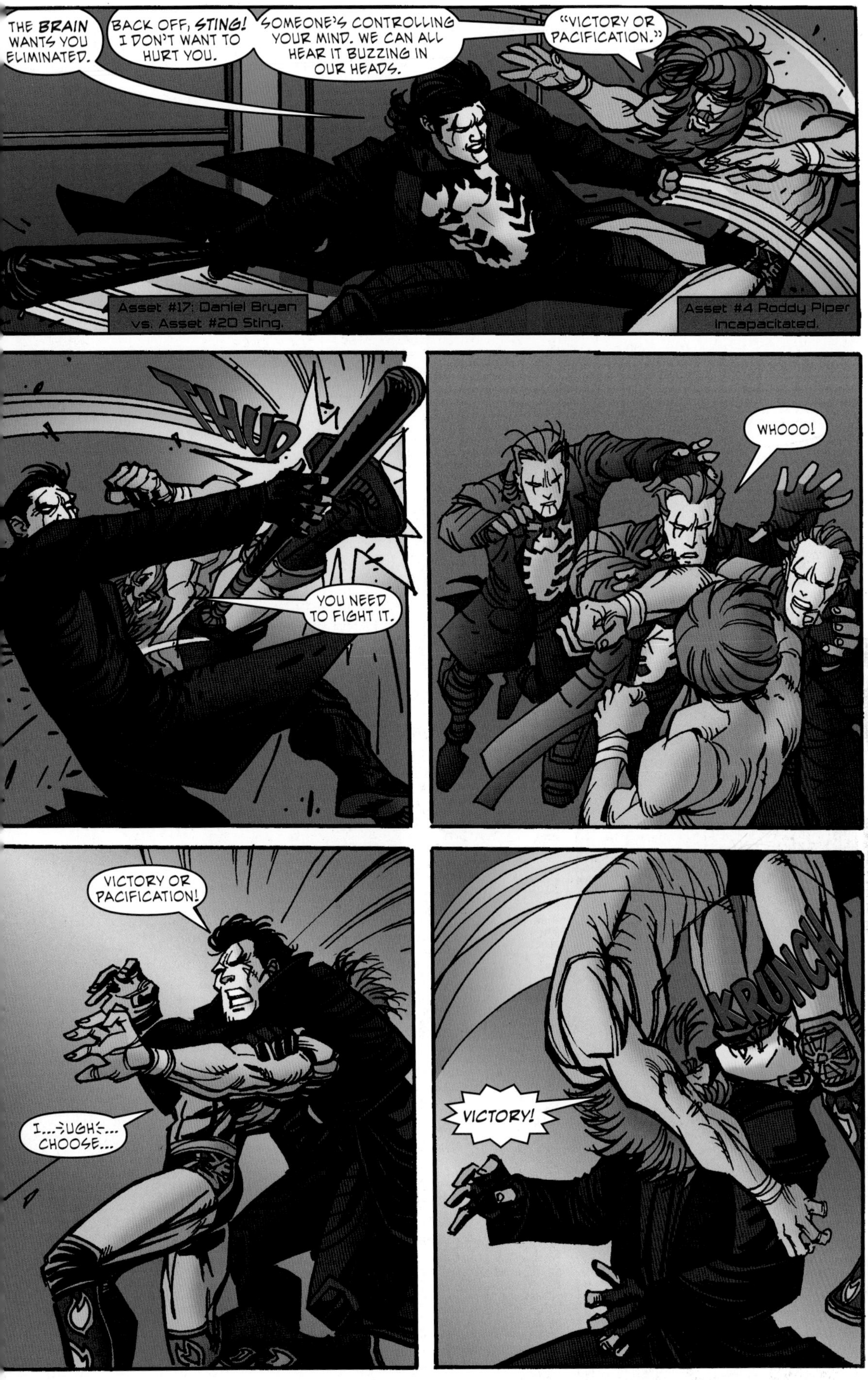
THE BRAIN WANTS YOU ELIMINATED.
BACK OFF, STING! I DON'T WANT TO HURT YOU.
SOMEONE'S CONTROLLING YOUR MIND. WE CAN ALL HEAR IT BUZZING IN OUR HEADS.
"VICTORY OR PACIFICATION."
Asset #17: Daniel Bryan vs. Asset #20 Sting.
Asset #4 Roddy Piper incapacitated.
THUD
YOU NEED TO FIGHT IT.
WHOOO!
VICTORY OR PACIFICATION!
I...UGH... CHOOSE...
KRUNCH
VICTORY!

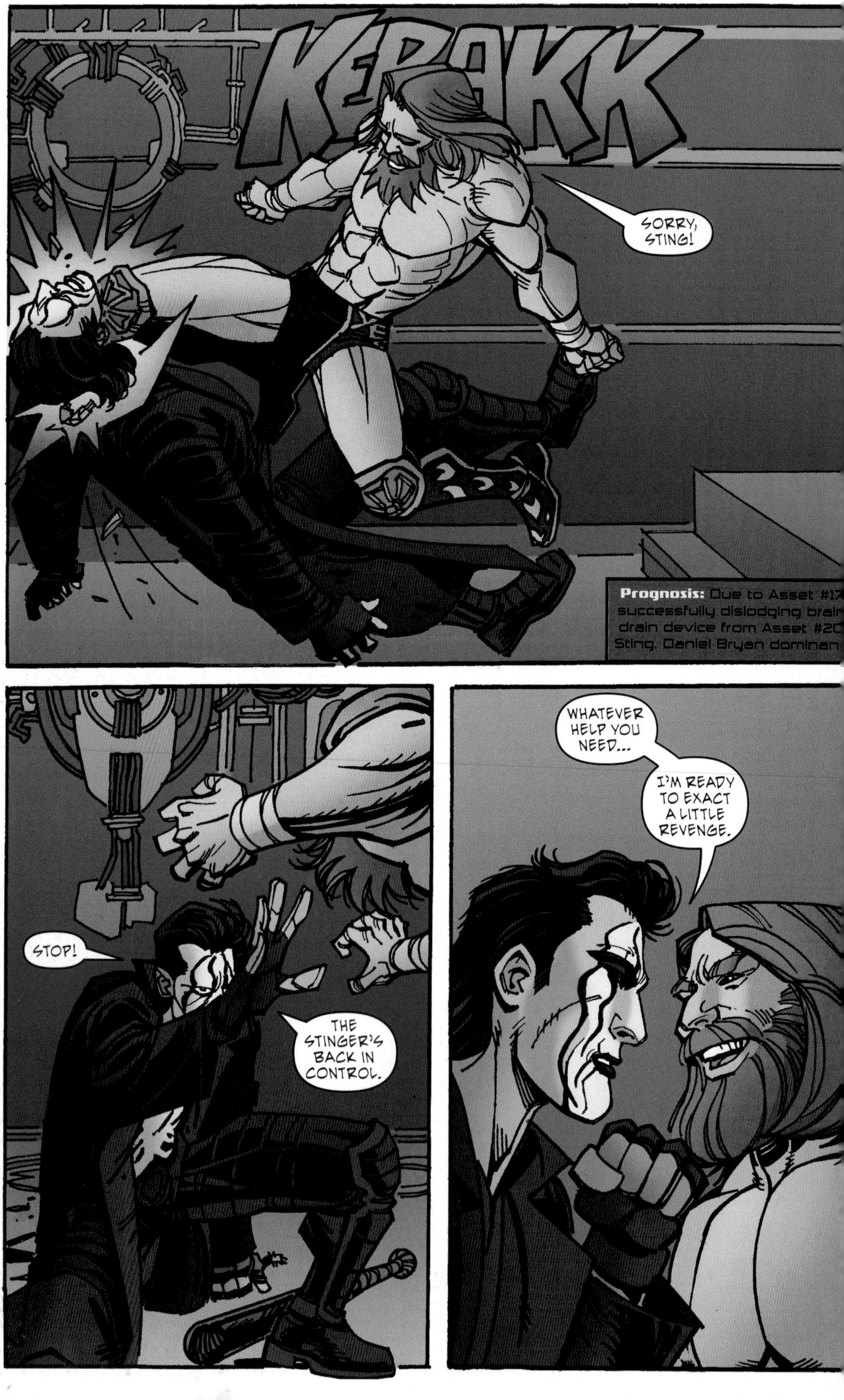
KERAKK
SORRY, STING!
Prognosis: Due to Asset #17 successfully dislodging brain drain device from Asset #20 Sting, Daniel Bryan dominan
STOP!
THE STINGER'S BACK IN CONTROL.
WHATEVER HELP YOU NEED...
I'M READY TO EXACT A LITTLE REVENGE.

"OH, WHAT A TANGLED WEB WE WEAVE, WHEN FIRST WE PRACTICE TO DECEIVE."

THAT'S A LITTLE SNAKESPEARE FOR YOU, UNDERTAKER.*

*ACTUALLY, IT'S SIR WALTER SCOTT. — JIM "THE EDITOR" SALICRUP

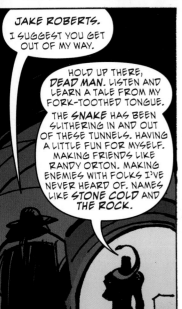

JAKE ROBERTS. I SUGGEST YOU GET OUT OF MY WAY.

HOLD UP THERE, DEAD MAN. LISTEN AND LEARN A TALE FROM MY FORK-TOOTHED TONGUE.

THE SNAKE HAS BEEN SLITHERING IN AND OUT OF THESE TUNNELS. HAVING A LITTLE FUN FOR MYSELF. MAKING FRIENDS LIKE RANDY ORTON. MAKING ENEMIES WITH FOLKS I'VE NEVER HEARD OF. NAMES LIKE STONE COLD AND THE ROCK.

ALL MY LIFE I'VE BEEN ON THE OTHER SIDE OF THE FENCE. THE DARK SIDE.

YOU SAY YOU'RE ON THE DARK SIDE, UNDERTAKER. BUT YOU'VE NEVER WALKED THE FEARLESS LINE I HAVE. THAT RAZOR'S EDGE. BUT NOW...

NOW I AM AFRAID.

THAT'S RIGHT. THE SNAKE IS SCARED. DAMIEN KNOWS IT'S TRUE.

LEAD THE WAY, ROBERTS.

BUT KNOW IF YOU BETRAY THE REAPER, I WILL SHOW YOU THE JUST HOW EVIL THE DARK SIDE CAN BE.

YOU DON'T WANT TO SEE MY FANGS.

I NEED YOUR HELP TO FREE THEM.

I THOUGHT I COULD RULE THIS WORLD. BUT I SAW CREATURES COME OUT OF THE DEPTHS OF HELL AND SWALLOW FRIENDS AND ENEMIES. ABSOLUTE HORRORS THAT WERE HALF HULK HOGAN, HALF I DON'T KNOW WHAT.

BUT NOW I KNOW WHERE THEY'RE HIDING THE BODIES, UNDERTAKER.

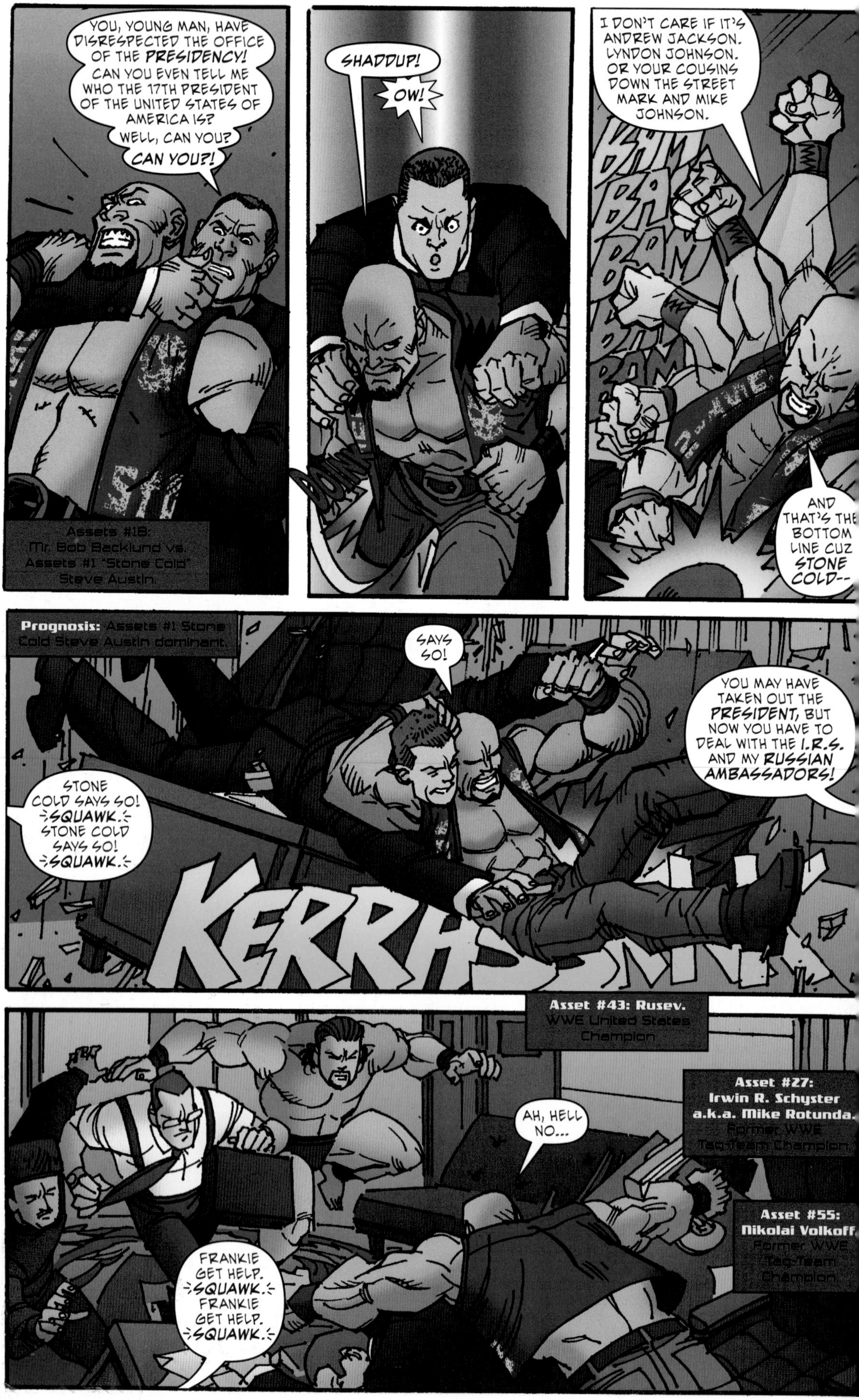

YOU, YOUNG MAN, HAVE DISRESPECTED THE OFFICE OF THE PRESIDENCY! CAN YOU EVEN TELL ME WHO THE 17TH PRESIDENT OF THE UNITED STATES OF AMERICA IS? WELL, CAN YOU? CAN YOU?!
Assets #18: Mr. Bob Backlund vs. Assets #1 "Stone Cold" Steve Austin.
SHADDUP!
OW!
I DON'T CARE IF IT'S ANDREW JACKSON. LYNDON JOHNSON. OR YOUR COUSINS DOWN THE STREET MARK AND MIKE JOHNSON.
AND THAT'S THE BOTTOM LINE CUZ STONE COLD--
Prognosis: Assets #1 Stone Cold Steve Austin dominant.
SAYS SO!
YOU MAY HAVE TAKEN OUT THE PRESIDENT, BUT NOW YOU HAVE TO DEAL WITH THE I.R.S. AND MY RUSSIAN AMBASSADORS!
STONE COLD SAYS SO! -SQUAWK.- STONE COLD SAYS SO! -SQUAWK.-
Asset #43: Rusev. WWE United States Champion
Asset #27: Irwin R. Schyster a.k.a. Mike Rotunda. Former WWE Tag-Team Champion.
AH, HELL NO...
Asset #55: Nikolai Volkoff. Former WWE Tag-Team Champion.
FRANKIE GET HELP. -SQUAWK.- FRANKIE GET HELP. -SQUAWK.-

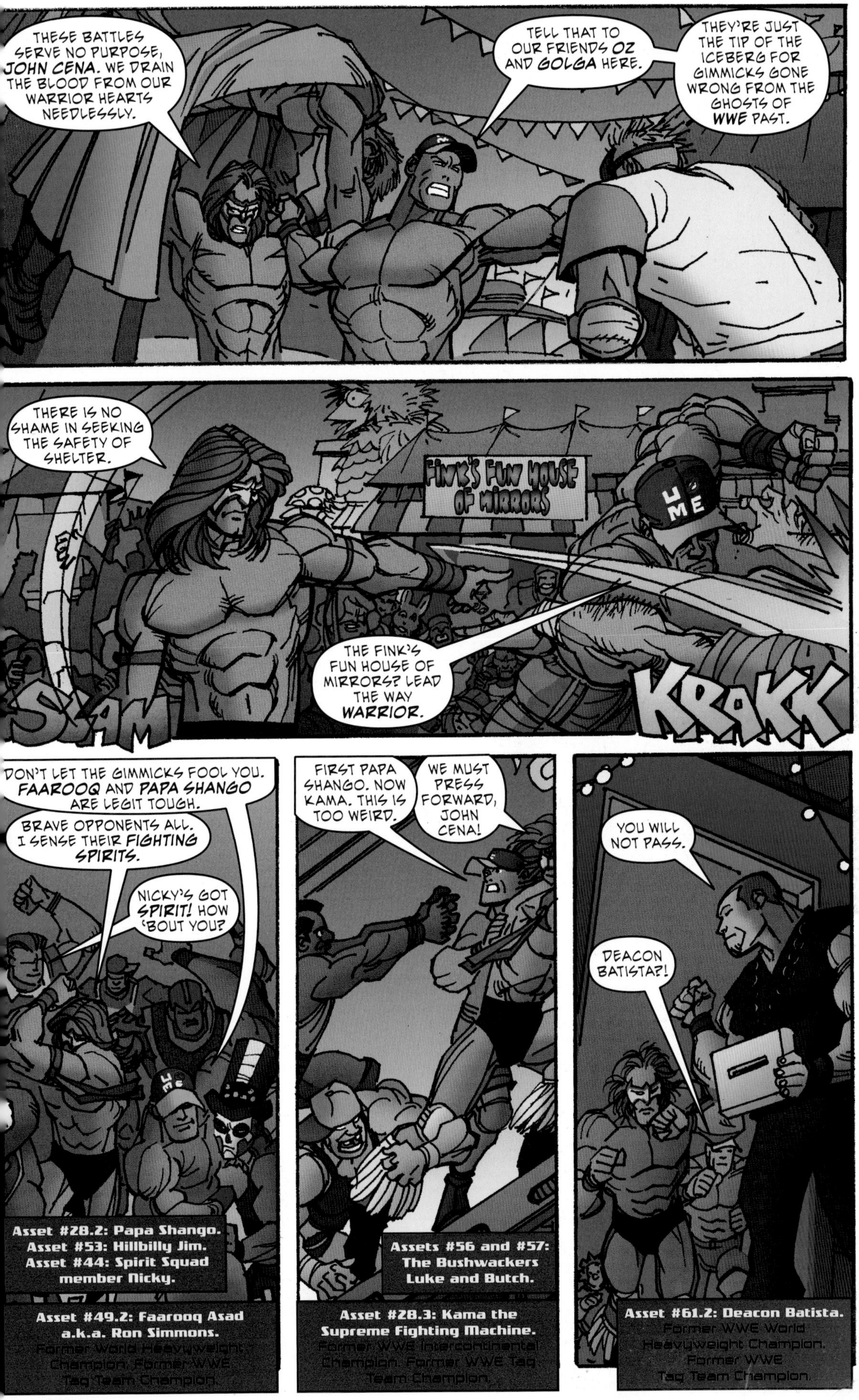
THESE BATTLES SERVE NO PURPOSE, JOHN CENA. WE DRAIN THE BLOOD FROM OUR WARRIOR HEARTS NEEDLESSLY.
TELL THAT TO OUR FRIENDS OZ AND GOLGA HERE.
THEY'RE JUST THE TIP OF THE ICEBERG FOR GIMMICKS GONE WRONG FROM THE GHOSTS OF WWE PAST.
THERE IS NO SHAME IN SEEKING THE SAFETY OF SHELTER.
FINK'S FUN HOUSE OF MIRRORS
THE FINK'S FUN HOUSE OF MIRRORS? LEAD THE WAY WARRIOR.
SLAM
KRAKK
DON'T LET THE GIMMICKS FOOL YOU. FAAROOQ AND PAPA SHANGO ARE LEGIT TOUGH.
BRAVE OPPONENTS ALL. I SENSE THEIR FIGHTING SPIRITS.
NICKY'S GOT SPIRIT! HOW 'BOUT YOU?
Asset #28.2: Papa Shango.
Asset #53: Hillbilly Jim.
Asset #44: Spirit Squad member Nicky.
Asset #49.2: Faarooq Asad a.k.a. Ron Simmons.
Former World Heavyweight Champion. Former WWE Tag Team Champion.
FIRST PAPA SHANGO. NOW KAMA. THIS IS TOO WEIRD.
WE MUST PRESS FORWARD, JOHN CENA!
Assets #56 and #57: The Bushwackers Luke and Butch.
Asset #28.3: Kama the Supreme Fighting Machine.
Former WWE Intercontinental Champion. Former WWE Tag Team Champion.
YOU WILL NOT PASS.
DEACON BATISTA?!
Asset #61.2: Deacon Batista.
Former WWE World Heavyweight Champion.
Former WWE Tag Team Champion.

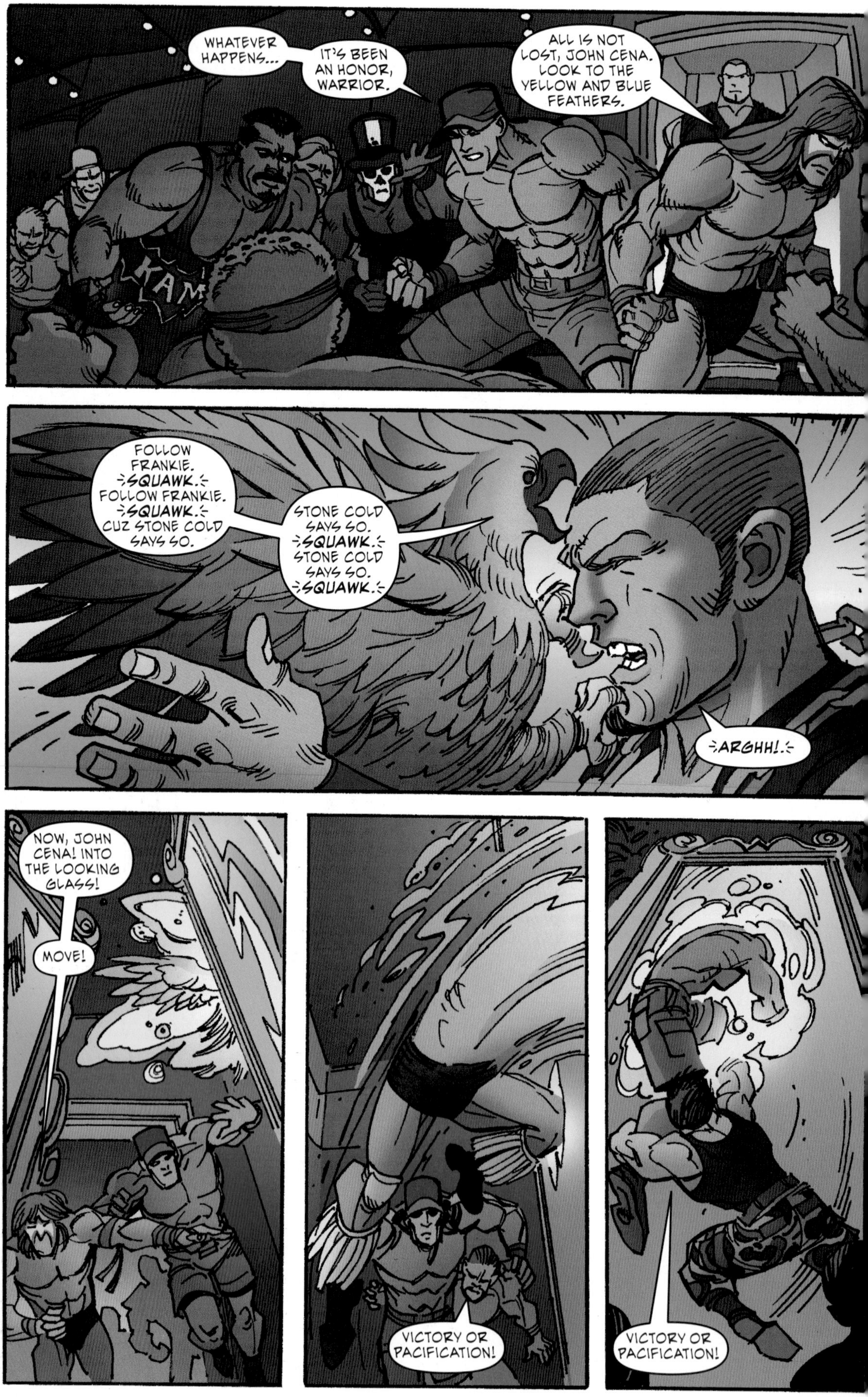
WHATEVER HAPPENS...
IT'S BEEN AN HONOR, WARRIOR.
ALL IS NOT LOST, JOHN CENA. LOOK TO THE YELLOW AND BLUE FEATHERS.
FOLLOW FRANKIE. -SQUAWK.- FOLLOW FRANKIE. -SQUAWK.- CUZ STONE COLD SAYS SO.
STONE COLD SAYS SO. -SQUAWK.- STONE COLD SAYS SO. -SQUAWK.-
-ARGHH!-
NOW, JOHN CENA! INTO THE LOOKING GLASS!
MOVE!
VICTORY OR PACIFICATION!
VICTORY OR PACIFICATION!

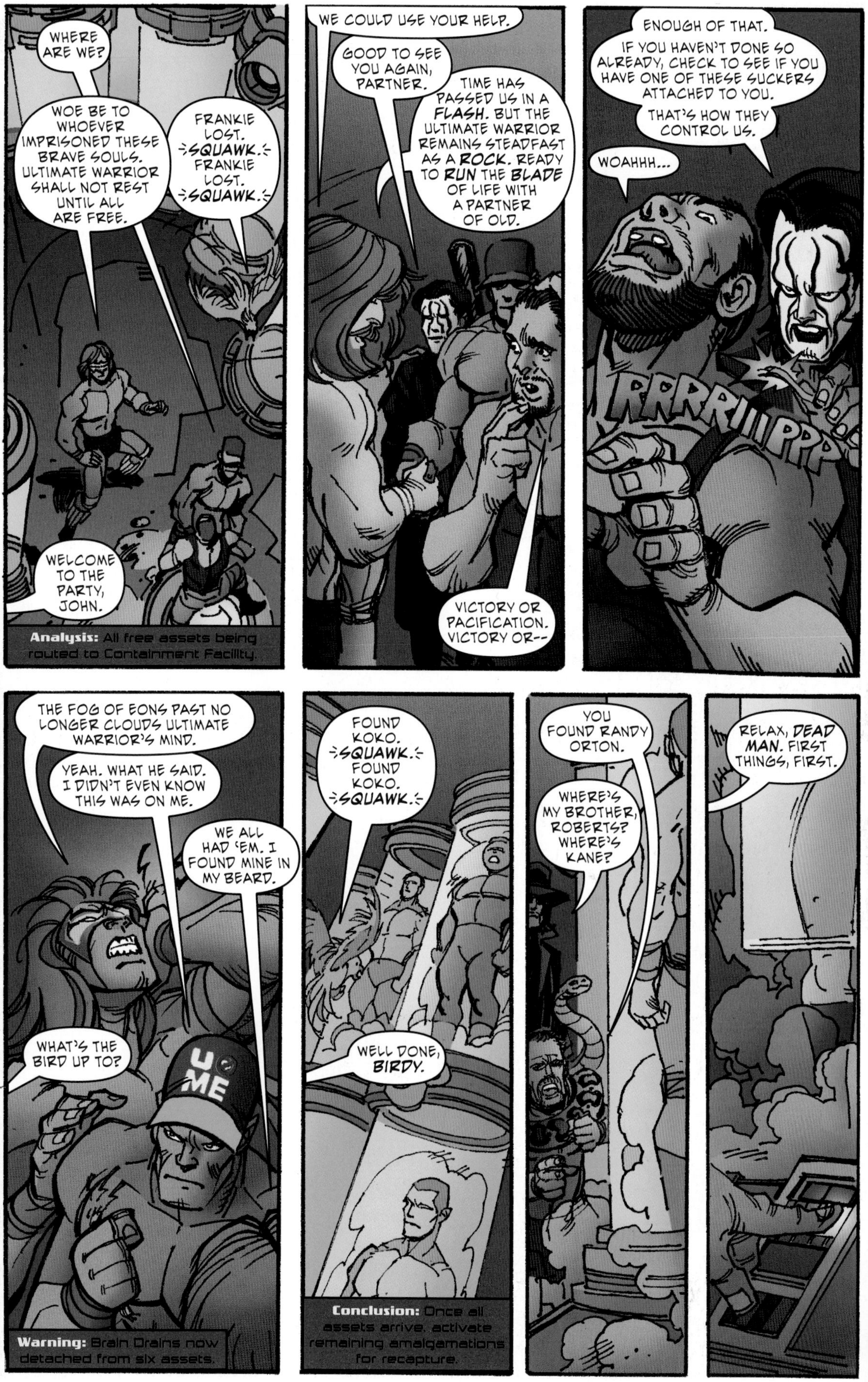

WHERE ARE WE?
WOE BE TO WHOEVER IMPRISONED THESE BRAVE SOULS. ULTIMATE WARRIOR SHALL NOT REST UNTIL ALL ARE FREE.
FRANKIE LOST. -SQUAWK.- FRANKIE LOST. -SQUAWK.-
WELCOME TO THE PARTY, JOHN.
Analysis: All free assets being routed to Containment Facility.
WE COULD USE YOUR HELP.
GOOD TO SEE YOU AGAIN, PARTNER.
TIME HAS PASSED US IN A FLASH. BUT THE ULTIMATE WARRIOR REMAINS STEADFAST AS A ROCK. READY TO RUN THE BLADE OF LIFE WITH A PARTNER OF OLD.
VICTORY OR PACIFICATION. VICTORY OR--
ENOUGH OF THAT.
IF YOU HAVEN'T DONE SO ALREADY, CHECK TO SEE IF YOU HAVE ONE OF THESE SUCKERS ATTACHED TO YOU.
THAT'S HOW THEY CONTROL US.
WOAHHH...
RRRRIIIPPP
THE FOG OF EONS PAST NO LONGER CLOUDS ULTIMATE WARRIOR'S MIND.
YEAH. WHAT HE SAID. I DIDN'T EVEN KNOW THIS WAS ON ME.
WE ALL HAD 'EM. I FOUND MINE IN MY BEARD.
WHAT'S THE BIRD UP TO?
U ME
Warning: Brain Drains now detached from six assets.
FOUND KOKO. -SQUAWK.- FOUND KOKO. -SQUAWK.-
WELL DONE, BIRDY.
Conclusion: Once all assets arrive, activate remaining amalgamations for recapture.
YOU FOUND RANDY ORTON.
WHERE'S MY BROTHER, ROBERTS? WHERE'S KANE?
RELAX, DEAD MAN. FIRST THINGS, FIRST.

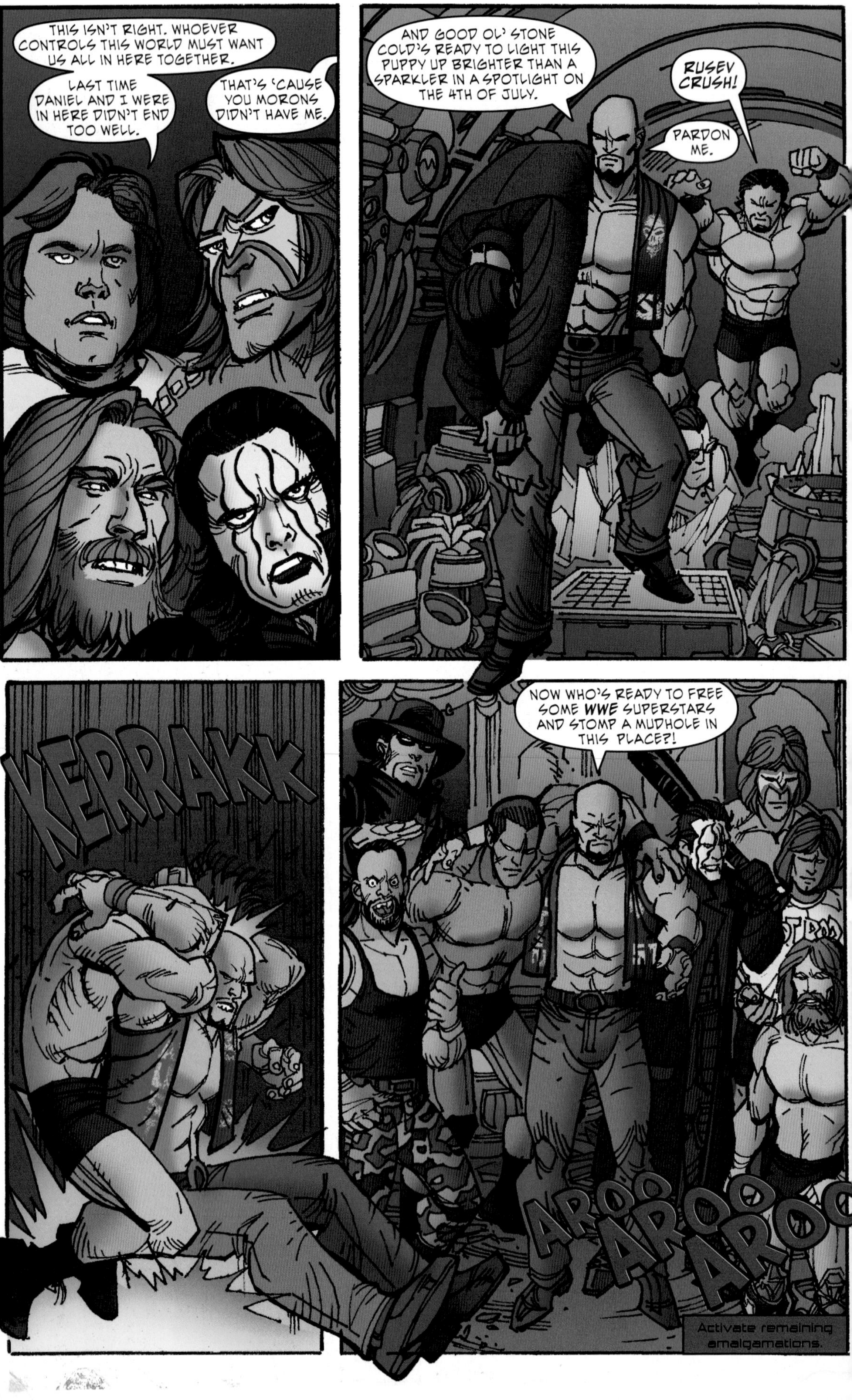
THIS ISN'T RIGHT. WHOEVER CONTROLS THIS WORLD MUST WANT US ALL IN HERE TOGETHER.
LAST TIME DANIEL AND I WERE IN HERE DIDN'T END TOO WELL.
THAT'S 'CAUSE YOU MORONS DIDN'T HAVE ME.
AND GOOD OL' STONE COLD'S READY TO LIGHT THIS PUPPY UP BRIGHTER THAN A SPARKLER IN A SPOTLIGHT ON THE 4TH OF JULY.
RUSEV CRUSH!
PARDON ME.
KERRAKK
NOW WHO'S READY TO FREE SOME WWE SUPERSTARS AND STOMP A MUDHOLE IN THIS PLACE?!
AROOO AROOO AROO
Activate remaining amalgamations.

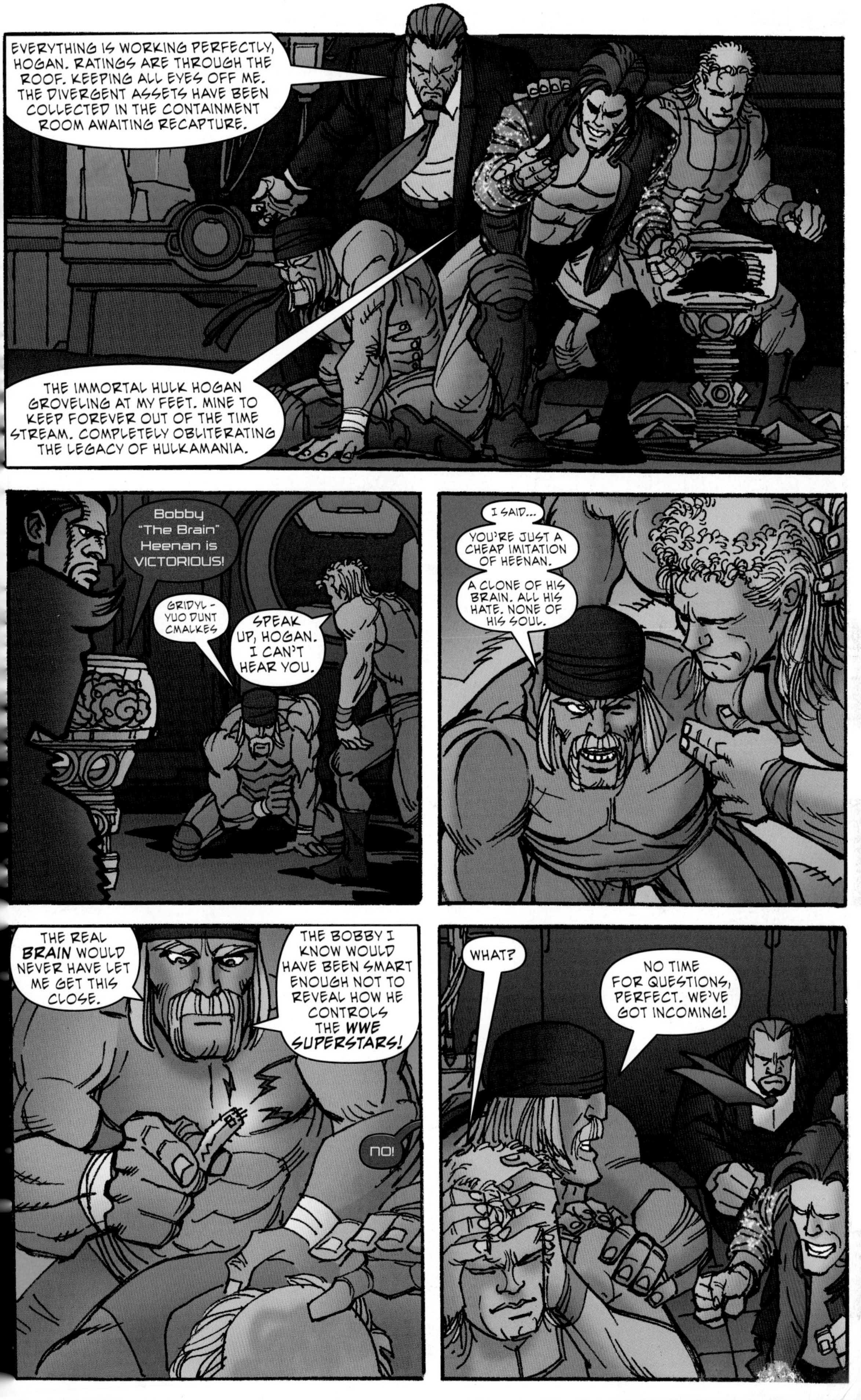
EVERYTHING IS WORKING PERFECTLY, HOGAN. RATINGS ARE THROUGH THE ROOF. KEEPING ALL EYES OFF ME. THE DIVERGENT ASSETS HAVE BEEN COLLECTED IN THE CONTAINMENT ROOM AWAITING RECAPTURE.
THE IMMORTAL HULK HOGAN GROVELING AT MY FEET. MINE TO KEEP FOREVER OUT OF THE TIME STREAM. COMPLETELY OBLITERATING THE LEGACY OF HULKAMANIA.
Bobby "The Brain" Heenan is VICTORIOUS!
GRIDYL - YUO DUNT CMALKES
SPEAK UP, HOGAN. I CAN'T HEAR YOU.
I SAID...
YOU'RE JUST A CHEAP IMITATION OF HEENAN.
A CLONE OF HIS BRAIN. ALL HIS HATE. NONE OF HIS SOUL.
THE REAL BRAIN WOULD NEVER HAVE LET ME GET THIS CLOSE.
THE BOBBY I KNOW WOULD HAVE BEEN SMART ENOUGH NOT TO REVEAL HOW HE CONTROLS THE WWE SUPERSTARS!
NO!
WHAT?
NO TIME FOR QUESTIONS, PERFECT. WE'VE GOT INCOMING!

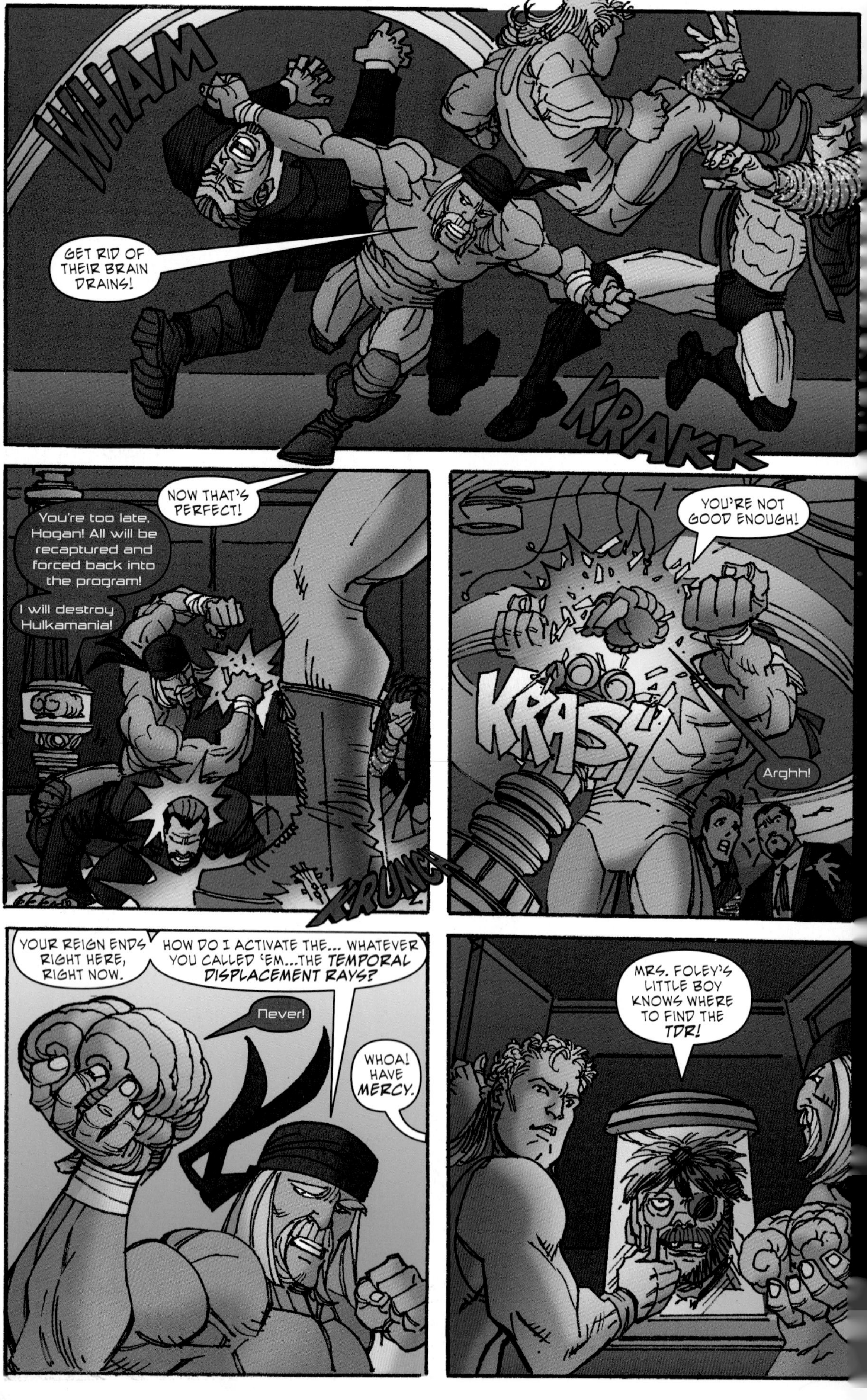
WHAM
GET RID OF THEIR BRAIN DRAINS!
KRAKK
NOW THAT'S PERFECT!
You're too late, Hogan! All will be recaptured and forced back into the program!
I will destroy Hulkamania!
KRUNCH
YOU'RE NOT GOOD ENOUGH!
KRASH
Arghh!
YOUR REIGN ENDS RIGHT HERE, RIGHT NOW.
HOW DO I ACTIVATE THE... WHATEVER YOU CALLED 'EM...THE TEMPORAL DISPLACEMENT RAYS?
Never!
WHOA! HAVE MERCY.
MRS. FOLEY'S LITTLE BOY KNOWS WHERE TO FIND THE TDR!

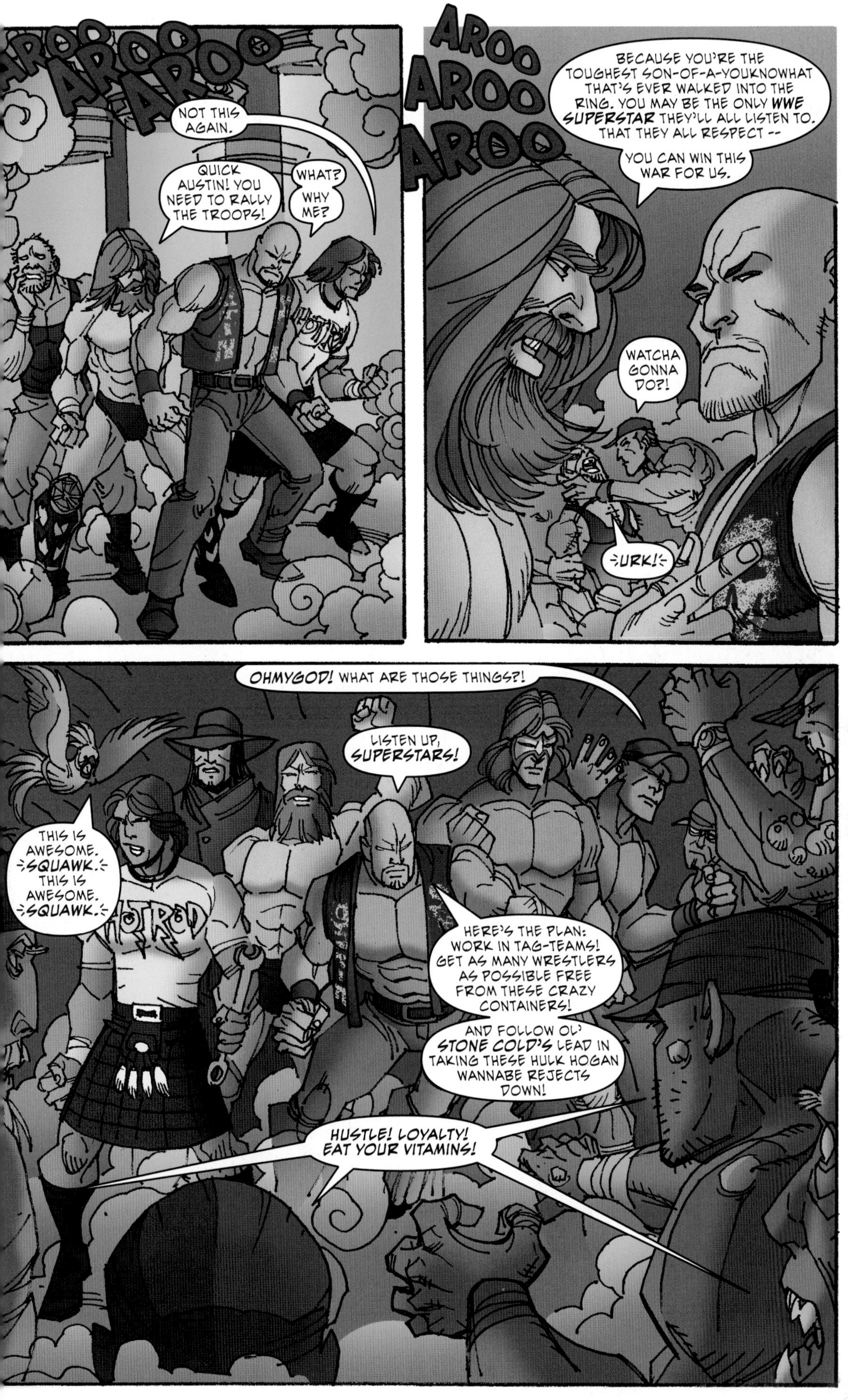
AROOO
AROOO
NOT THIS AGAIN.
QUICK AUSTIN! YOU NEED TO RALLY THE TROOPS!
WHAT?
WHY ME?
AROO
AROO
AROO
BECAUSE YOU'RE THE TOUGHEST SON-OF-A-YOUKNOWWHAT THAT'S EVER WALKED INTO THE RING. YOU MAY BE THE ONLY WWE SUPERSTAR THEY'LL ALL LISTEN TO. THAT THEY ALL RESPECT --
YOU CAN WIN THIS WAR FOR US.
WATCHA GONNA DO?!
URK!
OHMYGOD! WHAT ARE THOSE THINGS?!
LISTEN UP, SUPERSTARS!
THIS IS AWESOME. SQUAWK. THIS IS AWESOME. SQUAWK.
HERE'S THE PLAN: WORK IN TAG-TEAMS! GET AS MANY WRESTLERS AS POSSIBLE FREE FROM THESE CRAZY CONTAINERS!
AND FOLLOW OL' STONE COLD'S LEAD IN TAKING THESE HULK HOGAN WANNABE REJECTS DOWN!
HUSTLE! LOYALTY! EAT YOUR VITAMINS!

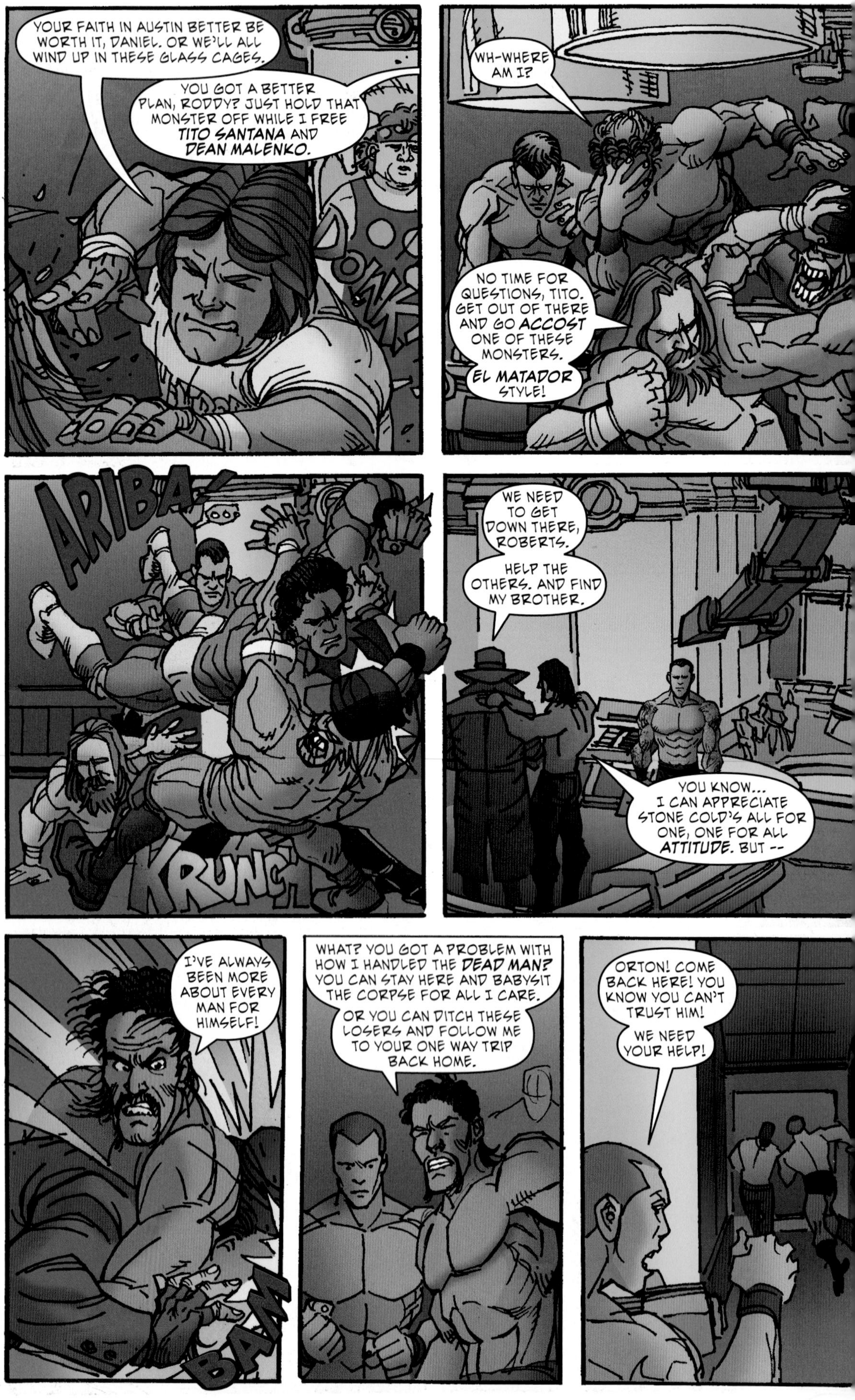
YOUR FAITH IN AUSTIN BETTER BE WORTH IT, DANIEL. OR WE'LL ALL WIND UP IN THESE GLASS CAGES.
YOU GOT A BETTER PLAN, RODDY? JUST HOLD THAT MONSTER OFF WHILE I FREE TITO SANTANA AND DEAN MALENKO.
WH-WHERE AM I?
NO TIME FOR QUESTIONS, TITO. GET OUT OF THERE AND GO ACCOST ONE OF THESE MONSTERS. EL MATADOR STYLE!
ARIBA!
KRUNCH
WE NEED TO GET DOWN THERE, ROBERTS.
HELP THE OTHERS. AND FIND MY BROTHER.
YOU KNOW... I CAN APPRECIATE STONE COLD'S ALL FOR ONE, ONE FOR ALL ATTITUDE. BUT --
I'VE ALWAYS BEEN MORE ABOUT EVERY MAN FOR HIMSELF!
BAM
WHAT? YOU GOT A PROBLEM WITH HOW I HANDLED THE DEAD MAN? YOU CAN STAY HERE AND BABYSIT THE CORPSE FOR ALL I CARE.
OR YOU CAN DITCH THESE LOSERS AND FOLLOW ME TO YOUR ONE WAY TRIP BACK HOME.
ORTON! COME BACK HERE! YOU KNOW YOU CAN'T TRUST HIM!
WE NEED YOUR HELP!

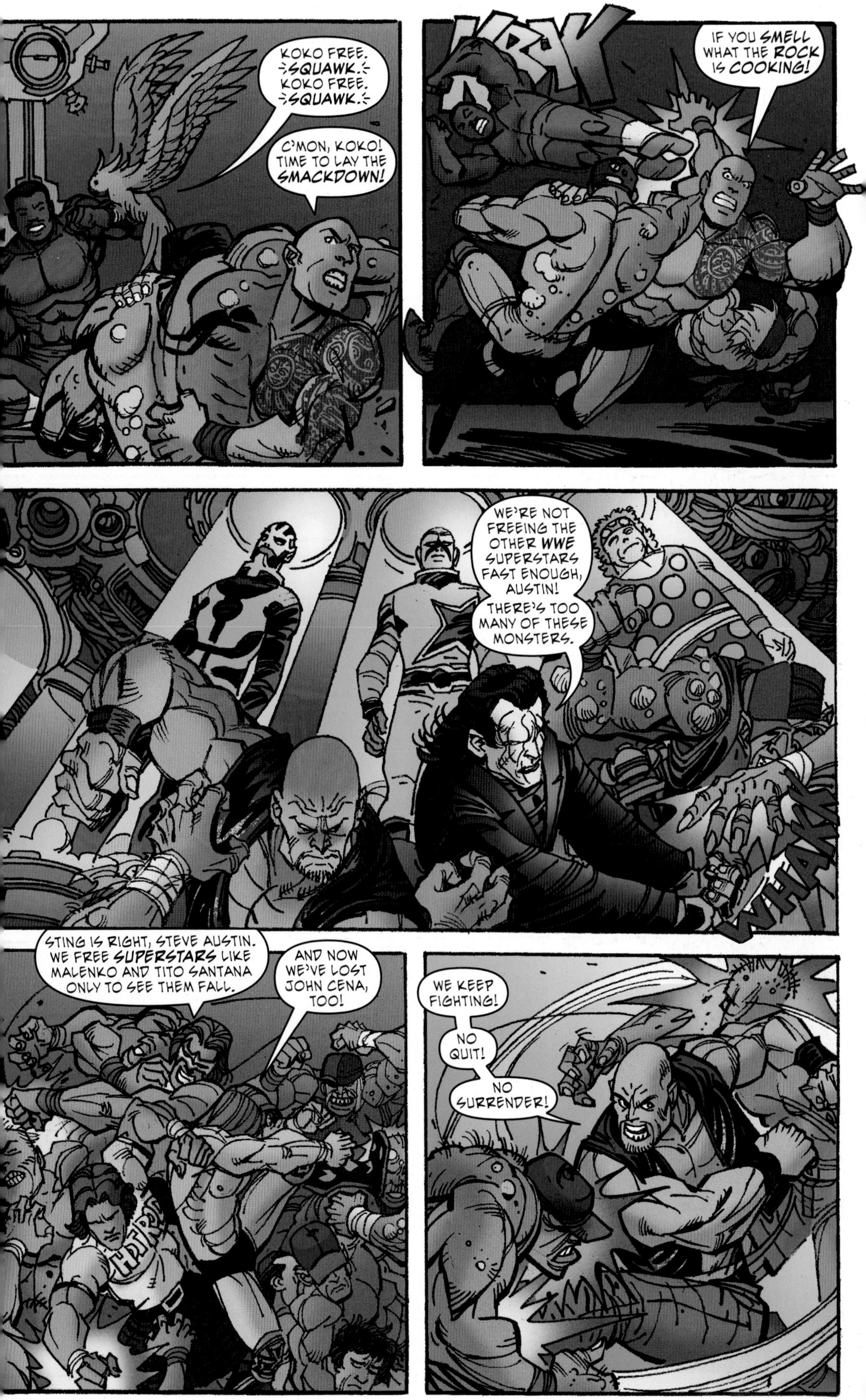
KOKO FREE. SQUAWK. KOKO FREE. SQUAWK.
C'MON, KOKO! TIME TO LAY THE SMACKDOWN!
KRAK
IF YOU SMELL WHAT THE ROCK IS COOKING!
WE'RE NOT FREEING THE OTHER WWE SUPERSTARS FAST ENOUGH, AUSTIN!
THERE'S TOO MANY OF THESE MONSTERS.
WHAK
STING IS RIGHT, STEVE AUSTIN. WE FREE SUPERSTARS LIKE MALENKO AND TITO SANTANA ONLY TO SEE THEM FALL.
AND NOW WE'VE LOST JOHN CENA, TOO!
WE KEEP FIGHTING!
NO QUIT!
NO SURRENDER!

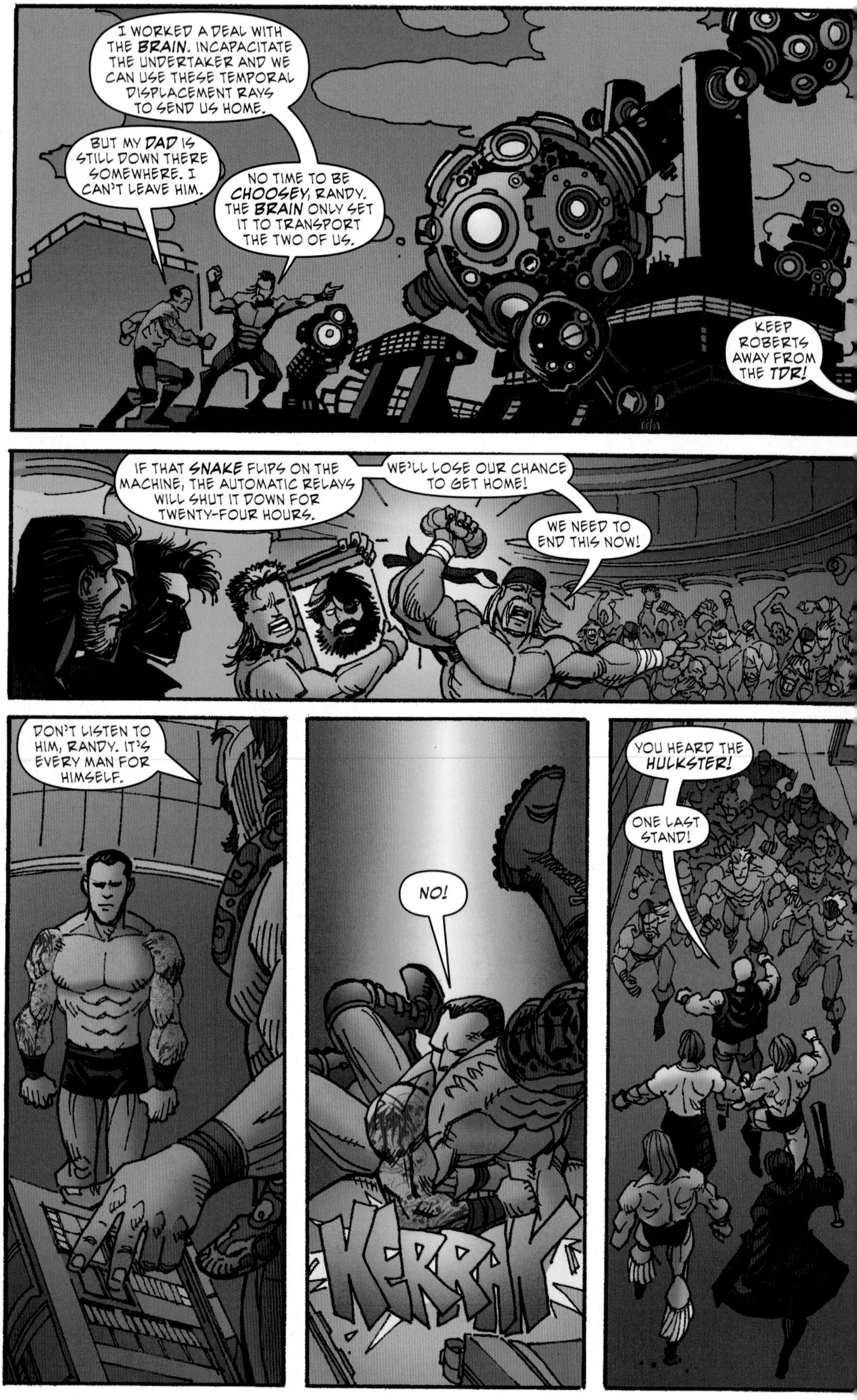
I WORKED A DEAL WITH THE BRAIN. INCAPACITATE THE UNDERTAKER AND WE CAN USE THESE TEMPORAL DISPLACEMENT RAYS TO SEND US HOME.
BUT MY DAD IS STILL DOWN THERE SOMEWHERE. I CAN'T LEAVE HIM.
NO TIME TO BE CHOOSEY, RANDY. THE BRAIN ONLY SET IT TO TRANSPORT THE TWO OF US.
KEEP ROBERTS AWAY FROM THE TDR!
IF THAT SNAKE FLIPS ON THE MACHINE, THE AUTOMATIC RELAYS WILL SHUT IT DOWN FOR TWENTY-FOUR HOURS.
WE'LL LOSE OUR CHANCE TO GET HOME!
WE NEED TO END THIS NOW!
DON'T LISTEN TO HIM, RANDY. IT'S EVERY MAN FOR HIMSELF.
NO!
KERRAK
YOU HEARD THE HULKSTER!
ONE LAST STAND!

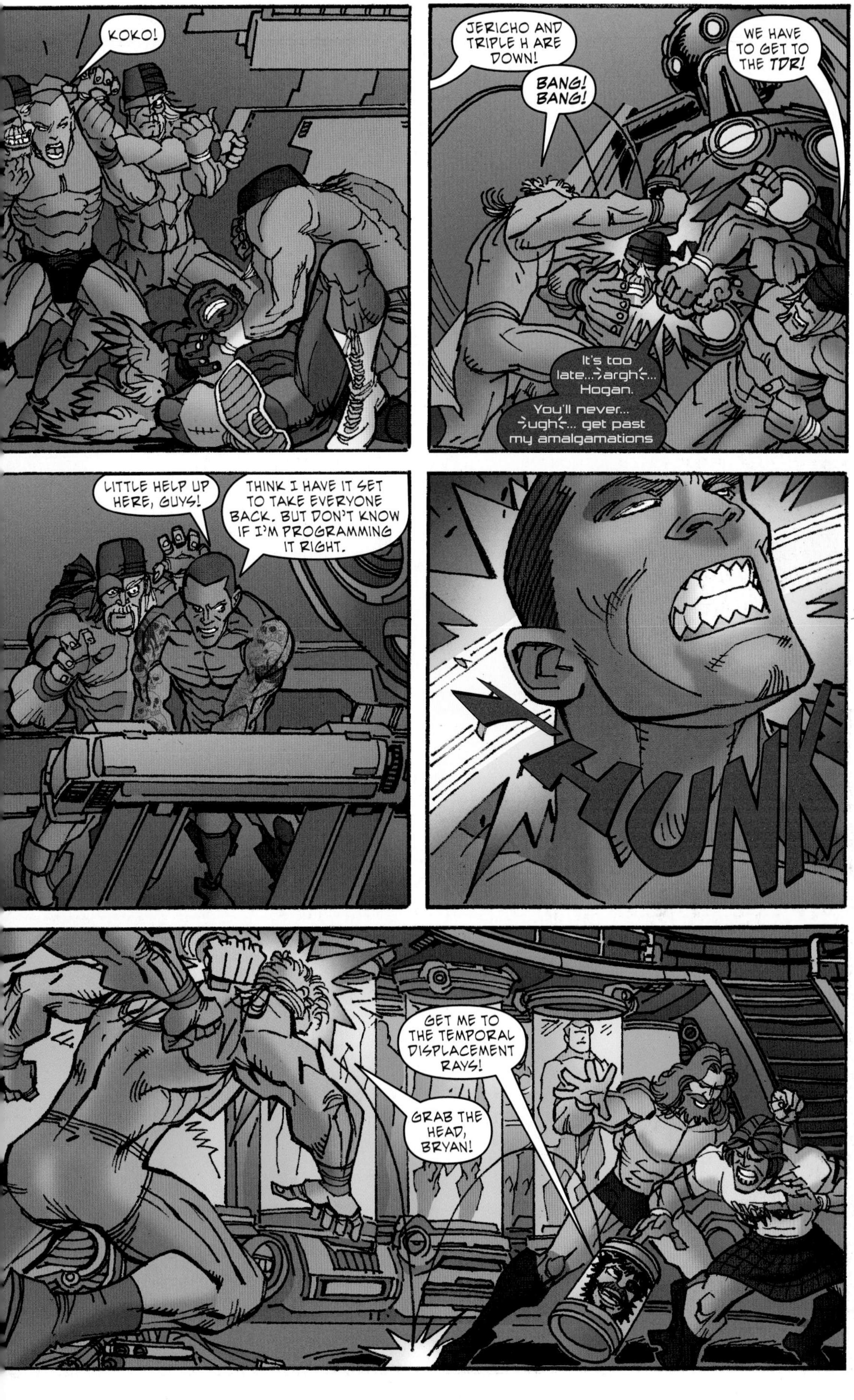
KOKO!
JERICHO AND TRIPLE H ARE DOWN!
BANG! BANG!
WE HAVE TO GET TO THE TDR!
It's too late...argh... Hogan.
You'll never... ugh... get past my amalgamations
LITTLE HELP UP HERE, GUYS!
THINK I HAVE IT SET TO TAKE EVERYONE BACK. BUT DON'T KNOW IF I'M PROGRAMMING IT RIGHT.
THUNK
GET ME TO THE TEMPORAL DISPLACEMENT RAYS!
GRAB THE HEAD, BRYAN!

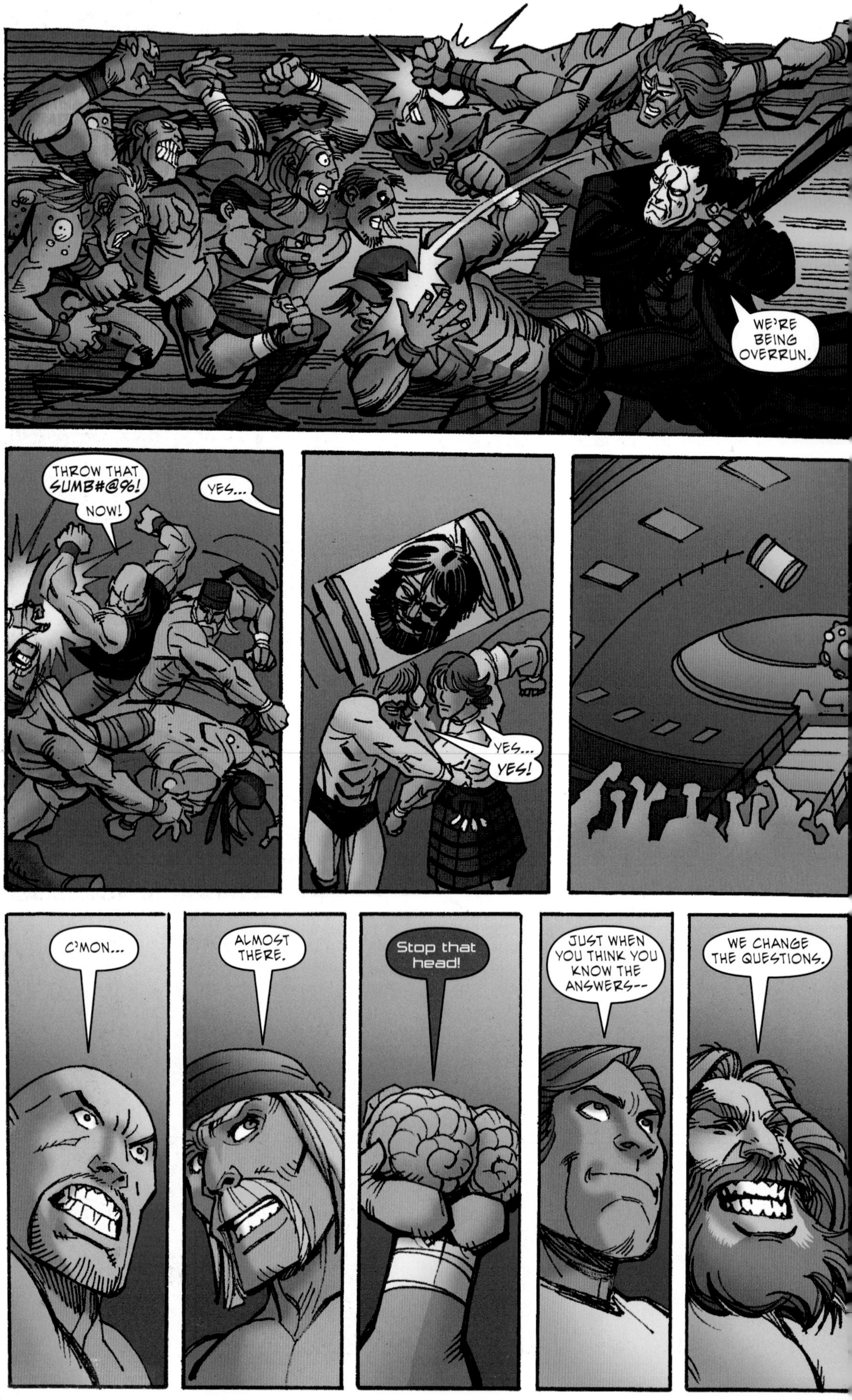
WE'RE BEING OVERRUN.
THROW THAT SUMB#@%! NOW!
YES...
YES... YES!
C'MON...
ALMOST THERE.
Stop that head!
JUST WHEN YOU THINK YOU KNOW THE ANSWERS--
WE CHANGE THE QUESTIONS.

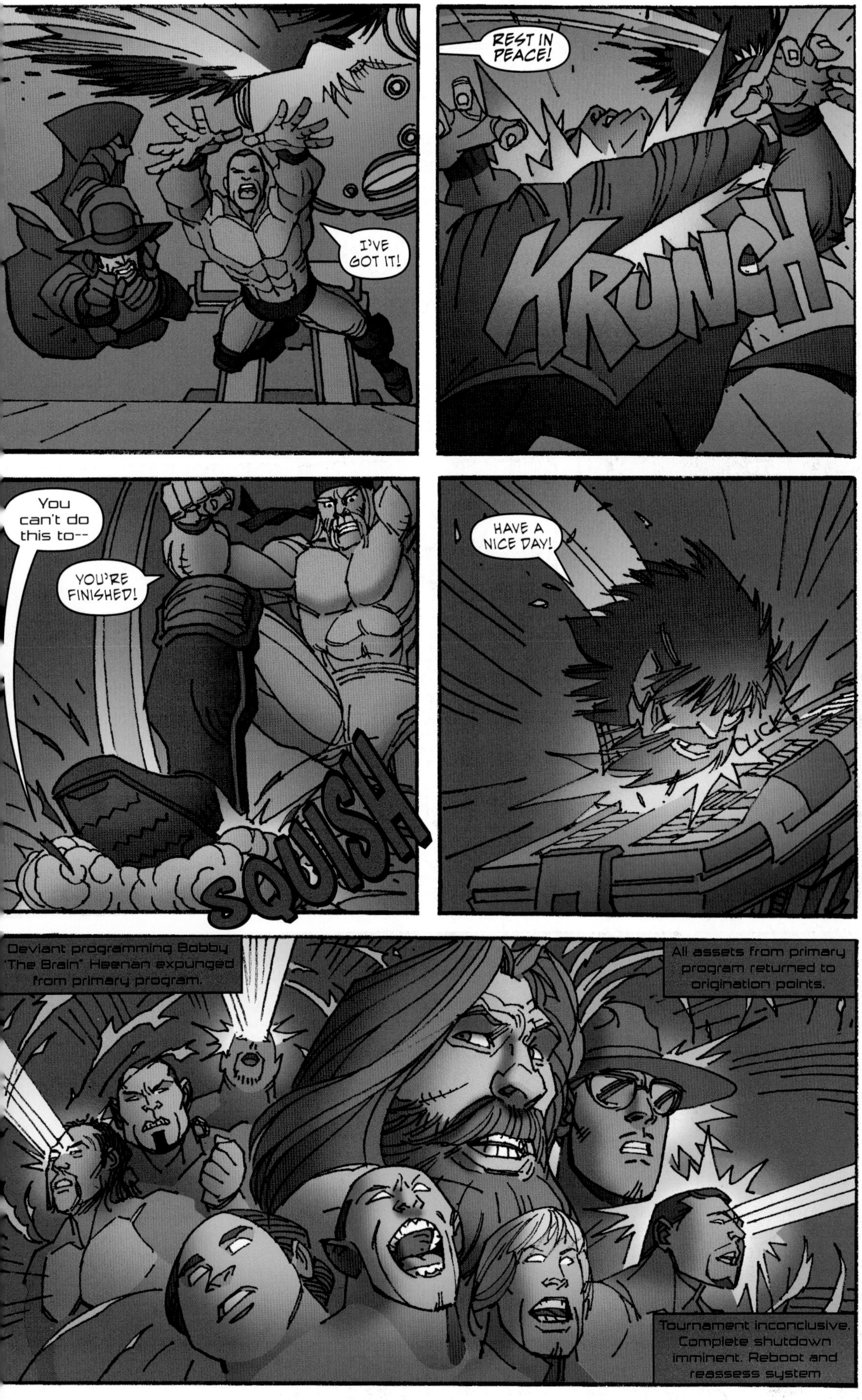
I'VE GOT IT!
REST IN PEACE!
KRUNCH
You can't do this to--
YOU'RE FINISHED!
SQUISH
HAVE A NICE DAY!
CLICK
Deviant programming Bobby "The Brain" Heenan expunged from primary program.
All assets from primary program returned to origination points.
Tournament inconclusive. Complete shutdown imminent. Reboot and reassess system

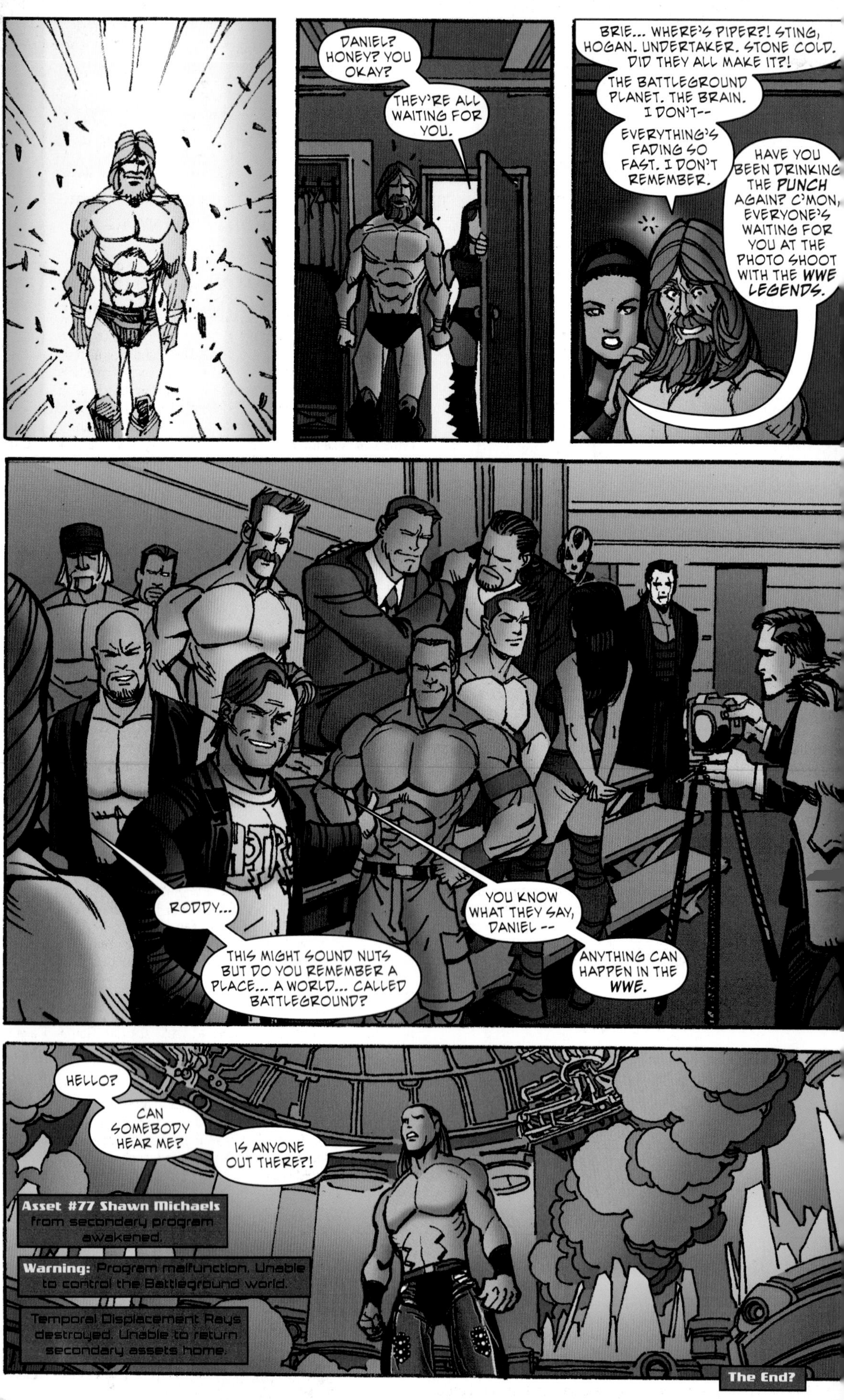
DANIEL? HONEY? YOU OKAY?
THEY'RE ALL WAITING FOR YOU.
BRIE... WHERE'S PIPER?! STING, HOGAN. UNDERTAKER. STONE COLD. DID THEY ALL MAKE IT?!
THE BATTLEGROUND PLANET. THE BRAIN. I DON'T--
EVERYTHING'S FADING SO FAST. I DON'T REMEMBER.
HAVE YOU BEEN DRINKING THE PUNCH AGAIN? C'MON, EVERYONE'S WAITING FOR YOU AT THE PHOTO SHOOT WITH THE WWE LEGENDS.
RODDY...
THIS MIGHT SOUND NUTS BUT DO YOU REMEMBER A PLACE... A WORLD... CALLED BATTLEGROUND?
YOU KNOW WHAT THEY SAY, DANIEL --
ANYTHING CAN HAPPEN IN THE WWE.
HELLO?
CAN SOMEBODY HEAR ME?
IS ANYONE OUT THERE?!
Asset #77 Shawn Michaels from secondary program awakened.
Warning: Program malfunction. Unable to control the Battleground world.
Temporal Displacement Rays destroyed. Unable to return secondary assets home.
The End?

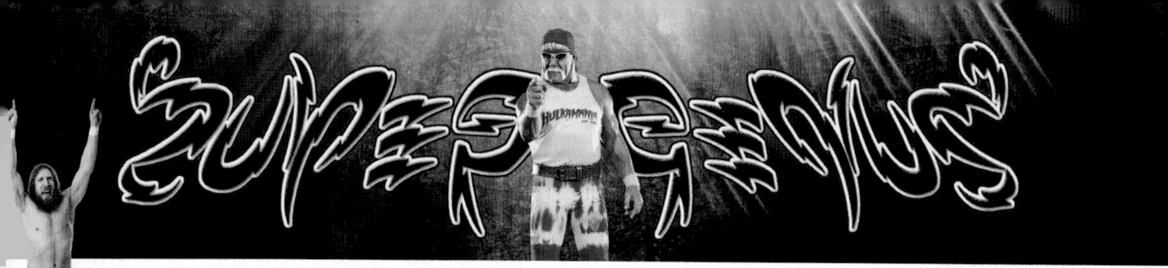
SUPER GENIUS

CONTACT INFO: EMAIL: salicrup@papercutz.com | WEB: supergeniuscomics.com
FANMAIL: Super Genius, 160 Broadway, Suite 700, East Wing, New York, NY 10038

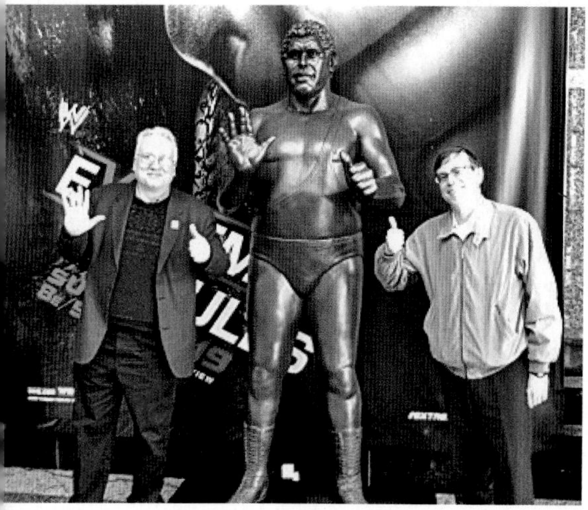
Jim & Terry at WWE Headquarters

THE LEGEND OF SUPER GENIUS

Take note, comics historians, that ten years ago, in 2005, graphic novel publishing pioneer Terry Nantier and me, humble best-selling comics editor, Jim Salicrup, launched a new comics company dedicated to publishing great graphic novels for all ages called Papercutz. You may be wondering what was so special about that? Would you believe that a decade ago the idea of a graphic novel publisher devoted to creating graphic novels for al-ages was unheard of! Graphic novels were mostly for adults, but we were dedicated to create graphic novels for kids too. Since then Papercutz has prospered, with such graphic novel series hits as THE SMURFS ANTHOLOGY, LEGO® THE LEGEND OF CHIMA, THEA STILTON, and TALES FROM THE CRYPT. A couple of years ago we decided to try something a little different. In 2013, we started the first Papercutz imprint, modestly titled Super Genius to publish comics and graphic novels for an older audience. Our debut Super Genius title was WWE SUPERSTARS and comics and sports entertainment history was made!

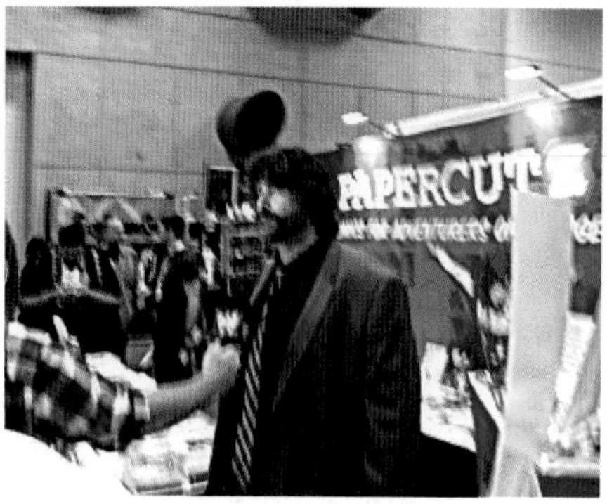
PAPERCUTZ

ENTER MICK FOLEY

Sure there were other comics that were published prior to WWE SUPERSTARS, but how many of them were lucky enough to get direct input from WWE Hall of Fame Inductee and real-life Super Genius Mick Foley, otherwise known as Dude Love, Cactus Jack, and Mankind (Yes, that's what that strange head in the bottle was in the preceding comics—the Four Faces of Foley!). Both the comics world and the WWE Universe were shocked when Mick Foley announced at the 2013 Comics Con International: San Diego that he would be writing the WWE SUPERSTARS comicbook.

Mick and his writing partner Shane Riches created the first four-part comicbook story "Money in the Bank," and that sent a message that these comics were not what everyone was expecting. I mean, were you expecting a film noir-like crime thriller in which all the characters were WWE Superstars? That was followed up with a comedy/adventure featuring the WWE Superstars trying to remember exactly why they ruined a taping of WWE RAW and to explain to Mr. McMahon why he shouldn't fire them. Just as "Money in the Bank" was collected in the first WWE SUPERSTARS trade paperback, so too was "Haze of Glory!" in the second collection.

LEGENDS CREATING LEGENDS

Now what could Foley and Riches possibly come up with that could create even more excitement than the previous two WWE epics? Well, you're looking at it! Not unlike the hit WWE video game, WWE2K15, the concept was to give you, the WWE Universe, the dream matches you've always wanted to see. Here was the opportunity to give you battles between WWE heroes and villains from every part of the WWE's rich history, and to have the Superstars all at their peak physical condition. But like the previous two WWE graphic novel adventures, we've taken the WWE Superstars out of the ring in the comics! Way, way out of the ring—all the way to Mars in fact! "Legends" has got to be the wildest WWE extravaganza that we've cooked up yet!

We also lucked out by getting Comic Art Legend Paris Cullins aboard to illustrate "Legends." Paris has been a superstar in his own right for years, still well-loved for his great work on DC's BLUE DEVIL and BLUE BEETLE comics. (Don't think we haven't thought about asking him to draw The Smurfs!)

WHAT'S NEXT?

The feedback to the "Legends" storyline has been overwhelming positive, with the only complaint being that the WWE Universe doesn't want the story to end. But as with all good things, everything must end, right? Well, yes and no. Yes, "Legends" is over, but "Last Man Standing," a star-studded continuation of "Legends," is coming soon!

But don't think we've forgotten about the dark, crime-filled world of Titan City, which was featured in "Money in the Bank." There's a follow-up to that in the works as well, starring Roman Reigns and Sting.

THE WRAP UP!

But while WWE SUPERSTARS was the premiere offering from Super Genius, it's not all we're planning to publish. Coming soon, from the mind of Super Genius Neil Gaiman is a special hardcover series collecting characters he created such as Lady Justice, Teknophage, and Mr Hero. These long-lost comics were created in the early 90s and have never been collected in book form... until now. So, as you can see, Super Genius is just getting started. We're lining up even more exciting titles to unleash on you in 2015, so keep an eye on our website, www.supergeniuscomics.com for exciting future announcements! So, until we meet again, like our friend Mick Foley always says, "Have a nice day!"

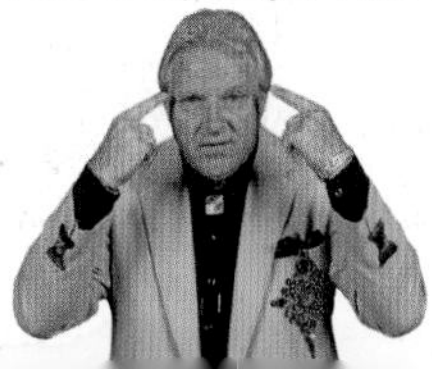

Jim Salicrup

IT'S PASS GO TIME!

FEATURES 6 CUSTOM TOKENS!

AVAILABLE NOW AT WWE.COM AND AMAZON.COM